Classic
Supercars

Classic Supercars

300 Amazing Automobiles

Richard Nicholls

amber
BOOKS

Amber Books Ltd
United House
North Road
London N7 9DP
United Kingdom
www.amberbooks.co.uk
Instagram: amberbooksltd
Facebook: amberbooks
Twitter: @amberbooks

ISBN: 978-1-78274-980-6

Project Editor: Chris Stone
Design: Stylus Design

Printed and bound in China

Picture credits:
Aerospace Publishing: all three-quarter views
All profile images courtesy of IMP Inc. except the following:
TRH Pictures 10, 13; TRH/John Cadman 6, 9, 11;

CONTENTS

Introduction

Carl Benz rolled out his first four-wheeled car, called the Victoria, in 1893, then a year later put his 1894 Benz Velo into production. It was one of the latter in which he entered the first recorded car race from Paris to Rouen. Ever since, people have been interested in tuning up their cars for performance.

The early 20th century saw racing become very popular as manufacturers and individuals competed for pride and prestige. Racing was extremely good for sales even back then, as competition cars captured the public's imagination and got them fired up about owning one of these new, rapid forms of horseless carriages. At the time, rapid meant a heady 50–60 mph (80–97 km/h) on pre-19th century vehicles, which rose to a scary 80–100 mph (129–160

Originally using the Ford Zephyr's straight-six for power, the AC Ace went on to become a firebreathing roadster when given Ford's 289 ci (4.8-litre) V8 by Carroll Shelby.

km/h) in Grand Prix racing of the first 20th-century decade, and this speed was constantly being raised by individuals who stripped and tuned their vehicles purely for the most miles or kilometers per hour. Such vehicles went on to be the Land Speed Record cars and, while they attained almost unheard-of speeds of 200 mph (320 km/h) just two decades on – sceptics had warned that man would not be able to live much over 100 mph (160 km/h)! – manufacturers continued to produce specially tuned cars for the road and track.

After World War I fuel shortage became a major concern for the growing car industry, which put a damper on sportscar production. During the 1920s many fast machines became available, but most to the wealthy only. The early 1930s saw the huge stockmarket crash of America, which sent shockwaves throughout the world and, again, restrained the car industry. Ford persevered through the bad times and in 1934 debuted the first mass-produced V8 car, which the public took to well.

POST-WORLD WAR II BOOM

World War II again saw cars on the decline as manufacturers both in Europe and the United States switched production to war machines or components thereof, though as peace was declared and the world economy got back on its feet, it was business as usual. Before long, Ford's Flathead V8, which had originated from their 1934 car, was being used in far more performance-biased cars, as it was cheap yet torquey. Allard of Great Britain was one such manufacturer using a derivative of the engine in its 1946 J1 machine, which could achieve 60 mph (97 km/h) in under 10 seconds and top 100 mph (160 km/h). The later J2 went on to be powered by more American muscle V8s from the likes of Chrysler, Cadillac or Oldsmobile, and these cars could easily leave a trail of dust for the famous 1948 Jaguar XK120 roadster which was capable of 120 mph (193 km/h).

The mere fact that many manufacturers were using US powerplants by the 1950s indicates the boom happening in the country. The American public liked their cars big and brash, but they also liked the reassuring torque of a V8, and this started the horsepower race of the 1950s and 1960s, in which many manufacturers partook. Chrysler were the first to kick-start it off in 1951 with their new 'Hemispherical' combustion chamber design, in a V8 configuration engine (most had previously used a straight eight). While this Hemi design had been used before in racing machines, Chrysler were the first to bring it to the public, but its cost meant it wasn't really for the masses, and just 87,000 cars came with that Firepower engine in 1951. In comparison, 1955 was a boom year for Chevrolet as they debuted their new 265 ci (4.3-litre) small-block Chevy V8. It was a massive hit, especially with America's youth, and model production soared to 1.7 million, a record for any vehicle manufacturer. Just two years on that engine was taken to 283 ci (4.6 litres) and given mechanical fuel-injection on the 1957 Chevy. Chevrolet claimed a groundbreaking one horsepower per cubic inch and independent testing backed this up to confirm the Chevy sedan as a muscular machine.

MUSCLE VERSUS EXOTICA

Chevrolet continued making high performance machines through the 1960s, going head-to-head with Chrysler's Dodge and Plymouth brands in what became known as the muscle-car era. This put the biggest production engines into intermediate-sized sedans and coupes, to make ever-faster accelerating cars. Dodge and Plymouth took a lot of the credit as they continued with the development of the Hemi engine until it hit 426 ci (6.9 litres) and a claimed 425 bhp (317 kW), which was underrated, as actual output was closer to 550 bhp (410 kW) on the Street Hemi dual carburettor models. Ford went to war in NASCAR against the Hemi-equipped Dodge Daytonas and Plymouth Roadrunners, with its 428 ci (7-litre) Super Cobra Jet Torino Talledegas, and won, even though it was by default when NASCAR virtually outlawed the Hemi engine in 1970 because it was too successful.

Meanwhile, Chevrolet was close in the street stakes with its big-block 454 ci (7.5-litre) V8, nicknamed the Rat motor by fans. This was the ultimate 400 bhp (298 kW) plus engine in their line-up, but not far behind was the 427 ci (6.9-litre) engine which was also capable of incredible power outputs in the likes of the Camaro and Corvette. In fact, during the late 1950s and early 1960s, the Corvette was the fastest sportscar in the world and was capable of beating the likes of Jaguar and Ferrari in European competition.

Enzo Ferrari, ex-racing driver and team manager for Alfa Romeo in the 1930s, had started producing road cars in the late 1940s, and while his machines were very expensive, their style and performance were second to none. Ferrari got a reputation not only for good-looking and fast street machines, but also for winning many sportscar races like Le Mans, and Grand Prix races with legends such as Stirling Moss and Juan Manuel Fangio behind the wheel. These races brought great respect to the model, but it didn't go unchallenged in Europe. Both Maserati and Lamborghini chased the same market, and indeed Maserati proved stiff competition when it launched the

The car manufacturer started by Sir Richard Lyons as SS Cars Ltd in 1933 (known as Jaguar from 1945), has survived through patchy times, but now under Ford's ownership its future looks bright.

170 mph (274 km/h) 5000GT and Bora (1971) models. But it was Lamborghini who ran neck-and-neck with Ferrari, and instantly made all cars from the Maranello factory seem dated when it debuted the first ever mid-engined supercar, the Miura, in 1966. The two companies would remain competitors over the following three decades, with Ferrari having high points such as the Dino, Daytona and 308, while Lamborghini won acclaim for the striking Countach in LP400 and LP500 guises.

Porsche launched its race-inspired 356 in 1948 and it was too tiny and underpowered to be considered in the super-exotica league. It was based on VW mechanicals, after all. However, the 356 developed and, by the early 1960s, had become considerably faster in the Carrera model. Then Porsche threw all its knowledge gained in its racing and road cars into the flat six-cylinder 911. This 1963 model continued largely unchanged, save for wider arches and ever-increasing power outputs, right through into the late 1980s, and though joined by other worthy Porsche models, it never was replaced,

The company said their Boxster would bring Porsche motoring to more people, but even so an initial price of $32,000 ($53,000) surprised many. The car has been a massive success since its launch in 1997.

which showed how much people enjoyed the high build quality and driving thrill of the rear-engined supercar.

BRITISH SPORTSCARS

In Great Britain there was one name which had become synonymous with performance and racing victories: Jaguar. In the post-World War II period, the company – started by Sir Richard Lyons as SS in 1931 and known as Jaguar from 1945 – produced its XK120. This roadster was good for an incredible 120 mph (192 km/h) and sold well throughout both Europe and the USA. The company's first racer was the C-Type and it was based on the XK model, and with a specially tuned 204 bhp (152 km/h) engine the C-Type took a win at Le Mans in 1951 and 1953. This was followed by the D-Type which sadly only saw 62 models produced. Far more successful and recognizable was the E-Type which came along in 1961. This was nothing short of a sensation when revealed at the British Motor Show and with the promised 150 mph (243 km/h) top speed tested on the British M1 motorway, the car soon became the sports machine to own, especially for the rich and famous. Beyond the E-Type the company was known for its sporty sedans, though the E-Type was superseded by the striking XJS in 1975, and this went on to see performance versions which marked high points in Jaguar car production.

Aside from Jaguar, the British car industry had many sports cars, but none were made in such high numbers. MG was the next biggest, but alas the performance of most models left a lot to be desired, especially as the 1960s turned into the 1970s and more practical, faster machines began to steal sales. It was only the development of the MG B, BGT Mk 2 and versions like the V8 which kept the name alive, at least until 1980, when British Leyland decided enough was enough. The heritage was, thankfully, more respected

Lamborghini's Diablo was particularly spacious, surpassing its forerunner the Countach not just in roominess but in its user-friendly nature too. Naturally, with a six-figure price tag, leather was standard.

by later management and at first the badge was simply put on sporting versions of sedans and hatchbacks from the Austin line, though during the 1990s it saw revival proper in the MGR V8 and MGF, the latter of which captured much of that early MG B model feeling.

The Triumph story tells in a similar fashion to MG, with progressive neglect through the 1960s and 1970s until the name was killed off in 1980, again by British Leyland. It was not before high points such as the TR range however, the hottest performers from there being the TR6 and V8-powered TR8.

TVR is the most inspiring of tales as the company came along in the 1960s and, through offering high-performance cars in low production, with regular updates, remained alive and profitable. This was even more evident in the 1990s as the company took its machines to a new level of supercar performance, but for a fraction of the price.

JAPANESE THREAT

While the rest of the world was busy getting on with the glitz and glamour of ever-more powerful machines, Japan was working intensely just to establish its brand names on the world's car market. Toyota might have been started in the 1930s, but it only built up influence during the 1960s and didn't attempt to hit the UK and USA markets with a sporty model until the 1970 Celica. Nevertheless, when this car did arrive, it surprised everyone with its rugged build and handsome, coupe styling. It led the way for models such as the mid-engined MR2 and muscular Supra coupe.

Nissan matched Toyota all the way with models in a similar vein, with the incredibly popular 240Z model (so popular in fact that Nissan remade the car in limited production in the late 1990s for the US only). This car paved the way for the Silvia Turbo and 300ZX Turbo of the 1980s, both representing opposite ends of the price spectrum whilst being quick machines. The turbo technology learned in these cars went on to become Nissan's forte in its 1990s models such as the limited-production rally-based GTiR hatchback, and the Skyline GTR, which launched the firm into the supercar league.

Mitsubishi wasn't far behind, though its name was only mentioned in the same sentence as performance come the 1990s. Models such as the FTO, Eclipse Spyder and Lancer Evo established the manufacturer and meant more choice for the power-hungry buyer.

With this book I hope we've covered an excellent cross-section of the type of vehicles which have long captured the imagination of driving enthusiasts. Every machine in this book has been built with some degree of performance bias, justifying the tag of 'supercar'. Sometimes this bias is merely in addition to the more important styling, but with the majority performance has been the first thought on the designer's mind, and that's what makes each entry a worthy supercar.

The Ginetta company was started by the Walklett brothers in the late-1950s and has survived, albeit in various hands, ever since – providing cars with no frills but plenty of thrills.

AC Ace

After a long battle in the boardroom, the AC Ace name was revived and the car launched in 1997. A version of the Ace had been designed by International Automotive Design in 1991, and the prototype used a Cosworth turbo four-cylinder engine, which was replaced in production with a modified Ford V6. The model didn't do well, with 48 sold before AC went into receivership. Pride Automotive Group later acquired the company and came up with the current Ace, with smoother body lines. The exterior was aluminium and composite, bonded to the stainless steel chassis to form a very stiff structure. Suspension consisted of double wishbones front and rear, with 10–inch (282mm) discs all around covered by wide 17-inch (436mm) alloys. Under the hood was all Mustang V8 again, as with the 1960s Shelby-built AC Cobra, though this time with sequential fuel injection and a supercharger.

Top speed:	165 mph (264 km/h)
0–60 mph (0–95 km/h):	5.5 sec
Engine type:	V8
Displacement:	302 ci (4,942 cc)
Transmission	5-speed manual
Max power:	340 bhp (254 kW) @ 5,700 rpm
Max torque:	385 lb ft (522 Nm) @ 3,500 rpm
Weight:	3,330 lb (1,514 kg)
Economy:	17 mpg (6 km/l)

AC Cobra 289

This car launched thousands of replicas and it was Carroll Shelby who started it all. He approached the Hurlock brothers at AC in 1961 – who were then producing the six-cylinder AC Ace – with the idea of putting Ford's compact and lightweight V8 into the car. AC jumped at the chance and in 1962 production began. At first, Shelby installed the 260ci (4.3-litre) but only the first 75 cars had this engine. In 1963 Shelby switched to the 289ci (4.7-litre) V8 and changed the steering to rack and pinion. The result in this lightweight roaster was sensational. The Cobra was the fastest accelerating car in the 1960s, but required nerves of steel because of the basic twin tube chassis. Its saving features were all-round independent wishbone suspension and large disc brakes. The bare essentials inside the roadster kept weight well under a ton and 100mph (160km/h) could be reached in just 14 seconds.

Top speed:	140 mph (224 km/h)
0–60 mph (0–95 km/h):	5.5 sec
Engine type:	V8
Displacement:	289 ci (4,735 cc)
Transmission	4-speed manual
Max power:	271 bhp (202 kW) @ 5,750 rpm
Max torque:	285 lb ft (386 Nm) @ 4,500 rpm
Weight:	2,024 lb (920 kg)
Economy:	15 mpg (5.3 km/l)

AC Cobra MkIV

The original AC Ace, modified by Shelby American to produce the AC Cobra in 1962, was every inch a muscle machine. In the mid-1980s AC Cars of Surrey, England, was emulating those early cars with a modern version of the Cobra, the MkIV. Still using a Mustang V8, this time it was the Phase 3 Mustang's 5.0 HO motor with sequential fuel injection and a lightweight engine block to keep the weight down. Through a manual gearbox it gave the MkIV almost the same acceleration as the original car, but with more fuel economy and better road manners. Underneath there were double wishbones front and rear to keep the suspension quick reacting, while 11-inch (280mm) discs provided awesome stopping ability on the roadster. Inside the car was hardly different even after all those years, with the bare minimum of analogue dials required just to keep the driver informed.

Top speed:	135 mph (216 km/h)
0–60 mph (0–95 km/h):	5.3 sec
Engine type:	V8
Displacement:	302 ci (4,942 cc)
Transmission	5-speed manual
Max power:	225 bhp (168 kW) @ 4,200 rpm
Max torque:	300lb ft (406 Nm) @ 3,200 rpm
Weight:	2,468 lb (1,122 kg)
Economy:	17 mpg (6 km/l)

AC Superblower

The Superblower was a re-creation of what Carroll Shelby had done in the early 1960s, only this time it had more bite. Like its predecessors, the Superblower was hand-built and even used a similar chassis with twin round tubes running the length of the car and smaller tubes between. Unequal-length wishbones front and rear made the handling good, and at each corner were huge discs. But most people were interested in the 'go' of the Superblower and the power was exceptional. Like the Cobras of the past, the car used a Mustang V8, this time the 5.0L from the 1987–1995 models, but with a Ford SVT (Special Vehicle Team) centrifugal blower to boost power up from the standard engine's 225bhp (167kW) and 300lb ft (406Nm) torque. The body was still hand-fabricated by craftsmen in aluminium alloy, while inside there was a modern interpretation of the original multi-dial dash.

Top speed:	155 mph (248 km/h)
0-60 mph (0–95 km/h):	4.2 sec
Engine type:	V8
Displacement:	302 ci (4,942 cc)
Transmission	5-speed manual
Max power:	355 bhp (250 kW) @ 5,700 rpm
Max torque:	385 lb ft (521 Nm) @ 3,750 rpm
Weight:	2,558 lb (1,163 kg)
Economy:	14 mpg (5 km/l)

Acura Integra Type R

The Integra Type R was launched in 1997, though its roots can be traced back years before that. In 1994 Honda debuted an all-wheel drive Integra prototype to the world's press, but it never went into production because of weight and cost. Instead, the design team concentrated on a lightweight, front-wheel-drive only vehicle and put into practice all their technology from the F1. The 110ci (1.8-litre) engine used their variable camshaft timing VTEC technology, low-friction pistons, high-volume intake, a bigger free-flow exhaust and a compression ratio of 11.1:1 for 195bhp (145kW), though being at 8,000rpm, the motor needed to be kept buzzing for best results. A stiffened bodyshell, full independent suspension with MacPherson struts up front, plus a helical gear-type limited-slip differential kept the power down and made it one of the best-handling front-wheel-drive cars ever.

Top speed:	143 mph (228 km/h)
0—60 mph (0–95 km/h):	6.7 sec
Engine type:	In-line four
Displacement:	105 ci (1,797 cc)
Transmission:	5-speed
Max power:	195 bhp (145 kW) @ 8,000 rpm
Max torque:	130 lb ft (176 Nm) @ 7,300 rpm
Weight:	2,427 lb (1,103 kg)
Economy:	26 mpg (9.2 km/l)

Alfa Romeo 1750 GTV

The forerunner to the 1967 1750 GTV, the Sprint Coupe, debuted in 1963 as part of the Giulia family of cars which included saloons and Spiders designed by Giorgetto Giugiaro, was distinctive and handsome. The GTV (GT Veloce) was the fast version of the Sprint and shared the same mechanicals as other models in the range. Independent front suspension using double wishbones and an anti-roll bar, together with a live axle with trailing arms and anti-roll bar, made for fantastic handling with just a slight hint of understeer. Best of all was the all-aluminium engine twin-overhead cam which used larger valves and a modified intake to increase power. Though it started out as a 98ci (1.6-litre), in 1967 the engine was increased to 120ci (1.7 litre) and this is regarded as the high point in its development; it was such a sweet revver, even if not as powerful as the 120ci (1.9-litre) unit of 1971.

Top speed:	116 mph (185 km/h)
0–60 mph (0–95 km/h):	9.3 sec
Engine type:	In-line four
Displacement:	108 ci (1,779 cc)
Transmission:	5-speed manual
Max power:	132 bhp (98 kW) @ 5,500 rpm
Max torque:	137 lb ft (186 Nm) @ 2,900 rpm
Weight:	2,239 lb (1,018 kg)
Economy:	20 mpg (7 km/l)

Alfa Romeo GTV6

Styling by Giorgetto Giugiaro made the GTV attractive and with its low front nose, steeply raked windscreen and sharply cut-off fastback, it was ahead of its time in the mid-1970s. Back then it ran a 122ci (2-litre) at best, but all changed in 1981 when the GTV6 joined the line-up. The following year a GTV6 won the first of four consecutive European Touring Car titles before production of the car came to an end in 1986. It was originally based on the 1972 Alfetta, with the wheelbase shortened by just over 4 inches (102mm) to suit the GT. The motor was first used in Alfa's Six saloon in 1979, and it became their defining modular engine of the 1980s. The all-alloy unit ran a single cam-per-bank, with Bosch multi-point fuel injection, and the spread of torque made the GTV6 so satisfying to drive, especially with the V6's high rpm howl. A rear-mounted gearbox kept weight distribution near perfect.

Top speed:	132 mph (211 km/h)
0–60 mph (0–95 km/h):	8.8 sec
Engine type:	V6
Displacement:	152 ci (2,492 cc)
Transmission	5-speed manual
Max power:	154 bhp (115 kW) @ 5,500 rpm
Max torque:	152 lb ft (206 Nm) @ 3,200 rpm
Weight:	2,840 lb (1,291 kg)
Economy:	25 mpg (8.8 km/i)

Alfa Romeo Spider

The wedge shape of the Spider can be traced back to the SZ which was launched in 1989, and more still to the Proteo concept car which Alfa showed at the Geneva Motor Show two years later. It was 1994 before the public got to see the actual Spider, but it was worth the wait. With a dramatic wedge waistline running down the car and beautifully sculptured grille flanked by twin headlamps (actually one big lamp behind), the Spider was instantly recognizable as an Italian classic. Even with front-wheel drive, unusual for an Alfa sports car, it used the power well, thanks to MacPherson struts at the front and a multi-link rear, again both new, as the cars previously used double wishbones and a live rear axle. The Twin Spark engine from other Alfa models was used and with balancer shafts plus 16 valves, it gave a smooth power delivery which would buzz eagerly to the 7,000rpm redline.

Top speed:	130 mph (208 km/h)
0–60 mph (0–95 km/h):	8.9 sec
Engine type:	In-line four
Displacement:	120 ci (1,970 cc)
Transmission	5-speed manual
Max power:	150 bhp (112 kW) @ 6,200 rpm
Max torque:	137 lb ft (185 Nm) @ 4,000 rpm
Weight:	3,020 lb (1,373 kg)
Economy:	29.4 mpg (10.4 km/l)

Alfa Romeo SZ

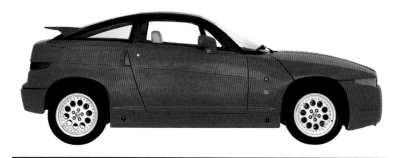

The bulldog looks promised much, but the SZ, Alfa's foray into sportscar territory in 1989, was not as quick many expected. However, what it lacked in out-and-out performance, the car more than made up for in handling and grip once out on the road. This it achieved through the rear-mounted transmission which distributed the weight perfectly. Based on the Alfa 75 Saloon, the SZ differed in that it used a composite body bonded to a steel frame, therefore making the chassis very solid, stable and predictable. The all-aluminium V6 ran a single cam-per-bank for 210bhp (175kW), and gave a glorious multi-cylinder howl. Combined with the torsion bar front suspension and de Dion rear end, the on-the-limit cornering ability of the Alfa is how it's best remembered. With less than 1,000 produced, the SZ was a rare sight on the road, but part of the attraction of the car was its exclusivity.

Top speed:	153 mph (245 km/h)
0–60 mph (0–95 km/h):	7.2 sec
Engine type:	V6
Displacement:	180ci (2,959 cc)
Transmission	5-speed manual
Max power:	210 bhp (157 kW) @ 6,200 rpm
Max torque:	181 lb ft (245 Nm) @ 4,500 rpm
Weight:	2,778 lb (1,263 kg)
Economy:	20.8 mpg (7.3 km/l)

Allard J2

The J2 was conceived after Sidney Allard made a visit to the USA in the late 1940s and saw how effective a powerful American V8 could be in a lightweight roadster. He chose the Mercury V8 modified by Ardun for 267ci (4.3 litres), though some cars were shipped to America without any engines and ended up with one of two favourites: the Cadillac V8 or 331ci (5.4-litre) Chrysler Hemi. While the J2 was a lightweight, its tubular cross-braced chassis was also flexible, and this didn't help handling. The other downfall was the split front axle which gave positive camber, though the de Dion rear improved things. The car was very quick and a handful on the circuit, with a huge steering wheel, widely spaced pedals and awkward gearshift hampering rapid progress in anything but a straight line. The later J2X, with its extended nose to house much-improved suspension, was a better machine.

Top speed:	110 mph (176 km/h)
0–60 mph (0–95 km/h):	8.0 sec
Engine type:	V8
Displacement:	267ci (4,375 cc)
Transmission	3-speed manual
Max power:	140 bhp (104 kW) @ 4,000 rpm
Max torque:	225 lb ft (305 Nm) @ 2,500 rpm
Weight:	2,072 lb (942 kg)
Economy:	14 mpg (5 km/l)

AM General Hummer

The High Mobility Multi-purpose Wheeled Vehicle, otherwise known as the HMMWV or Humvee for short, started life in 1980 with tests in the Nevada desert after being designed just 11 months earlier. The American Army were so impressed they ordered 55,000 vehicles in 1983, but it wasn't until 1993, after the Gulf War where the Humvee starred, that the car was sold to the general public. It started public life with a gasoline small-block Chevy engine, but this was replaced in 1994 by GM's new 378ci (6.4-litre) turbo diesel V8 which gave out massive torque. The car was designed to be tough for military use, so weight was not an issue, hence there's a massive ladder-style chassis. Independent suspension is used with a lot of travel and huge ground clearance, while four-wheel drive was mandatory with a four-speed auto transmitting to a two-speed transfer case and centre differential.

Top speed:	87 mph (140km/h)
0–60 mph (0–95 km/h):	17.3 sec
Engine type:	V8 diesel
Displacement:	395 ci (6,472 cc)
Transmission	4-speed auto
Max power:	195 bhp (145 kW) @ 3,400 rpm
Max torque:	430 lb ft (582 Nm) @ 1,700 rpm
Weight:	6,620 lb (3,009 kg)
Economy:	10.7 mpg (3.8 km/l)

AMC AMX

The 1968 AMX was basically a shortened Javelin, and was the first American two-passenger steel-bodied production sportscar since the 1957 Ford T-bird. AMX stood for 'American Motors Experimental' and it came in base-model form with a 290ci (4.8-litre) V8, though did have a 343ci (5.6-litre) option and monster 390ci (6.6-litre) V8 which turned it into a screamer. When Craig Breedlove took a 390ci AMX to Goodyear's Texas test track in February 1968, he established 106 World Speed Records. AMC even made 50 Breedlove specials with red, white and blue paint jobs to celebrate, but they only came with the 290ci (4.75-litre) engine. Independent front suspension with an anti-roll bar were part of the good handling set-up, along with quick-rack power steering, front disc brakes and a limited-slip differential, so the AMX was as capable through the twists as pounding down the drag strip.

Top speed:	125 mph (200 km/h)
0–60 mph (0–95 km/h):	6.6 sec
Engine type:	V8
Displacement:	390 ci (6,390 cc)
Transmission	3-speed auto
Max power:	315 bhp (235 kW) @ 4,600 rpm
Max torque:	425 lb ft (575 Nm) @ 3,200 rpm
Weight:	3,400 lb (1,545 kg)
Economy:	13 mpg (4.6 km/l)

Anglia Gasser

As drag-racing grew ever-more popular in the 1950s, racers looked for smaller and lighter cars in which to put big engines. Ford's little 'sit-up-and-beg' car, which began life in 1939 as the Anglia EO4A and went through from 1953 to 1959 as the Popular, proved to be ideal for the big engine swap. Its already basic interior could easily be replaced with aluminium panels to lose weight, while inside the front was deceptively large once the inner wings were cut away. With basic suspension, racers could get their car's weight right down, and modifying a V8 would see the power-to-weight ratio way beyond any supercar. As cars and racing developed, roll cages were added for safety, special drag-racing suspension was installed and the power increased with either superchargers or nitrous oxide. Such cars represent a nod to past racers, giving as much excitement, but more safety.

Top speed:	170 mph (272 km/h)
0–60 mph (0–95 km/h):	2.4 sec
Engine type:	V8
Displacement:	350 ci (5,735 cc)
Transmission	4-speed clutchless manual
Max power:	775 bhp (578 kW) @ 6,200 rpm
Max torque:	680 lb ft (921 Nm) @ 4,000 rpm
Weight:	1,870 lb (850 kg)
Economy:	4 mpg (1.4 km/l)

Aston Martin DB5

Most famous for its role in the James Bond film 'Goldfinger' the DB5 was more than just a movie star. It is widely regard as one of the most beautiful Astons and was an exceptional grand tourer, thanks to its power ride. Underneath was a strong steel platform with steel tubes to support the hand-formed aluminium bodywork. A double wishbone front with coil springs and telescopic dampers was complemented by a live rear axle well located with a Watts linkage and radius arms, again using coils. The all-alloy straight-six engine was first debuted in the DB4, but engineer Tadek Marek reworked it for 244ci (4-litre) displacement in the DB5. With twin overhead camshafts and triple SU carburettors, it was powerful enough, but with triple Webers, its output was raised to 314bhp (234kW) in the Vantage. All after the first 90 cars used a ZF five-speed transmission, and had front/rear disc brakes.

Top speed:	143 mph (229 km/h)
0–60 mph (0–95 km/h):	8.6 sec
Engine type:	In-line six
Displacement:	244 ci (3,995 cc)
Transmission	5-speed manual
Max power:	282 bhp (210 kW) @ 5,550 rpm
Max torque:	280 lb ft (379 Nm) @ 4,500 rpm
Weight:	3,450 lb (1,568 kg)
Economy:	15 mpg (5.3 km/l)

Aston Martin DB6

The 1966 DB6 replaced the DB5 and was a much updated car. Underneath, out went the steel platform construction and in came a modern monocoque design with steel inner panels and floorpan covered with the aluminium body. Though longer by 3.7 inches (94mm) in the wheelbase, which gave a slightly better ride quality, the DB6 used the same suspension layout as the DB5 with double wishbones at the front and a Watts linkage/trailing arm live axle rear. The engine was also the DB5's, but slightly up in power especially in Vantage form which had 325bhp (242kW). While similar in the nose, the DB6 had a distinct cut-off rear which was accentuated by a raised rear lip which doubled as a spoiler. It made the car more aerodynamic, increasing downforce and high speed stability. The interior had Wilton carpet, leather seats, multiple gauges and a wood/aluminium wheel.

Top speed:	150 mph (240 km/h)
0—60 mph (0–95 km/h):	6.7 sec
Engine type:	In-line six
Displacement:	244 ci (3,995 cc)
Transmission	5-speed manual
Max power:	325 bhp (242 kW) @ 5,750 rpm
Max torque:	290 lb ft (393 Nm) @ 4,500 rpm
Weight:	3,417 lb (1,553 kg)
Economy:	10.7 mpg (3.8 km/l)

Aston Martin Virage

Aston's 1988 Virage was the successor to the DBS which had been introduced in the late1960s. The chassis was modernized using a steel semi-monocoque frame to make it stiffer. However, the suspension configuration was much the same as previous Astons with double wishbones and an alloy de Dion rear with Watts linkage and alloy trailing arms. Massive 13 and 11-inch (330 and 279mm) discs were fitted to cope with the extra pace available from the heavyweight tourer. The engine's head were re-designed by Corvette tuner Reeves Calloway, who put the valves closer together to improve flow and packaging of the huge V8. The modifications gave an extra 32bhp (24kW) through a heavy-shifting ZF five-speed manual. Luxury was evident inside with leather and walnut, and the outer styling won many fans, despite Audi 100 headlights and VW Scirocco tail lamps.

Top speed:	157 mph (251 km/h)
0–60 mph (0–95 km/h):	7.0 sec
Engine type:	V8
Displacement:	326 ci (5,340 cc)
Transmission	5-speed manual
Max power:	330 bhp (360 kW) @ 6,000 rpm
Max torque:	340 lb ft (246 Nm) @ 3,700 rpm
Weight:	3,940 lb (1,791 kg)
Economy:	13.1 mpg (4.6 km/l)

Aston Martin DB7

A takeover of Aston Martin by Ford in 1992, and the subsequent access to plenty of development cash, meant Aston Martin could at long last produce a worthy successor to the famed DB6 model. Underneath, the DB7 was closely related to the XJS of Jaguar, also owned by Ford, though the engine was all new. Developed with the help of famed motorsport company TWR, the 195ci (3.2-litre) all-alloy straight-six produced more than 100bhp (74kW) per litre thanks to four valves per cylinder, sequential fuel injection and an Eaton supercharger. The body broke from Aston Martin tradition in that instead of hand-formed aluminium, it used composite panels, though it featured retro touches such as the vents behind the front wheels. Massive vented discs behind 18-inch (457mm) alloy rims ensured speed was wiped off quickly, while leather and wood were inside as a benchmark of British quality.

Top speed:	157 mph (251 km/h)
0–60 mph (0–95 km/h):	6.0 sec
Engine type:	In-line six
Displacement:	198 ci (3,239 cc)
Transmission	5-speed manual
Max power:	335 bhp (250 kW) @ 5,750 rpm
Max torque:	400 lb ft (542 Nm) @ 3,000 rpm
Weight:	3,859 lb (1,754 kg)
Economy:	13.8 mpg (4.7 km/l)

Aston Martin Zagato

The first Zagatos were produced in the early 1960s, and a meeting in 1984 between AM chairman Victor Gauntlett and Gianni Zagato led to the idea of re-creating that Zagato styling magic on a new Aston to revive the line-up. It was 1986 that production of the Zagato began, with almost $7 million taken in orders based on the sketches alone. Underneath the car used the V8 Vantage floorpan shortened by 16 inches (406mm). It had a double wishbone front and a de Dion rear, which allowed the huge rear vented discs to be moved inboard for quicker suspension movement. The short-stroke all-alloy V8 dated back to 1969 but had been steadily improved, featuring twin overhead chain-driven camshafts, four Weber carbs, Cosworth pistons and a less restrictive intake and exhaust. The Zagato was every bit a supercar with a claimed 180mph (290km/h) top speed, but only 75 were produced.

Top speed:	183 mph (292 km/h)
0–60 mph (0–95 km/h):	4.8 sec
Engine type:	V8
Displacement:	326 ci (5,340 cc)
Transmission	5-speed auto
Max power:	432 bhp (322 kW) @ 6,200 rpm
Max torque:	395 lb ft (534 Nm) @ 5,100 rpm
Weight:	3,630 lb (1,650 kg)
Economy:	12 mpg (4.2 km/l)

Audi A4 BTCC

The British Touring Car Championship was the most hotly contested race series of the 1990s, so when Audi decided to compete, they had to be good. They entered in 1996 and instantly made an impression with a pole position and two wins at the opening rounds, then that season dominated with eight wins, twice as many as any other manufacturer. The secret to Audi's success was their 4WD system which offered immense traction and cornering speed, even with a 275lb (125kg) weight penalty over other cars with 2WD only. The car used an ultra stiff multi-point roll cage with double wishbones and struts, plus 13-inch (330mm) disc brakes with alloy callipers that gave immensely powerful yet lightweight brakes. The all-alloy engine displaced 122ci (1.9 litres) and used four valves per cylinder. Wheels were 8.2x19-inch (208x483mm) OZ forged alloys with slick Dunlops.

Top speed:	152 mph (243 km/h)
0–60 mph (0–95 km/h):	4.9 sec
Engine type:	In-line four
Displacement:	122ci (1,998 cc)
Transmission	6-speed sequential
Max power:	296 bhp (221 kW) @ 8,250 rpm
Max torque:	189 lb ft (225 Nm) @ 7,000rpm
Weight:	2,292 lb (1,042kg)
Economy:	5 mpg (1.8 km/l)

Audi Quattro SWB

Highly regarded as the car of the 1980s, the cutting-edge Quattro turbo brought 4WD to the sportscar market in 1983. In 1981 the car had been homologated for rallying and it took fifth place that year, going on to win Audi its first constructor's rally championship in 1982. The Quattro dominated mid-1980s rally action, especially with this later short wheelbase 306bhp (228kW) 20-valve Sport Quattro. The road-going car was put together using many parts already in the Audi range, such as a 200 turbo front end, the Coupe floorpan and the rear differential from sister company VW. The combination of MacPherson strut suspension all-around plus four-wheel drive made it virtually impossible to unstick a Quattro on the road. The Sport Quattro used Kevlar and glass-fibre panels to reduce weight, while underneath it had Porsche brakes to cope with the extreme performance.

Top speed:	154 mph (246 km/h)
0-60 mph (0–95 km/h):	5.0 sec
Engine type:	In-line five
Displacement:	130 ci (2,133 cc)
Transmission	5-speed manual
Max power:	306 bhp (228 kW) @ 6,700 rpm
Max torque:	258 lb ft (349 Nm) @ 3,700 rpm
Weight:	2,867 lb (1,303 kg)
Economy:	13.1 mpg (4.6 km/l)

Audi RS2

Most remember the RS2 so well that few can recall its predecessor, the 230bhp (172kW) S2 Avant which made the Audi 80 wagon into a very quick yet practical car. However, the RS2 took performance to a whole new level with much involvement from Porsche in its engineering. Starting with an Audi 80 wagon, Porsche tweaked the all strut suspension and added race-spec anti-roll bars and Bilstein shocks. The permanent four-wheel drive system used a central Torsen-type differential to ensure the best grip, and a six-speed close-ratio gearbox was fitted. The brakes were vented discs with four-pot callipers, all from Porsche's 968 model, while the 8x17-inch (203x432mm) rims were straight off a 911. The five-cylinder was Audi, but Porsche added a larger intercooler on the KKK turbo (giving out 16psi boost), larger injectors, a 911 fuel pump, high-lift cams and a low-pressure exhaust.

Top speed:	158 mph (253 km/h)
0–60 mph (0–95 km/h):	4.8 sec
Engine type:	In-line five
Displacement:	136 ci (2,226 cc)
Transmission	6-speed manual
Max power:	315 bhp (235 kW)@ 6,500 rpm
Max torque:	302 lb ft (409 Nm) @ 3,000 rpm
Weight:	3,510 lb (1,595 kg)
Economy:	20 mpg (7.1 km/l)

Audi S4

As Audi's 4WD cars developed, it became apparent they were shooting at a more performance-orientated market. The S4 was one of the most recent cars to harness all-wheel power and it was also one of their most powerful yet stress-free drives. It was basically an A4 sedan, but with the transverse engine removed and a longitudinal V6 mounted in its place. Audi concentrated on making low down power with the new motor, so gave it a small turbo per bank and thus made lag non-existent. It had over 250lb ft (338Nm) from 1,850 through to 3,600 where most street driving is done. Power was put down through a Torsen centre differential and rear limited-slip differential. Double wishbones and fully independent suspension ensured the best cornering on the six-spoke 7.5x17 (203x431mm) alloys with 45-series tyres, while 10 -and 12-inch (254 and 305mm) vented and ABS-assisted discs stopped it very rapidly.

Top speed:	143 mph (230 km/h)
0—60 mph (0–95 km/h):	5.9 sec
Engine type:	V6
Displacement:	163 ci (2,671 cc)
Transmission:	6-speed manual
Max power:	250 bhp (186 kW) @ 5,800 rpm
Max torque:	258 lb ft (349 Nm) @ 1,850 rpm
Weight:	3,593 lb (1,633 kg)
Economy:	22 mpg (7.8 km/l)

Audi TT

Fitting a shortened Golf floorpan underneath their sportscar, Audi created a masterpiece in design with the TT. From the sharp-edged looks through to the heavily stitched leather interior, the car was instantly recognizable as Audi in design. The exterior harked back to the pre-WW2 Auto Union racers, while huge 17-inch (432mm) diameter rims pushed to each corner gave the car an almost futuristic feel. The base engine in the TT was the 110ci (1.8-litre) turbo unit as used in the VW and Audi range, though top was the Quattro with five-valves per cylinder, a KKK K04 turbocharger, new intake manifolds plus a six-speed gearbox to make the most of the 225bhp (168kW). MacPherson struts and a double wishbone rear on the Quattro made for fantastic handling with tremendous grip. However, even the base model offered good road-holding and performance from the punchy turbo motor.

Top speed:	130 mph (208 km/h)
0–60 mph (0–95 km/h):	7.4 sec
Engine type:	In-line four
Displacement:	109 ci (1,781 cc)
Transmission	5-speed manual
Max power:	180 bhp (134 kW) @ 5,500 rpm
Max torque:	173 lb ft (234 Nm) @ 1,950 rpm
Weight:	2,910 lb (1,323 kg)
Economy:	31 mpg (11 km/l)

Audi V8 Quattro

With its successful 4WD system proven years earlier, Audi applied its technology to the interesting V8 Quattro in 1989. The world-class sports saloon took on the competition from BMW and Mercedes and offered a fantastic package. While the body and chassis' roots could be traced back to the early 1980s, the Quattro four-wheel-drive system with front and rear differentials connected via a viscous coupling was state-of-the-art. Same goes for the engine, Audi's first eight-cylinder engine in a mainstream production car. The technological masterpiece was all-aluminium with four belt-driven overhead camshafts and 32 valves. Originally in 225ci (3.7-litre) form, it went to 256ci (4.2 litres) in later models. Wide BBS cross-spoked alloys distinguished the later Quattro V8 4.2 models available from 1992 to 1994, and these represented good value for money as a sport/luxury saloon built for all seasons.

Top speed:	145 mph (232 km/h)
0–60 mph (0–95 km/h):	6.6 sec
Engine type:	V8
Displacement:	217 ci (3,562 cc)
Transmission	4-speed auto
Max power:	240 bhp (179 kW) @ 5,800 rpm
Max torque:	245 lb ft (331 Nm) @ 4,400 rpm
Weight:	3,898 lb (1,772 kg)
Economy:	16 mpg (5.7 km/l)

AUSTIN

Austin Healey 3000

The Donald Healey Motor Company debuted its stunning little sportscar, the 100, at the 1952 Earls Court Motor Show. Using the four-cylinder 159ci (2.6-litre) Austin Atlantic engine, the roadster was competition to Triumph's TR2. Four years later the 100 turned into the 100-Six using Austin's six-cylinder 159ci (2.6-litre) engine. The Austin Healey 3000 MkI came in 1959 with an output of 124bhp (92.5kW). While looking like a sports roadster, Pat Moss proved what a worthy rally car the Healey was too by winning the Liege-Rome-Liege Rally. A re-styled MkII followed for 1961 with a curved screen, wind-up side windows and vertical grille slats. The final MkIII version (1964–1969) was the best, with 150bhp (112kW) and servo brakes. All the Healeys used a ladder-frame cross-braced chassis with wishbone and hard leaf spring suspension. They were a handful, with understeer which could very quickly switch to oversteer.

Top speed:	121 mph (193 km/h)
0–60 mph (0–95 km/h):	10.1 sec
Engine type:	In-line six
Displacement:	178 ci (2,912 cc)
Transmission	4-speed manual with overdrive
Max power:	148 bhp (110 kW) @ 5,250 rpm
Max torque:	165 lb ft (223 Nm) @ 3,500 rpm
Weight:	2,549 lb (1,159 kg)
Economy:	16.8 mpg (5.9 km/l)

Bentley Azure

Using the Continental R as a base, Bentley collaborated with the Italian stylist Pininfarina to come up with the luxurious 1995 two-door convertible Azure. Pininfarina also helped design the folding roof which stowed away neatly behind the rear seats. The car used a strengthened version of the Continental R's monocoque chassis, and to keep their new ideal of 'spirited driving' alive, Bentley put adaptive shock absorbers at each corner and self-levelling suspension at the rear. Braking was handled by 13.4-inch (340mm) discs brakes which were assisted by Bosch ABS. The engine was all about torque, being a turbocharged version of the long-running Cosworth tuned Rolls Royce V8, the Garret turbo running an intercooler too. This remains one of the torquiest production engines ever. It was also one of the biggest four seaters you could buy, being 17.5ft (5.3m) long.

Top speed:	150 mph (240 km/h)
0–60 mph (0–95 km/h):	6.3 sec
Engine type:	V8
Displacement:	412 ci (6,750 cc)
Transmission	4-speed auto
Max power:	385 bhp (287 kW) @ 4,000 rpm
Max torque:	553 lb ft (748 Nm) @ 2,000 rpm
Weight:	5,754 lb (2,615 kg)
Economy:	16 mpg (5.7 km/l)

Bentley Continental R

The handsome 1952 Continental R's fastback styling stopped show-goers in their tracks at the London Motor Show that same year. Such was the cost at the time, however, being many times the average annual wage, it was out of reach to all but the super rich, and in three years of production just 207 were made. The Continental shared its underpinnings with the MkVI Bentley saloon. Independent wishbones suspension at the front and leaf springs out back made a ride that was leisurely, though the car could turn on the pace when required and was remarkably quiet with it, even over the 100mph (160km/h) mark. A 280ci (4.6-litre) straight-six with intake valves mounted overhead and exhaust valves to the side was described by Bentley as 'adequate' and that it was, within a swift but silent grace. Inside was typically gentleman's club, awash with hide and walnut, and extreme luxury.

Top speed:	117 mph (187 km/h)
0–60 mph (0–95 km/h):	13.5 sec
Engine type:	In-line six
Displacement:	278 ci (4,566 cc)
Transmission	4-speed manual
Max power:	N/A
Max torque:	N/A
Weight:	3,543 lb (1,610 kg)
Economy:	16 mpg (5.7 km/l)

Bentley Turbo R/T

Bentley's history is associated with luxury and grace, but another attribute that could be added is high performance. Up until 1982 the company had been more concerned with producing the best car money could buy, but then it turbocharged the Mulsanne. The car was a phenomenal performer for such a heavyweight, and the R/T continued that tradition. To make such a big, luxurious and heavy car go so fast, a lot of power was needed, and thanks to a V8, albeit a basic one with a single in-block cam and two overhead valves per cylinder, displacing close to 427ci (7 litres) and breathed on by a Garret turbo, the R/T goes at the pace you'd expect of a low-slung supercar. Stiff suspension and electronically controlled shocks kept the ride smooth, though the handling was exceptional too. Big 18-inch (457mm) rims went against tradition, but run 265/45 ZR-rated tyres in the R/T's sporting theme.

Top speed:	152 mph (243 km/h)
0–60 mph (0–95 km/h):	6.7 sec
Engine type:	V8
Displacement:	412 ci (6,750 cc)
Transmission	4-speed auto
Max power:	400 bhp (298 kW) @ 4,000 rpm
Max torque:	490 lb ft (663 Nm) @ 2,000 rpm
Weight:	5,450 lb (2,477 kg)
Economy:	12.4 mpg (4.4 km/l)

BMW 2002 Turbo

It was in 1969 that BMW won the European Touring Car Championship with their turbocharged 2002, and it was from that car they developed a street-going version with the 2002 Turbo. The flared arches and racing stripes made it very obviously a circuit-inspired street car, and this was one of few cars at the time to use fuel injection. The street manners weren't so good and tractability wasn't the car's strong point, with the large turbo giving little power until the engine hit 3,800rpm, though by then it summoned an extra 46lb ft (63Nm) of torque (one-third more power) for an incredible hit in the back. This put the car into sub-8-sec territory for the 0–60mph dash, almost unheard of then from anything but a top sportscar. Suspension – MacPherson struts up front and a semi-trailing arm rear with anti-roll bars both ends – kept the car planted on the street, as did the wide alloy wheels.

Top speed:	130 mph (208 km/h)
0–60 mph (0–95 km/h):	7.6 sec
Engine type:	In-line four
Displacement:	121 ci (1,990 cc)
Transmission	5-speed manual
Max power:	170 bhp (126 kW) @ 5,800 rpm
Max torque:	177 lb ft (240 Nm) @ 4,500 rpm
Weight:	2,381 lb (1,082 kg)
Economy:	18.1 mpg (6.4 km/l)

BMW 3.0 CSL

The 1971 CSL was the ultimate derivative of the handsome CSi coupe, made for the European Touring Car Championship. Just 1,000 street versions were needed for homologation and they made them lightweight. An alloy hood, trunk lid and door skins saved weight, while inside fixed bucket seats were fitted along with a sport wheel. The independent suspension was as per the CSi, with MacPherson front struts and a trailing arm rear plus anti-roll bars both ends. The straight-six engine used a single overhead cam and Bosch fuel injection to get 200bhp (268kW), though later racer versions with twin cams and 24 valves had 370bhp (276kW). The aerodynamics were where this car scored best with a huge trunk spoiler to give downforce. The front air dam limited air flow under the car, rubber fins over the hood. Wide 7x14-inch (178x356mm) alloys and 195 tyres gave great roadholding.

Top speed:	133 mph (212 km/h)
0–60 mph (0–95 km/h):	7.6 sec
Engine type:	in-line six
Displacement:	183 ci (3,003 cc)
Transmission	4-speed manual
Max power:	200 bhp (149 kW) @ 5,500 rpm
Max torque:	199 lb ft (269 Nm) @ 4,300 rpm
Weight:	2,889 lb (1,313 kg)
Economy:	16.8 mpg (6 km/l)

BMW 850i

As a grander replacement for the 6-series coupe, the 1989 850i ended up bigger, heavier and more powerful. BMW designed the car to be easy to drive and virtually foolproof. It had both Automatic Stability Control and Traction Control to keep the car on the street in all situations. The former controlled the rear suspension as it incorporated a passive rear-steer system which eliminated any oversteer. The new engine for the flagship model was the same basic unit used in McLaren's F1, albeit a little de-tuned with just under half the output at 300bhp (223kW). In the 850 it was designed to be understressed, smooth and quiet. The swoopy coupe body used pillarless construction but to make up for the loss in strength, it featured longitudinal roll-over bars built into the roof. The underbody was smoothed also, helping produce the excellent 0.29 drag coefficient.

Top speed:	160 mph (256 km/h)
0–60 mph (0–95 km/h):	7.4 sec
Engine type:	V12
Displacement:	304 ci (4,988 cc)
Transmission	Six-speed manual
Max power:	300 bhp (224 kW) @ 5,200 rpm
Max torque:	335 lb ft (456 Nm) @ 4,100 rpm
Weight:	4,149 lb (1,886 kg)
Economy:	20 mpg (7.1 km/l)

BMW Alpina B10

In 1988 BMW launched their all-new 5 Series and soon after that Alpina, a German tuning firm specializing in BMWs, set about a 535i model. Starting with the suspension, they lowered it by half an inch then added Bilstein shocks and stronger anti-roll bars. To further improve the handling, Alpina 8x17-inch (203x432mm) 20-spoke alloys were fitted, which made the car stand out as the 535i came with 15-inch (381mm) wheels. Body styling was kept to a minimum, with a deep front spoiler and subtle trunk spoiler plus Alpina badges. The drive train was modified by taking the engine up in compression and giving it a hotter camshaft and hand-ported cylinder head. A twin turbocharged Bi-Turbo version was available which made 360bhp (268kW). To further improve acceleration, the rear end gears were changed, bringing the top end speed down, but it was still a very capable high-speed tourer.

Top speed:	157 mph (251 km/h)
0–60 mph (0–95 km/h):	7.0 sec
Engine type:	In-line six
Displacement:	209 ci (3,430 cc)
Transmission	5-speed manual
Max power:	254 bhp (189 kW) @ 6,000 rpm
Max torque:	240 lb ft (325 Nm) @ 4,000 rpm
Weight:	3,395 lb (1,543 kg)
Economy:	21 mpg (7.4 km/l)

BMW M Roadster

When BMW launched the Z3 in 1995, it came with a 140bhp (104kW) four-cylinder engine. People complained that a more powerful version wasn't available, and BMW answered their calls the following year by launching the 171ci (2.8-litre) straight-six model, then hinted at what could be with a concept M Roadster at the Geneva Motor Show, Switzerland. A year later with strong demand, the M Roadster was in production with the M3's straight-six under the hood. The BMW theory of keeping the driving and steering wheels separate continued with this model which had M3 front suspension, rear suspension from the previous 3 Series BMW and uprated springs and shocks. The double VANOS system varied both intake and exhaust timing, for greater flexibility. The car was limited to 240bhp (179kW) in the USA but the same as the M3, 321bhp (239kW), in European versions.

Top speed:	137 mph (220 km/h)
0–60 mph (0–95 km/h):	5.2 sec
Engine type:	In-line six
Displacement:	192 ci (3,152 cc)
Transmission	5-speed manual
Max power:	240 bhp (179 kW) @ 6,000 rpm
Max torque:	236 lb ft (320 Nm) @ 3,800 rpm
Weight:	3,084 lb (1,402 kg)
Economy:	27 mpg (9.6 km/l)

BMW M1

Started in 1972 with the intention of making a Group 4 endurance racing car, the M1 stumbled off the blocks with a re-design just months after the original concept drawings. Giorgetto Giugiaro came up with the M1's production look and it was launched in 1978. Unfortunately, due to the steel chassis and sheet steel reinforcement, even with a glass-fibre body the car was too heavy for competition. On the street the mid-mounted engine was mildly tuned to 277bhp (207kW), being the straight-six from the 1960s models, which had proved immensely strong. In race tune up to 700bhp (522kW) was possible in turbo form for Group 5 racing. Race suspension on the M1 consisted of adjustable double wishbones all around, and though the clutch and brake pedals were hard, the steering feel and response was typically BMW, and so very good, while the ride quality was firm.

Top speed:	162 mph (260 km/h)
0–60 mph (0–-95 km/h):	5.7 sec
Engine type:	In-line six
Displacement:	211 ci (3,453 cc)
Transmission	5-speed manual
Max power:	277 bhp (207 kW) @ 6,500 rpm
Max torque:	239 lb ft (323 Nm) @ 5,000 rpm
Weight:	3,122 lb (1,419 kg)
Economy:	12.9 mpg (4.6 km/l)

BMW M3

Originally launched in 1988 as a homologation special bred for the track, the M3 developed in the 1990s with the 1993 E36 3-series. The combination of refinement, handling, plus awesome power made it immensely sellable. A MacPherson strut front and multi-link rear suspension did most of the work, but wide 17-inch (432mm) alloys and ultra-low profile tyres sharpened the car's steering without compromising ride quality. The powerplant was very high-tech, featuring twin overhead camshafts and BMW's VANOS variable valve timing to improve low-end torque whilst allowing 7,500rpm, even though the torque peak was much lower. Helping make the most of the power was a six-speed manual gearbox and traction control, but even with the latter switched off, the car remained very controllable in a slide. Few sports coupes have offered such performance and practicality.

Top speed:	140 mph (224 km/h)
0-60 mph (0-95 km/h):	5.6 sec
Engine type:	In-line six
Displacement:	195 ci (3,201 cc)
Transmission:	6-speed manual
Max power:	321 bhp (239 kW) @ 7,400 rpm
Max torque:	258 lb ft (349 Nm) @ 3,250 rpm
Weight:	3,352 lb (1,523 kg)
Economy:	19.6 mpg (6.9 km/l)

BMW M3 1987

To homologate their car for Group A racing, BMW were required to build 5,000 road-going versions of their M3. The car appeared with a 192bhp (143kW) four-cylinder and was a success. The independent suspension layout is the same as the regular 3 Series, with MacPherson struts and a semi-trailing arm rear design, but the springs, shocks and bushes were uprated, along with the anti-roll bars, while up front the castor was increased to improve high-speed stability. The vented disc brakes were also increased in size and finally a limited slip differential was added. The engine had a forged steel crank, all-new alloy head with four valves per cylinder, and with short stroke/ large bore design, it could rev beyond 7,000 rpm. Side blister helped cover the wider wheels, but what isn't so obvious is the re-angled rear screen and fatter pillars, which gave a stiffer bodyshell.

Top speed:	141 mph (225 km/h)
0–60 mph (0–95 km/h):	6.9 sec
Engine type:	In-line four
Displacement:	140 ci (2,302 cc(
Transmission	5-speed manual
Max power:	192 bhp (143 kW) @ 6,750 rpm
Max torque:	170 lb ft (230 Nm) @ 4,750 rpm
Weight:	2,857 lb (1,299 kg)
Economy:	22 mpg (7.8 km/l)

BMW

BMW M5

With the launch of the second-generation 5-Series, BMW created a much better car with a more rigid bodyshell and excellent MacPherson strut/semi trailing arm front and rear suspension. It was a great basis on which to model the new M5 too, as all the M division had to do was lower and uprate the springs and shocks, plus fit thicker anti-roll bars, for a brilliant handling machine. Larger 8x17-inch (203x432mm) wheels at each corner allowed the fitting of 12-inch (305mm) brakes all around, which gave near-perfect brakes for the heavyweight sedan. The engine was another derived from BMW's M1 supercar, with a new forged crankshaft but the same twin-cam 24v alloy head which allowed it to rev past 7,000rpm. Post-1992 cars had 232ci (3.8 litres) and 340bhp (254kW), plus a six-speed transmission, larger brakes and 18-inch (257mm) wheels, formidable road cars, yet relaxing if required.

Top speed:	155 mph (248 km/h)
0–60 mph (0–95 km/h):	6.5 sec
Engine type:	In-line six
Displacement:	216 ci (3,535 cc)
Transmission	5-speed manual
Max power:	310 bhp (231 kW) @ 6,900 rpm
Max torque:	266 lb ft (360 Nm) @ 4,750 rpm
Weight:	3,804 lb (1,729 kg)
Economy:	16 mpg (5.7 km/l)

BMW M5 1985

Though an M535i was launched in 1980 with the same body style, it had very little Motorsport division technical input. That version had only a single cam, but for the 1985 M5, the engine from the M1 supercar was used, albeit without dry sump lubrication. It had a high compression ratio, cross-flow aluminium cylinder head with larger inlet and exhaust ports, twin overhead camshafts, Bosch fuel injection, an oil cooler and low restriction dual exhaust. It was too much for the standard 5-speed, so BMW had Getrag produce a special close-ratio version with dog-leg first gear. The suspension used a patented Track Link system at rear, but was conventional MacPherson strut up front with shorter springs and uprated shocks all around. Massive four-wheel vented discs with ABS meant excellent stopping power. Inside the driving position was perfect and there were power seats plus air-con.

Top speed:	147 mph (235 km/h)
0–60 mph (0–95 km/h):	6.0 sec
Engine type:	In-line six
Displacement:	210 ci (3,453 cc)
Transmission	5-speed manual
Max power:	256 bhp (191 kW) @ 6,500 rpm
Max torque:	243 lb ft (329 Nm) @ 4,500 rpm
Weight:	3,420 lb (1,554 kg)
Economy:	20 mpg (7.1 km/l)

BMW M6

BMW's top 6-series model, the 635CSi, was a looker and performer when it was launched in 1983. Using that car as a basis, BMW's Motorsport division revamped it and produced the M6, also known as the M635CSi throughout Europe. Underneath the suspension was re-calibrated with Bilstein gas shocks, stiffer springs and anti-roll bars. A lower ride-height increased stability in corners and a re-located battery (to the trunk) helped weight distribution. The 24-valve engine, taken from the defunct M1 supercar, used a light-alloy head with central spark plugs for maximum combustion power. MacPherson struts and a multi-link rear kept the handling predictable, while a close-ratio transmission kept the engine in the power band. Bringing the most powerful BMW of the 1980s down in speed was the job of 11-inch (280mm) discs. Inside the car had air-con, on-board computer and leather.

Top speed:	158 mph (253 km/h)
0–60 mph (0–95 km/h):	6.0 sec
Engine type:	In-line six
Displacement:	210 ci (3,453 cc)
Transmission	5-speed manual
Max power:	286 bhp (213 kW) @ 6,500 rpm
Max torque:	251 lb ft (340 Nm) @ 4,500 rpm
Weight:	3,329 lb (1,513 kg)
Economy:	18 mpg (6.4 km/l)

BMW Z3

While the Z1 roadster concept had had 8,000 cars built in 1986, it was only ever really a testbed for BMW's Z-axle arrangement. It did show, however, that people were keen for the Munich-based company to produce a roadster for the masses. Competition from the likes of Mazda and Toyota with their roadsters also meant the time was right for the 1996 Z3. Using the usual BMW layout of a front-engined, rear-drive layout, the long and sloping Z3 hood hid a 116ci (1.8-litre) engine. The car cleverly used parts from other BMWs including the front suspension from the 3-series sedan and the rear semi-trailing arm set-up from the 3-Series Compact, though both were modified for a wider track. The 24-valve engine had adjustable intake runners to promote torque at low rpm and extra bhp higher up. It also was designed to minimize friction and gave the roadster good fuel economy.

Top speed:	116 mph (185 km/h)
0–60 mph (0–95 km/h):	8.2 sec
Engine type:	In-line four
Displacement:	116 ci (1,895 cc)
Transmission:	5-speed manual
Max power:	138 bhp (103 kW) @ 6,000 rpm
Max torque:	133 lb ft (180 Nm) @ 4,300 rpm
Weight:	2,732 lb (1,242 kg)
Economy:	29.4 mpg (10.4 km/l)

BMW M Coupe

Adding a roof to an already successful Z3 roadster seemed logical, yet the almost estate-like M Coupe didn't win over everyone straight away. The proportions took some getting used to, though this was better in 'M' guise. The roof also added rigidity to the structure, making it some 2.5 times stiffer torsionally than the roadster. The effect was to sharpen up the car's responses dramatically. Understeer was built in, but with so much power it could be corrected quickly with the traction control off. The engine used twin overhead camshafts and BMW's VANOS variable valve system, and could make 321bhp (239kW) in Europe. Huge 12.4-inch (315mm) vented discs were fitted all around and inspired much confidence, as did the anti-roll bars front and rear which keep the body virtually horizontal. Inside the car was typically 'M', with figure-hugging seats, and sports wheel in leather and Alcantara.

Top speed:	139 mph (222 km/h)
0–60 mph (0–95 km/h):	5.1 sec
Engine type:	In-line six
Displacement:	192 ci (3,152 cc)
Transmission	5-speed manual
Max power:	240 bhp (179 kW) @ 6,000 rpm
Max torque:	236 lb ft (320 Nm) @ 3,800 rpm
Weight:	3,131 lb (1,423 kg)
Economy:	21 mpg (7.4 km/l)

Buick GNX

Onlookers could be fooled into thinking the Buick GNX was just another US coupe-styled car without a performance bias. That's without knowing it had help from ASC/McLaren in developing its turbocharged V6 engine, which put out a lot of horsepower and even bigger surge of torque. Initially, the car started life in 1978 as a Buick Regal with turbo V6 producing just 150hp (112kW). Four years later just 215 Grand Nationals (the 'GN' in the name) made it on the street and by 1984 power was up to 200bhp (149kW). Revised engine management and an intercooler pushed output to 235bhp (175kW) for 1986, then a year later came the association with McLaren and push to 276bhp (206kW) with huge torque. Although just 547 made it in this guise, the GNX was worth finding. It had modified uprated suspension for better handling, and a Panhard rod to increase cornering capability.

Top speed:	124 mph (198 km/h)
0–60 mph (0–95 km/h):	5.5 sec
Engine type:	V6
Displacement:	231 ci (3,785 cc)
Transmission:	4-speed auto
Max power:	276 bhp (206 kW) @ 4,400 rpm
Max torque:	360 lb ft (487 Nm) @ 3,000 rpm
Weight:	3,545 lb (1,611 kg)
Economy:	23 mpg (8.1 km/l)

Buick GS 400

Buick loaded its GS model with luxuries, but also gave it a powerful engine so it could hold its own amongst the street-fighter muscle cars of 1969. The drive was leisurely and the handling would turn to understeer when pushed, but in a straight line, it was incredible. Its 400ci (6.6-litre) 'Nailhead' engine is a bored and stroked version of the 340. The 400 got 11:1 compression ratio, a four-barrel carb, low-restriction exhaust and cold-air hood induction which was claimed to an 8 per cent increase in power. An uprated GM Turbo-Hydramatic three-speed auto was the transmission, and further back was a Positraction limited-slip differential to help put the power down through skinny bias-ply tyres. The fastback coupe was the most body style, though the convertible has remained the most desirable, as just 1,776 were made. In 1970, the GS 400 was replaced by the GS 455.

Top speed:	125 mph (200 km/h)
0–60 mph (0–95 km/h):	5.8 sec
Engine type:	V8
Displacement:	400 ci (6,555 cc)
Transmission	3-speed auto
Max power:	345 bhp (257 kW) @ 4,800 rpm
Max torque:	440 lb ft (595 Nm) @ 3,200 rpm
Weight:	3,594 lb (1,633 kg)
Economy:	14 mpg (5 km/l)

Buick GSX

While the mid-sized GS 455 was enough for some, for others it was too sedate, so Buick launched the fearsome 1970 GSX. This car had all the power of the regular GS 455, but had improved suspension and more dynamic looks, with Magnum 500 wheels, spoilers, scoops and stripes. The suspension used independent wishbones at the front and coil springs out back (all uprated), but anti-roll bars at both ends improved cornering while 11-inch (279mm) discs and finned rear drums upgraded the brakes. While the 455ci (7.5-litre) was the biggest engine Buick produced, and standard in the base GSX, the majority of buyers went for the Stage 1 option, which had a four-barrel Quadrajet carb, high-lift camshaft, larger valves and a 10.5:1 compression ratio. With a true rating of 400bhp (298kW) and massive torque of over 500lb ft (677Nm), it was one of the most powerful in the muscle-car era.

Top speed:	123 mph (197 km/h)
0–60 mph (0–95 km/h):	5.5 sec
Engine type:	V8
Displacement:	455 ci (7,456 cc)
Transmission	4-speed manual
Max power:	360 bhp (268 kW) @ 4,600 rpm
Max torque:	510 lb ft (690 Nm) @ 2,800 rpm
Weight:	3,561 lb (1,618 kg)
Economy:	7.1 mpg (2.5 km/l)

Buick Riviera Gran Sport

Designed by Jerry Hirshberg, the 1971 Riviera broke away from Buick's conservative look which had been associated with their previous cars. It was bigger and heavier than previous models, but the dramatic styling which brought the car to a point at eight ends, more prominent at the rear, led to the car being nicknamed the 'boat tail Buick'. It rode on a separate perimeter chassis, with an independent wishbone front and live axle rear supported on coil springs. The Gran Sport package meant stiffer springs, revised shock valving, and a thick front anti-roll bar, With fuel at just 30 cents a gallon, Buick had no qualms putting in their 455ci (7.5-litre) big-block engine, which with its long stroke made a lot of torque and the car more of a luxury cruiser than straight-line performer. The car lived for just two years before being re-styled, then dropped altogether.

Top speed:	120 mph (192 km/h)
0–60 mph (0–95 km/h):	8.1 sec
Engine type:	V8
Displacement:	455 ci (7,456 cc)
Transmission	3-speed auto
Max power:	330 bhp (246 kW) @ 4,600 rpm
Max torque:	455 lb ft (616 Nm) @ 2,800 rpm
Weight:	4,325 lb (1,965 kg)
Economy:	8 mpg (2.8 km/l)

Cadillac Series 62

General Motors needed a response to Chrysler's growing fins on the 1950s cars, and they had famous Stylist Harley Earl apply his ideas to a new Cadillac model, called the Series 62. Earl took much of his influence from the aero industry, and it showed. Huge tail fins, the biggest to appear on any car ever, stood to a point and featured bullet tail light lenses, while the front fender and grille looked like a reflection of itself, with four shotgun-style lenses, the upper two of which automatically came on at dusk and dipped from high to low beam when they detected oncoming traffic. The car used coil springs and telescopic shocks, but the top Eldorado models could be ordered with air suspension. The all-cast iron big block was enlarged for 1959 and came in two states of tune, either a 325bhp (242kW) single carb version, or the 345bhp (257kW) triple carb unit.

Top speed:	121 mph (194 km/h)
0–60 mph (0–95 km/h):	11.0 sec
Engine type:	V8
Displacement:	390 ci (6,390 cc)
Transmission	3-speed auto
Max power:	325 bhp (242 kW) @ 4,800 rpm
Max torque:	435 lb ft (589 Nm) @ 3,400 rpm
Weight:	4,885 lb (2,220 kg)
Economy:	13 mpg (4.6 km/l)

Callaway Corvette Speedster

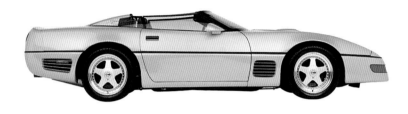

Reeves Callaway's fitting of twin turbos to an Alfa Romeo GTV6 impressed Chevrolet bosses. With his Alfa boasting an output of 230bhp (172kW), well up on the standard car, he was asked to do the same to a Corvette. Three years later the Callaway 'Sledgehammer' appeared, an 880bhp (656kW) supercar with the body re-designed by French-Canadian stylist, Paul Deutschman. The Speedster's debut at the Los Angeles Auto Show in 1991 led to 50 orders. Underneath the dramatic low body, with 7 inches (178mm) chopped out of the stock Corvette's screen, was adjustable coilover suspension at each corner, plus uprated Callaway/Brembo brakes using vented discs and four-piston callipers. The engine was stripped and fitted with an upgraded crankshaft and new pistons to allow the fitting of twin RotoMaster turbos with intercooling. Callaway continues his modified Corvette business today.

Top speed:	185 mph (296 km/h)
0–60 mph (0–95 km/h):	4.5 sec
Engine type:	V8
Displacement:	350 ci (5,700 cc)
Transmission	6-speed manual
Max power:	420 bhp (313 kW) @ 4,250 rpm
Max torque:	562 lb ft (761 Nm) @ 2,500 rpm
Weight:	3,200 lb (1,455 kg)
Economy:	10.4 mpg (3.7 km/l)

Caterham 21

It was like a Seven with clothes on, and was the Surrey, UK-based manufacturer's attempt at a more civilized version of the roadster, without losing any of the driving thrill of the 'naked' Seven. The composite body hid a tubular steel spaceframe just like the Seven's, the only difference being increased front track width to match the rear. Adjustable slim-line front wishbones with a coil-over shock arrangement, plus de Dion rear with A-frame, kept handling responsive and to the weight goal of two-thirds of a ton. The convertible has a sparse but comfortable interior, but there was no doubt about the intentions of this car, with Rover's highly acclaimed K-series unit up front. It was available in basic 97ci (1.6-litre) 118bhp (88kW) form right up to a 110ci (1.8-litre) 190bhp (141kW) VHPD (Very High Performance Derivative) version, the 'slower' doing 6.7 seconds in the 60mph dash.

Top speed:	127 mph (203 km/h)
0–60 mph (0–95 km/h):	6.7 sec
Engine type:	In-line four
Displacement:	97 ci (1,588 cc)
Transmission	6-speed manual
Max power:	136 bhp (102 kW) @ 7,000 rpm
Max torque:	115 lb ft (155 Nm) @ 5,000 rpm
Weight:	1,466 lb (666 kg)
Economy:	23.5 mpg (8.3 km/l)

Caterham Seven JPE

The Super 7 version of Caterham's lightweight roadster steadily developed through the 1970s and 1980s, but in 1992 the Surrey, UK-based company pulled out all the stops with their limited edition Seven JPE. The car used a tubular steel spaceframe chassis with much triangulation to create a rigid structure. Double wishbones up front and a de Dion rear with lower A-frame was used as per other Sevens, while steering was quick with a rack and pinion that needed two turns lock to lock. The highly tuned Vauxhall 122ci (2-litre) 16v engine, developed with the help of F1 driver Jonathan Palmer, hence the 'JP' in the title ('E' for Evolution), used Weber fuel injection, and each motor was built at Swindon Racing Engines. The car held the world record for 0–60mph (0–95km/h) for some time, and could do the dash and brake back to a standstill again before a Ferrari F40 hit 60mph (95km/h).

Top speed:	147 mph (235 km/h)
0–60 mph (0–95 km/h):	3.7 sec
Engine type:	In-line four
Displacement:	122 ci (1,998 cc)
Transmission	5-speed manual
Max power:	250 bhp (186 kW)@ 7,750 rpm
Max torque:	186 lb ft (252 Nm) @ 6,250 rpm
Weight:	1,169 lb (531 kg)
Economy:	20 mpg (7.1 km/l)

Caterham Super 7 HPC

Much the same as Caterham's other models in the chassis and body, the Super 7 HPC differed in that it used a Vauxhall engine for the first time, having used mostly Ford and Rover powerplants prior to the HPC's launch in 1992. The Surrey, England based company utilized their strong steel spaceframe chassis under the HPC, with built-in roll-over bar that also serves to stiffen the rear end. The all-independent suspension used a double A-arm front set-up and de Dion rear axle, and while there were vented discs all around, they weren't huge because the car was so lightweight. Alloy 7x 16-inch (178x406mm) rims with Goodyear Eagle tyres provided all the road-contact the car needed; it took an awful lot to unstick it in corners. Power came from GM's British arm Vauxhall, the 122ci (2-litre) 16v being torquey and with twin Weber sidedraught carburettors to rev easily to 7,500rpm.

Top speed:	126 mph (202 km/h)
0–60 mph (0–95 km/h):	5.4 sec
Engine type:	In-line four
Displacement:	122 ci (1,998 cc)
Transmission	5-speed manual
Max power:	175 bhp (130 kW) @ 6,000 rpm
Max torque:	155 lb ft (210 Nm) @ 4,800 rpm
Weight:	1,385 lb (630 kg)
Economy:	19.5 mpg (6.9 km/l)

Chevrolet 454SS

With fuel concerns diminishing in the mid-1980s, manufacturers began to produce more powerful cars again and with America's pick-up obsession, a new market was soon born: the muscle truck. Chevrolet, having long been a maker of pick-ups, was one of the first to get a grip on the market with their 1989 454 C1500 truck, which had been re-styled just a year before, so looked bang up to date. Underneath the SS454 was still very trucklike, with a strong ladder frame chassis and carlike double wishbone suspension, but a leaf spring rear. All spring rates were uprated and Bilstein shocks took place of the stock ones. Also modified was the steering, with quicker gearing to help the handling. The 454ci (7.4-litre) came from the standard C/K 3/4 and 1-ton pick-ups, and with its long stroke was designed for low rpm torque delivery. Rear end 4.10:1 gears were good for rapid acceleration.

Top speed:	120 mph (193km/h)
0–60 mph (0–95 km/h):	7.2 sec
Engine type:	V8
Displacement:	454 ci (7,440 cc)
Transmission	4-speed auto
Max power:	255 bhp (190 kW) @ 4,000 rpm
Max torque:	405 lb ft (548 Nm) @ 2,400 rpm
Weight:	4,535 lb (2,061 kg)
Economy:	10 mpg (3.5 km/l)

Chevrolet Bel Air 409

Everything about the 1962 Bel Air looked plain, but to drive it was far different. Chevrolet brought it out as the horsepower wars were hotting up in the early 1960s, fitting the 409ci (6.7-litre) big-block V8 and creating a car which could chirp the tyres in every gear. In 1962 the engine was rated at 380bhp (283kW), but with twin four-barrel carburettors this went to 409bhp (305kW). Though the 409 could be ordered in any body style, most chose the coupe because of its 'bubble-top' looks and light weight. More pounds could be shed by ordering aluminium front panels from the factory; in fact Chevy made 12 cars like this which were aimed squarely at drag racers. Inside, the car was sparse as most buyers were interested only in speed, though there was a small steering column-mounted 7,000rpm rev counter. The car was so good it won the NHRA S/S (Super Stock) drag-racing championship in 1962.

Top speed:	115 mph (184 km/h)
0–60 mph (0–95 km/h):	7.3 sec
Engine type:	V8
Displacement:	409 ci (6,702 cc)
Transmission	4-speed manual
Max power:	380 bhp (283 kW) @ 6,000 rpm
Max torque:	420 lb ft (569 Nm) @ 3,200 rpm
Weight:	3,480 lb (1,582 kg)
Economy:	14 mpg (5 km/l)

Chevrolet Bel Air 1957

Stylist Harley Earl was responsible for the 1957 Chevy, and he created a car which became an American icon. His philosophy was to make cars lower, wider and longer, but he still showed aeroplane influence at this time, with the large rear fins, hood fins and large side spears. The grille looked like a huge, gaping mouth sucking in air for the engine, though that sat back some way from the front. Perhaps the most famous V8 of all time, the small-block Chevy, was used under the hood, having grown in size by then to 283ci (4.6-litre) from the original 265ci (4.3-litre). It gave the Bel Air exceptional performance, and even the handling was ahead of the competition, despite basic underpinnings of a double-wishbone front and leaf sprung live rear axle. While the Bel Air had many options, one popular one was the continental kit which extended the rear fender and re-located the licence plate.

Top speed:	115 mph (184 km/h)
0–60 mph (0–95 km/h):	8.5 sec
Engine type:	V8
Displacement:	283 ci (4,637 cc)
Transmission	3-speed manual
Max power:	220 bhp (164 kW) @ 4,800 rpm
Max torque:	270 lb ft (366 Nm) @ 2,800 rpm
Weight:	3,409 lb (1,550 kg)
Economy:	20 mpg (7.1 km/l)

Chevrolet Bel Air Modified

Because of its iconic nature and easy tuneability, the 1957 Chevy was modified from the day it was produced. However, a tell-tale sign of Harley Earl's timeless design is that few people chose to heavily modify the bodywork, instead concentrating on making the car go, stop and corner better. This car retains the original chassis, albeit restored, but has new suspension arms and 2-inch (51mm) drop spindles, as well as lowering springs to get the nose down. Custom semi-elliptical leaf springs drop the rear to match while lowering the centre of gravity to aid handling. Powering the car is still the job of a small-block Chevy, though it's heavily modified with a B&M Roots-type supercharger. To help put the power down, a narrowed 9-inch (228mm) Ford axle with Posi-traction limited-slip differential sits at the rear, along with 13-inch (330mm) wide Mickey Thompson street/strip tyres.

Top speed:	147 mph (235 km/h)
0–60 mph (0—95 km/h):	3.9 sec
Engine type:	V8
Displacement:	350 ci (5,735 cc)
Transmission	3-speed auto
Max power:	420 bhp (313 kW) @ 5,400 rpm
Max torque:	435 lb ft (589 Nm) @ 2,500 rpm
Weight:	3,197 lb (1,453 kg)
Economy:	9.4 mpg (3.3 km/l)

Chevrolet Camaro Z28 1968

General Motors designed the Camaro to compete with Ford's Mustang, but with the likes of the Shelbys around, GM needed more power in their car. Also, in order to race in the Trams Am series, GM had to build 1,000 road models, though at the end of 1968 the new Z28 had gone well past 7,000 sales. The car needed a high-rpm race-type engine with less than 305ci (5 litres) so Chevrolet combined their 4-inch (102mm) bore 327 block with a short-stroke 3-inch (76mm) forged crank, similar to the one in their 283. With a high compression of 11:1, large valve heads and high-lift cam, it revved well, and though rated at 290bhp (216kW), output was closer to 350bhp (261kW). Handling was improved by quickening the steering, fitting harder brake-linings, stiffening the rear leaf springs, and uprating shocks. The car had a three-speed auto but the Muncie four-speed manual was often fitted.

Top speed:	123 mph (197 km/h)
0–60 mph (0–95 km/h):	6.5 sec
Engine type:	V8
Displacement:	302 ci (4,948 cc)
Transmission	4-speed manual
Max power:	290 bhp (216 kW) @ 5,800 rpm
Max torque:	290 lb ft (393 Nm) @ 4,200 rpm
Weight:	3,528 lb (1,604 kg)
Economy:	15.7 mpg (5.6 km/l)

Chevrolet Camaro Z28 1992

The third-generation Camaro came in 1982 and lasted for 10 years, growing in power during that period and having many of the traits which made the Camaro popular from its launch in 1967. As always, the Z28 was the performance option, and in 1992, the 25th anniversary of the model, the car got a Heritage appearance package in either red, white or black, and continued the use of bolt-on spoilers and side skirt to modernize its appearance. The live rear axle had a limited-slip differential and 3.42:1 gears, and was located on longitudinal links plus a Panhard rod for improved cornering. The 305ci (5-litre) V8 had electronic Tuned Port fuel injection with an individual runner for each cylinder, and Chevrolet made the car into more of a driver's machine by fitting a 5-speed manual gearbox as standard. Production cars could do 14-second quarter-miles.

Top speed:	137 mph (219 km/h)
0–60 mph (0—95 km/h):	6.5 sec
Engine type:	V8
Displacement:	305 ci (4,998 cc)
Transmission	5-speed manual
Max power:	235 bhp (175 kW) @ 4,400 rpm
Max torque:	300 lb ft (406 Nm) @ 3,200 rpm
Weight:	3,105 lb (1,411 kg)
Economy:	13.8 mpg (4.9 km/l)

Chevrolet Camaro Z28 1997

By 1993 it was the turn of the fourth-generation Camaro to carry the torch for the long-lived muscle car. Chevrolet gave the buyer a lot of bang-for-the-buck with an original sale price of under $20,000. While still featuring monocoque construction with chassis subframes at each end, the Z28 did use gas shocks all around and a torque arm, plus Panhard rod at the rear to locate the live axle very well. The small-block Chevy under the hood was the very same which had appeared for years in the Chevrolet line-up, though in this LT1 guise it was somewhat modernized with multi-point fuel injection, aluminium heads, roller cam, 10.4:1 compression and an Optispark ignition system. Best of all, the car came with a six-speed manual to exploit all the available power. To keep the Z28 lightweight, all bar the rear fenders, hood and roof were plastic.

Top speed:	155 mph (248 km/h)
0–60 mph (0–95 km/h):	6.1 sec
Engine type:	V8
Displacement:	350 ci (5,735 cc)
Transmission:	6-speed manual
Max power:	275 bhp (205 kW) @ 5,000 rpm
Max torque:	325 lb ft (440 Nm) @ 2,400 rpm
Weight:	3,475 lb (1,580 kg)
Economy:	19 mpg (6.7 km/l)

Chevrolet Camaro SS 1998

T he 'SS' stood for Super Sport and the name had been used some years previous to the 1998 Camaro SS. Back in 1967 the original Camaro SS got you the 295bhp (220kW) Turbo-Fire 350ci (5.7-litre) V8 engine and special SS hood, badges and stripes. In the more recent version, output didn't seem much higher, but the all new aluminium engine could scream the Camaro SS to 60mph (95km/h) in a shade over 5 seconds and down the quarter-mile in 13 seconds. The aluminium LS1 engine featured ram air on the SS to help boost power from the usual 305bhp (227kW). At the rear the live axle remained which could upset handling, but only on the worst streets. Up front it used unequal-length wishbones, and with uprated suspension plus the 9x17-inch (229x432mm) alloys and 275/40 tyres, this could pull 0.9gs on the skid pad. It is one of Chevrolet's fastest muscle cars of all time.

Top speed:	161 mph (258 km/h)
0–60 mph (0–95 km/h):	5.2 sec
Engine type:	V8
Displacement:	347 ci (5,686 cc)
Transmission	6-speed manual
Max power:	320 bhp (238 kW) @ 5,200 rpm
Max torque:	325 lb ft (440 Nm) @ 4,400 rpm
Weight:	3,593 lb (1,633 kg)
Economy:	27 mpg (9.6 km/l)

Chevrolet Camaro ZL1

This car represented the zenith of Chevy's muscle cars. It's one of the most powerful Camaros ever, and also the most exclusive, with a production numbering just 69. In the 1960s Chevrolet supported the Automotive Manufacturers Association's ban by using over 400ci (6.9-litre) engines only in Corvettes or its full-size cars. However, one of Chevrolet's employees, Vince Piggins, found a loophole in the ban and created the ZL1. The car started as an SS396 model, with F41 uprated suspension, front discs, a cowl induction hood and exclusive engine unlike anything else Chevrolet had. It was an all-aluminium 427ci (7.2-litre) V8 which weighed the same as a small-block, hence the handling remained very good. However, the awesome power meant the car could run 11-second quarter-miles with racing tyres. Collectors have paid anything from $150,000 to $250,000 for a ZL1.

Top speed:	125 mph (201 km/h)
0–60 mph (0–95 km/h):	5.3 sec
Engine type:	V8
Displacement:	427 ci (6,997 cc)
Transmission	4-speed manual
Max power:	430 bhp (321 kW) @ 5,200 rpm
Max torque:	450 lb ft (609 Nm) @ 4,400 rpm
Weight:	3,300 lb (1,500 kg)
Economy:	7 mpg (2.5 km/l)

Chevrolet Corvette 1953–1955

The Corvette didn't make a great start sales-wise, but GM persevered. It debuted at the 1953 GM Motorama Show, and production began later that year, all cars being white. In 1954 several more colours were available plus the car had an increase in power. The Corvette was the world's first production car to be made out of glass-fibre and it was a daring move. Underneath it used a separate steel chassis with an X-brace which added stiffness along with the one-piece floor moulding. Also new in the Corvette were the leaf springs mounted outside the chassis rails. The straight-six engine came from the sedan range, and under the name 'Blue Flame Special' it used a high-lift cam, higher compression ratio, modified head and double valve springs to cope with increased rpm use. The car was almost shelved in 1954, and it was only the new small-block V8 engine that saved it.

Top speed:	107 mph (172 km/h)
0–60 mph (0–95 km/h):	11.0 sec
Engine type:	In-line six
Displacement:	235 ci (3,850 cc)
Transmission	2-speed auto
Max power:	150 bhp (112 kW) @ 4,200 rpm
Max torque:	223 lb ft (302 Nm) @ 2,400 rpm
Weight:	2,851 lb (1,295 kg)
Economy:	16 mpg (5.7 km/l)

Chevrolet Corvette 1956–1962

Introduced in 1956 in V8 form, the Corvette established Chevrolet as kings of the US automotive world with a range of cars to suit every taste and pocket. By 1958 the car had been re-styled more aggressively and was both wider and longer. The famous small-block Chevy engine, which started out at 265ci (4.5 litres) V8, grew to 283ci (4.6 litres) by 1958, and by 1962 it was bored and stroked to 327ci (5.4 litres). The significance of this V8 engine can't be underestimated as, in fuel injected form at least, it made the Corvette one of the most powerful sportscars in the world and certainly one of the quickest at the time. Unfortunately the brakes and handling didn't match, though the steering was precise enough to catch the sudden oversteer the Corvette suffered from when pushed. But the 1956–1962 car was more about style, being inspired by fighter planes of the time.

Top speed:	135 mph (217 km/h)
0–60 mph (0–95 km/h):	6.1 sec
Engine type:	V8
Displacement:	327 ci (5,385 cc)
Transmission	4-speed manual
Max power:	360 bhp (268 kW) @ 6,000 rpm
Max torque:	352 lb ft (476 Nm) @ 4,000 rpm
Weight:	2,942 lb (1,337 kg)
Economy:	12.4 mpg (4.4 km/l)

Chevrolet Corvette Grand Sport

With a fifth-generation Corvette about to be launched, Chevrolet had to send off the previous car in style, thus the 1996 Grand Sport was conceived. It harked back to the 1960s' Grand Sport race cars which had success in the SCCA circuit series, with a striped paint scheme and many upgrades. The suspension used thicker anti-roll bars, firmer springs and shocks to create more sure-footed handling. Larger 315/35 tyres at the rear were fitted to cope with the extra power and, to get these on, special arch extensions were needed. The 405bhp (302kW) LT-5 engine would have been ideal, had it not been dropped by Chevrolet the previous year. Hence, they used the 350ci (5.7-litre) LT-4 and added modified pistons, large valves, modified cylinder heads, a hot cam and roller rockers. Behind it a ZF six-speed manual transmission was deemed necessary, and it suited the new engine perfectly.

Top speed:	168 mph
0–60 mph (0–95 km/h):	4.7 sec
Engine type:	V8
Displacement:	350 ci (5,735 cc)
Transmission:	6-speed manual
Max power:	330 bhp (246 kW) @ 5,800 rpm
Max torque:	340 lb ft (460 Nm) @ 4,500 rpm
Weight:	3,298 lb (1,499 kg)
Economy:	21 mpg (7.4 km/l)

Chevrolet Corvette Sting Ray 1963

Using a chassis from the cancelled Corvette SS racing programme, GM Chief stylist Bill Mitchell and designer Larry Shinoda styled their own body, called it the Stingray, then campaigned it with their own money. It was to be the shape that defined the 1963 second-generation Corvette, right down to the split rear window which Mitchell fought hard to keep. The Sting Ray came in both hardtop or open top form, and was the first Corvette to use fully independent suspension which dramatically improved the handling, allowing it to compete with the Jaguar XKE race cars. The rear used a single transverse leaf spring which ran either side of the differential, which itself could be ordered with anything from 3.08:1 to 4.56:1 gearing. The base engine was the 327ci (5.3-litre), but potential racers could order the 'Fuelie' fuel injected 360bhp (268kW) with four-speed manual and Posi rear.

Top speed:	118 mph (189 km/h)
0–60 mph (0–95 km/h):	6.1 sec
Engine type:	V8
Displacement:	327 ci (5,358 cc)
Transmission	4-speed manual
Max power:	300 bhp (223 kW) @ 5,000 rpm
Max torque:	360 lb ft (487 Nm) @ 3,200 rpm
Weight:	3,160 lb (1,436 kg)
Economy:	18 mpg (6.4 km/l)

Chevrolet Corvette ZR1

Easily the most technologically advanced engine ever put in a Corvette, the LT5 was only part of the ZR1 package. The car entered production in 1990 after much hype, and immediately looked different, thanks to the wide rear bodywork, to allow fitting of 11x17-inch (276x432mm) alloys with 315/35 tyres. Lotus designed the engine and based it on Chevy's small-block V8, but started with an aluminium-alloy block. Completely new heads used two-cams-per-bank operating four valves per cylinder. The induction used two ports and injectors per cylinder and only one of each operated below 3,500rpm. Above this with the throttle floored the other port and injector would open up and allow the full 405bhp (302kW) on later models to be unleashed. Other high-tech gadgetry included the suspension on which the driver could select a setting: Touring, Sport or Performance.

Top speed:	180 mph (288 km/h)
0–60 mph (0–95 km/h):	5.0 sec
Engine type:	V8
Displacement:	350 ci (5,735 cc)
Transmission	6-speed manual
Max power:	405 bhp (302 kW) @ 5,800 rpm
Max torque:	371 lb ft (502 Nm) @ 4,800 rpm
Weight:	3,519 lb (1,600 kg)
Economy:	14.7 mpg (5.2 km/l)

Chevrolet Corvette C5

With a presence on the US scene for nearly 50 years, the Corvette has the longest production run of any supercar, the 1997 C5 being the fifth generation. An all-new small-block V8 engine called the LS1 was designed for the C5, and it returned to pushrods. With new cylinder heads, a composite induction system, electronic fuel injection plus electronic throttle control, the motor revved in an instant like a race car and was strong throughout the range. Having a glass-fibre body and magnesium wheels, the Corvette stayed relatively lightweight. The floor was balsa wood sandwiched between steel sheets to help stiffen the structure, while the steel chassis had a few tricks up its sleeve, with alloy suspension arms and a composite monoleaf rear spring. The gearbox was part of the transaxle at the rear, thus distributing the weight evenly and making the handling superb.

Top speed:	175 mph (281 km/h)
0–60 mph (0–95 km/h):	4.7 sec
Engine type:	V8
Displacement:	347 ci (5,686 cc)
Transmission	6-speed manual
Max power:	345 bhp (257 kW) @ 5,400 rpm
Max torque:	350 lb ft (474 Nm) @ 4,400 rpm
Weight:	3,220 lb (1,464 kg)
Economy:	20.2 mpg (7.2 km/l)

Chevrolet Coupe 1940

When Chevrolet launched their new model in 1940 it was significant. It was their first car to use both plastics and stainless steel, and, interestingly, while being very basic underneath, famous racing driver Juan Manual Fangio managed to win the 6,000-mile (9654km) Gran Primo Internacional Del Norte race in Argentina, South America in a Business Coupe just like this. Chevrolets often come second in popularity to Ford when creating street rods, but not in this case. This version has had a separate chassis built based on the original rails, with independent A-arm front and Jaguar independent rear suspension. The brakes are large discs all around with powerful four-pot callipers. The engine is a Corvette small-block Chevy with three two-barrel carburettors, which uses the centre carb on light throttle then all three on full throttle. It has all-electric Corvette seats.

Top speed:	125 mph (201 km/h)
0–60 mph (0–95 km/h):	6.8 sec
Engine type:	V8
Displacement:	327 ci (5,358 cc)
Transmission	4-speed auto
Max power:	300 bhp (223 kW) @ 5,000 rpm
Max torque:	321 lb ft (434 Nm) @ 3,200 rpm
Weight:	2,900 lb (1,318 kg)
Economy:	14.7 mpg (5.2 km/l)

Chevrolet C10 1973

In 1973, Chevrolet's light trucks were radically altered for a much smoother and modern appearance. The roof rails went in favour of doors which opened into the roof, and curved side glass was fitted. Along the waist line of the car was a sculpted curve, which gave the truck a wide feel. With their huge engine bays and brutish looks, the 1973 C10s soon became favourites for modification. This vehicle has had the ride height reduced with lowering springs at the front and block between the leafs and axle at the rear to effectively raise the axle up to the bodywork, thus lowering the rear. Also fitted were modern wheels and tyres to further enhanced handling. Under the hood the truck was fitted with a 1970 454ci (7.4-litre) Corvette big-block and with high-flow heads plus a high-lift cam, it has been known to cover the quarter-mile in 15 seconds.

Top speed:	122 mph (195 km/h)
0–60 mph (0–95 km/h):	7.8 sec
Engine type:	V8
Displacement:	454 ci (7,439 cc)
Transmission	3-speed auto
Max power:	425 bhp (317 kW) @ 6,200 rpm
Max torque:	500 lb ft (677 Nm) @ 3,400 rpm
Weight:	4,045 lb (1,838 kg)
Economy:	7 mpg (2.5 km/l)

Chevrolet El Camino SS454

Many muscle cars are remembered because they represent the pinnacle of the model, and the 1970–only El Camino SS454 is no different. The El Camino had seen a break of four years earlier in the 1960s, but was back by 1964 with a 396ci (6.5-litre) top engine option. It went through a major facelift in 1968 with softer, more rounded lines but still the 396ci (6.5 litre) remained. In 1970 the El Camino followed the line of the Chevelle SS by being available with the 454ci (7.4-litre) big-block 'Rat' V8. The engine came in two different versions, the mild one being the LS5 with 10.25:1 compression and 360bhp (268kW), while the wild one was the LS6 with forged aluminium pistons, a special cam, forged steel crank and rods and 11.5:1 compression for 450bhp (336kW). With a Positraction live axle and very little rear weight, the back wheels would easily light up under provocation.

Top speed:	130 mph (208 km/h)
0–60 mph (0–95 km/h):	7.0 sec
Engine type:	V8
Displacement:	454 ci (7,439 cc)
Transmission:	3-speed auto
Max power:	360 bhp (268 kW) @ 4,400 rpm
Max torque:	500 lb ft (677 Nm) @ 3,200 rpm
Weight:	4,270 lb (1,941 kg)
Economy:	14 mpg (5 km/l)

Chevrolet II SS

With plain styling, the Chevy II was more often regarded as a leisurely old people's car. That all changed when Chevrolet installed their L79 Corvette 350ci (5.7-litre) V8 into the 1966 SS model. Having a lightweight body, the SS could easily mix it up with the best muscle cars, though looked more sedate than any with just the badges giving it away. Underneath, it relied on drum brakes which could get frightening given the performance which was on tap, and wheel hop was a problem under acceleration because of the simple leaf spring rear end. The transmission to have was the close-ratio four-speed manual which could get it easily into the 14-second range on the quarter mile, though the auto wasn't far behind. There was a base L-30 275bhp (205kW) engine too, which had double the production run of the L-29, though the latter is more collectable.

Top speed:	123 mph (197 km/h)
0–60 mph (0–95 km/h):	6.5 sec
Engine type:	V8
Displacement:	327 ci (5,358 cc)
Transmission	4-speed manual
Max power:	350 bhp (261 kW) @ 5,800 rpm
Max torque:	360 lb ft (487 Nm) @ 3,600 rpm
Weight:	3,140 lb (1,427 kg)
Economy:	14 mpg (5 km/l)

Chevrolet Impala SS 1996

Debuted as a concept in 1993, the Impala SS received an excellent response from the US public, so GM gave it the green light for production soon after. It hit the showroom floors in 1996 and proved that modern technology could produce a better muscle car. It may have only run the small-block 350ci (5.7-litre) V8, but thanks to multi-point fuel injection, engine management and excellent torque, the de-tuned Corvette motor could propel the Impala to sub-7 second 0–60mph (0–95 km/h) times and an impressive top speed, while returning 21mpg (7.5km/l). The car was no lightweight at just under two tons, yet it could be thrown around, thanks to thicker anti-roll bars, stiffer springs and de Carbon shocks. Heavy-duty police front spindles and huge 12-inch (305mm) disc brakes all around helped the inspiring feel. The interior was fully loaded; the car was way ahead of its ancestors in the luxury stakes.

Top speed:	140 mph (224 km/h)
0–60 mph (0–95 km/h):	6.6 sec
Engine type:	V8
Displacement:	350 ci (5,735 cc)
Transmission:	4-speed auto
Max power:	260 bhp (194 kW) @ 5,000 rpm
Max torque:	330 lb ft (447 Nm) @ 3,200 rpm
Weight:	4,230 lb (1,923 kg)
Economy:	21 mpg (7.5 km/l)

Chevrolet Impala SS427

Chevrolet marketed their new-for-1967 Impala 427 with the slogan 'For the man who'd buy a sports car if it had this much room'. The theory was good, and by dropping in the big-block engine from the Corvette, the result was impressive. The engine had been released the year before and from the outset the famous 'Rat' motor was designed to produce big numbers. Staggered valves in the heads created better flow and power (at the cost of size and weight), while the torque was staggering which made hauling along the Impala easy. The Impala used a wider front track than early 1960s models and, because of the 1967 fastback coupe shape, the bodyshell was required to be very strong, which also helped handling. The SS also had superior rear-axle location with four, rather than three, links, making it one of the best-handling large muscle cars. The SS model was retired in 1968.

Top speed:	132 mph (211 km/h)
0–60 mph (0–95 km/h):	7.1 sec
Engine type:	V8
Displacement:	454 ci (7,439 cc)
Transmission:	3-speed auto
Max power:	360 bhp (269 kW) @ 4,400 rpm
Max torque:	500 lb ft (677 Nm) @ 3,200 rpm
Weight:	3,860 lb (1,755 kg)
Economy:	11.5 mpg (4.1 km/l)

Chevrolet Impala 1958

Following on from the successful 'Tri-Chevys' of 1955–1957 was tough but Chevrolet did a fine job with the 1958 Impala. It was the first they'd used the name on any cars in their range, though it was a new model supplementing the regular Bel Air, Biscayne and Delray variants. They wanted a lower look for 1958 and this required a new chassis of X-frame design with the main rails joined in the middle. Because of the lack of connection to the body sides, more mounting points were needed to the body elsewhere, and this improved structural rigidity a lot. The car ran a new W-Series engine initially designed for light truck duty. It was relatively compact and made 250bhp (186kW), though if fitted with the triple carb option could muster 315bhp (234kW). Also optional was air suspension with four rubber bellows replacing the sprigs and running off a self-levelling compressor. which was self levelling.

Top speed:	115 mph (184 km/h)
0–60 mph (0–95 km/h):	10.5 sec
Engine type:	V8
Displacement:	348 ci (5,702 cc)
Transmission	3-speed auto
Max power:	250 bhp (186 kW) @ 4,400 rpm
Max torque:	355 lb ft (454 Nm) @ 2,800 rpm
Weight:	3,459 lb (1,572 kg)
Economy:	14 mpg (5 km/l)

Chevrolet Impala 1960

The Impala was Chevrolet's top-of-the-range model in 1959, and it had everything. Huge fins, wild styling, plenty of horsepower and luxury fittings galore. It wasn't about handling, more about comfort, so it ran a basic separate chassis with double wishbones up front and a coil sprung live rear axle. It was offered with a choice of engines from a straight-six right up to the 348ci (5.7 litre) this car is equipped with. Designers concentrated on making it long and low, and gave the buyer a huge options list with which to 'customize' their vehicle. This particular car has side skirts, spot lights, a continental kit, fender guards, remote trunk release, cruise control, air-conditioning and power-assisted everything. Inside it can carry six with comfort. Due to its custom nature, it has become a firm favourite with lowrider fans in more recent times.

Top speed:	144 mph (230 km/h)
0–60 mph (0–95 km/h):	4.8 sec
Engine type:	V8
Displacement:	468 ci (7,669 cc)
Transmission	3-speed auto
Max power:	525 bhp (391 kW) @ 6,200 rpm
Max torque:	520 lb ft (704 Nm) @ 4,200 rpm
Weight:	3,250 lb (1,477 kg)
Economy:	6 mpg (2.1 km/l)

Chevrolet Monte Carlo SS454

On the design brief the 1970 Monte Carlo was required to be luxurious. It was built on the Chevelle platform but used a longer wheelbase. It had extra rubber mounts fitted between the body and chassis to reduce vibration from the street, plus extra sound-deadening inside. Ticking RPO Z20 on the options list gave you the SS454 model and for that you got the largest big-block Chevy had on offer, the infamous 'Rat'. The long stroke of the LS-5 motor produced the torque, giving the car endless pull anywhere in the rev range. The following year's version of the same engine, coded the LS-6, produced even more power with 450bhp (336kW). Underneath the car ran with the Chevelle's wishbone front and coil sprung rear suspension, with an Automatic Level Control system and on-board air compressor. Inside it was equipped with soft vinyl bucket seats and simulated walnut burr dash.

Top speed:	132 mph (211 km/h)
0–60 mph (0–95 km/h):	7.1 sec
Engine type:	V8
Displacement:	454 ci (7,439 cc)
Transmission	3-speed auto
Max power:	360 bhp (268 kW) @ 4,400 rpm
Max torque:	500 lb ft (677 Nm) @ 3,200 rpm
Weight:	3,860 lb (1,755 kg)
Economy:	11.5 mpg (4.1 km/l)

Chevrolet Nomad 1956

The Nomad was the top-of-the-range Chevy available from 1955 to 1957. The hottest news in 1955 was the use of the all-new small-block V8 which, displacing 265ci (4.3-litre), turned the sedans and station wagons into some of the best performers of their day. The Nomad was different to other station wagons because it was a two-door body with lifting tailgate, but its was sportingly handsome. The original car used leaf springs at the rear and double wishbones at the front, and pushed out just 162bhp (121kW) from its V8. This car has gone someway further, using 1986 Corvette front and rear suspension plus a lowered ride height for excellent handling, while the old 265 has been replaced by a fully-balanced 358ci (5.8-litre) small-block Chevy with ported heads and a B&M supercharger. So good are the Nomad's lines, little has changed except custom paint and Boyds alloys.

Top speed:	131 mph (210 km/h)
0–60 mph (0–95 km/h):	5.5 sec
Engine type:	V8
Displacement:	358 ci (5,866 cc)
Transmission:	3-speed auto
Max power:	400 bhp (298 kW) @ 4,800 rpm
Max torque:	420 lb ft (568 Nm) @ 3,000 rpm
Weight:	3,352 lb (1,523 kg)
Economy:	8.4 mpg (3 km/l)

Chevrolet Nova SS 1973

For 1968 the Nova filled out considerably, more towards an intermediate car. It also looked much more like many of the muscle cars of the time thanks to its fastback styling. Though the car was available with a big-block V8, by 1973 when this car was produced only the small-block V8 was on the option list. The Novas make great drag cars as they have much room under the hood for big engines and the owner of this car has chosen to install a 454ci (7.4-litre) big-block, bored out to 468ci (7.6 litres) and fully balanced. It has an Iskendarian high-lift cam, rare L88 manifold and a high-flow four-barrel Holley carburettor. Regular 454s are only rated at 450bhp (335kW), so it's no surprise this one will do the quarter-mile in 12.5 seconds. It uses the stock suspension, albeit lowered, with a pair of traction bars at the rear to help launch the car off the line.

Top speed:	144 mph (230 km/h)
0–60 mph (0–95 km/h):	4.8 sec
Engine type:	V8
Displacement:	468 ci (7,669 cc)
Transmission	3-speed auto
Max power:	525 bhp (391 kW) @ 6,200 rpm
Max torque:	520 lb ft (704 Nm) @ 4,200 rpm
Weight:	3,250 lb (1,477 kg)
Economy:	6 mpg (2.1 km/l)

Chevrolet Yenko Chevelle

Don Yenko was better known for his highly-tuned Camaros, but during 1969 he also turned his hand to the Chevelle, the result being an incredible street racer. He removed the 375bhp (280kW) 390ci (6.6-litre) big-block engine and replaced it with a 427ci (7.2-litre). To cope with the straight-line performance the car was fitted with disc brakes as standard, plus a Muncie four-speed manual, or GM TH400 if you preferred an auto. At the rear end the car also came with a strengthened GM 12-bolt live axle with 4.10:1 gearing as standard for maximum acceleration. It used heavy-duty suspension with coil springs at the rear and independent A-arms up front. Externally the cars were identified with 'Yenko SC' (Super Car) logos and black stripes, but even so, you rarely saw them on the street, as just 99 were built in 1969, being replaced by the Yenko Chevelle SS454 in 1970.

Top speed:	110 mph (176 km/h)
0–60 mph (0–95 km/h):	5.7 sec
Engine type:	V8
Displacement:	427 ci (6,997 cc)
Transmission:	3-speed auto
Max power:	450 bhp (335 kW) @5,000 rpm
Max torque:	460 lb ft (623 Nm) @ 4,000 rpm
Weight:	3,800 lb (1,727 kg)
Economy:	8 mpg (2.8 km/l)

Citroën SM

Citroën of France took over Italian firm Maserati in 1969 and provided much-needed financial support. It also requested of Maserati that they supply the engine and transmissions for a new, rather self-indulgent Citroën supercar, the SM. Many of the SM's parts underneath were from the Citroën DS model to keep costs down, parts such as the hydro-pneumatic suspension and ultra-sensitive four wheel-disc brakes. The V6 was produced by Maserati chopping two cylinders off their 183ci (3-litre) V8 and taking it out to 163ci (2.6 litres), though later versions had 183ci (3 litres). The gearbox was fitted in front of the engine to allow the engine to sit back as far as possible in the chassis for better weight-distribution. In 1971 Citroën put four cars into the Morocco Rally and gained first, third and fourth places. Peugeot bought Citroën in 1974, and the following year the SM finished.

Top speed:	142 mph (227 km/h)
0–60 mph (0–95 km/h):	8.5 sec
Engine type:	V6
Displacement:	163 ci (2,670 cc)
Transmission	5-speed manual
Max power:	178 bhp (133 kW) @ 5,500 rpm
Max torque:	171 lb ft (232 Nm) @ 4,000 rpm
Weight:	3,197 lb (1,453 kg)
Economy:	12.4 mpg (4.4 km/l)

Cosworth Vega

The Cosworth Vega was ahead of its time and had it appeared five years later it may well have had better sales. Chevrolet brought out the compact sedan/coupe in 1970 to battle with imports. It came with a top engine option of the 110bhp (82kW), 140ci (2.3-litre) four-cylinder, which was criticized as being coarse. In 1973 Chevy had Cosworth develop the fastest Vega yet to enhance its sporty-yet-economical nature, vital in the fuel conscious mid-1970s. Cosworth used the alloy block but with a shorter stroke for 122ci (2-litre), then added an alloy twin-cam 16v head. Special pistons and electronic fuel injection saw output at 130bhp (97kW) initially, though production versions actually only managed 110bhp (82kW), due to lower compression. Uprated suspension, quicker steering and low axle gears of 3.73:1 in 1975 helped acceleration; 6x13-inch (152x330mm) alloys aided handling.

Top speed:	112 mph (180 km/h)
0–60 mph (0–95 km/h):	12.3 sec
Engine type:	In-line four
Displacement:	122 ci (1,998 cc)
Transmission	4-speed manual
Max power:	110 bhp (82 kW) @ 5,600 rpm
Max torque:	107 lb ft (145 Nm) @ 4,800 rpm
Weight:	2,639 lb (1,200 kg)
Economy:	19.6 mpg (6.9 km/l)

Dale Earnhardt's Chevy Lumina

The late Dale Earnhardt, known as 'The Intimidator', had long been a Chevrolet NASCAR driver and started with the Lumina in 1992. That turned out to be a dismal year for the team, so Chevy doubled its efforts for 1993 and was rewarded with the Winston Cup Championship. The Lumina, like all NASCARs, had to run the same shape as the street car, but underneath there was nothing of the stock sedan. A full metal spaceframe filled the inside, with trailing arms and Panhard rod locating the live rear axle. At the front it used adjustable double wishbones and huge anti-roll bar. The car used different springs rates and tyre sizes because of travelling around to the left constantly. The small-block Chevy with a compression ratio of 13:1 had a carburettor restriction plate to even out competition and to keep weight to 3,500lb (1587kg), Kevlar body panels and Lexan windows were used.

Top speed:	200 mph (320 km/h)
0–60 mph (0–95 km/h):	3.5 sec
Engine type:	V8
Displacement:	358 ci (5,866 cc)
Transmission	4-speed manual
Max power:	680 bhp (507 kW) @ 7,000 rpm
Max torque:	N/A
Weight:	3,500 lb (1,590 kg)
Economy:	N/A

Datsun 240Z

Aimed directly at the American market, the 1969 Datsun 240Z had the looks, the handling thanks to independent suspension all around, a powerful free-revving engine plus a build quality which few could match for the money. It offered a monocoque design chassis/body, and whereas most cars of the era were still using leaf springs, the 240Z had struts all around, making it outstanding in corners. The straight-six engine was based on the Bluebird four-cylinder and was exceptionally strong, giving out plenty of power and torque while returning good economy and reliability that would see it go past 150,000 miles (241,350km) if properly serviced. Although having just two seats, it was practical with the hatchback rear. It also had a very high build quality which way surpassed anything else at its $3,526 price. The car sold over 150,000 models in 4 years.

Top speed:	125 mph (200 km/h)
0–60 mph (0–95 km/h):	8.7 sec
Engine type:	In-line six
Displacement:	146 ci (2,393 cc)
Transmission	5-speed manual
Max power:	150 bhp (112 kW) @ 6,000 rpm
Max torque:	148 lb ft (200 Nm) @ 4,400 rpm
Weight:	2,355 lb (1070 kg)
Economy:	25 mpg (8.9 km/l)

Datsun 280 ZX Turbo

While the original 1969 240Z was simple and effective, Datsun tried to make it more refined in later years. It gained weight which meant it wasn't quite as nimble and lost power. Physically it felt bigger too, but throughout the Z and ZX's history, all models offered much scope for tuning. This particular car was put together in Essex, UK, and starting with a 1979 model the owner has increased the intercooled turbocharger's boost and re-mapped the fuelling and timing for a power increase which allows 14.0 sec quarter-mile times. It uses adjustable shocks, motorsport springs, urethane bushes, uprated anti-roll bars and 9-inch/11-inch (229/279mm) alloys to maximize cornering potential, plus four-piston callipers on larger vented discs up front to increase braking power. Externally it features the IMSA arches from the ZX-R homologation special, only available in the USA.

Top speed:	144 mph (230 km/h)
0–60 mph (0–95km/h):	6.0 sec
Engine type:	In-line six
Displacement:	168 ci (2,753 cc)
Transmission	5-speed manual
Max power:	260 bhp (194 kW) @ 5,800 rpm
Max torque:	295 lb ft (399 Nm) @ 3,000 rpm
Weight:	2,850 lb (1,295 kg)
Economy:	20 mpg (7.1 km/l)

Datsun B-510

Datsun was little aware of the little racer it was producing when it turned out the new B-510 (known as Bluebird outside the USA) in 1967. They equipped the lightweight car well, giving it MacPherson front struts and an independent rear with trailing arms so it could really be thrown into bends with confidence. It came with a 97ci (1.5-litre) single SU-carb engine as standard and made 90bhp (67kW), but it was very useable, with little weight to carry around. This particular 510 has had a six-point cage and strut brace fitted to stiffen the chassis considerably, and the interior has been stripped in favour of aluminium panels and a single bucket seat. The engine sports twin Mikuni carbs, flat top pistons for higher compression, a gas-flowed head and high-lift cam. Vented discs, adjustable suspension and wide alloys help complete it as a street and track racer.

Top speed:	111 mph (178 km/h)
0–60 mph (0–95 km/h):	7.6 sec
Engine type:	In-line four
Displacement:	97 ci (1,595 cc)
Transmission	4-speed manual
Max power:	150 bhp (112 kW) @ 5,600 rpm
Max torque:	156 lb ft (211 Nm) @ 3,600 rpm
Weight:	2,130 lb (968 kg)
Economy:	20 mpg (7.1 km/l)

Datsun Fairlady

It was the 1961 Datsun Fairlady which started Japan's foray into the worldwide sportscar market. Its lightweight bodyshell coupled with a buzzy 122ci (2-litre) four-cylinder engine competed with British sportscars and had the MG beat on performance, if not character. The car used a separate box-section chassis, with double wishbone front suspension and a leaf sprung live rear axle on radius arms. While the car started out with drums brakes and 71bhp (53kW), by 1967 it had disc brakes up front, which offered superb stopping power. By then the Fairlady also had a new 2-litre OHC engine with 135bhp (101kW). It went through a five-speed all-syncromesh gearbox, which was leagues ahead of its rivals' transmissions. The Fairlady name was later used on Japan's limited edition version of the 240Z with 122ci (2-litre) straight six engine and excellent all-round independent suspension.

Top speed:	114 mph (182 km/h)
0–60 mph (0–95 km/h):	10.2 sec
Engine type:	In-line four
Displacement:	121 ci (1,982 cc)
Transmission	5-speed manual
Max power:	135 bhp (101 kW) @ 6,000 rpm
Max torque:	145 lb ft (196 Nm) @ 4,000 rpm
Weight:	2,115 lb (961 kg)
Economy:	26 mpg (9.2 km/l)

De Tomaso Mangusta

Designed to challenge Ferrari in the late 1960s, the Mangusta was Argentine Alexjandro de Tomaso's first volume production car, with mid-mounted Ford V8 mated to a ZF transmission. More technically advanced than the later Pantera, the Mangusta used folded and welded sheet steel to make a box-section central backbone. The over-light front end used double wishbone suspension but couldn't quite get the grip the car needed, while the rear used a reversed lower wishbone, single transverse link plus twin radius arms per side. The wheels were magnesium to keep weight down, but the Mangusta wasn't a great handling machine. It was, however, quick in a straight line thanks to the Ford V8 which was also used in Mustangs, the Shelby GT350 and AC Cobras. It was the latter the Mangusta aimed for, as its name meant 'Mongoose', the animal which ate Cobras.

Top speed:	130 mph (208 km/h)
0–60 mph (0–95 km/h):	6.3 sec
Engine type:	V8
Displacement:	302 ci (4,950 cc)
Transmission	5-speed manual
Max power:	230 bhp (171 kW) @ 4,800 rpm
Max torque:	310 lb ft (419 Nm) @ 2,800 rpm
Weight:	2,915 lb (1,325 kg)
Economy:	13 mpg (4.6 km/l)

De Tomaso Pantera

Thanks to Ford's funds, the Pantera saw light of day in 1969, and while Alexjandro de Tomaso owned the rights to sell it in Europe, Ford retained them in the USA. Unlike the Mangusta before it, the Pantera used a steel monocoque structure because it was to be sold through Ford dealerships and thus needed to be high volume, hence fast, in production. Double wishbones were mounted at each corner and remained for the car's life, as did Ford power. In 1982 the updated GT5 was launched, with wheel arch extensions allowing 10-inch (254mm) and 13-inch (330mm) wide wheels and massive Pirelli tyres, for better cornering. The mid-mounted Cleveland V8 (named after the plant where it was built) offered much scope in tuning, as did the later 5.0 HO V8, which had twin turbochargers bolted and mustered over 180mph (289km/h) in the Gandini-styled 450 of 1990.

Top speed:	165 mph (264 km/h)
0–60 mph (0–95km/h):	5.6 sec
Engine type:	V8
Displacement:	351 ci (5,763 cc)
Transmission	5-speed manual
Max power:	350 bhp (261 kW) @ 6,000 rpm
Max torque:	333 lb ft (451 Nm) @ 3,800 rpm
Weight:	3,219 lb (1,463 kg)
Economy:	13.1 mpg (4.6 km/l)

DeLorean DMC

Founder John DeLorean, former Pontiac chief engineer and the man responsible for the GTO muscle car, started his company in 1974, though production of the DMC didn't begin until 1981 in Belfast, Ireland, in a factory paid for by the British Government. The startling body, actually brushed stainless steel over glass-fibre, made the car look exotic, but it was let down by the bought-in all-alloy V6 jointly developed by Peugeot, Renault and Volvo. The motor was never developed as a sporty performer and even though it later used Renault Alpine A 310 and A610 in turbocharged form, DeLorean never got that far, making only one prototype twin-turbo car which, ironically, worked very well. A lack of sales caused the company to close just one year after production had started, still with 2,000 cars unsold which were – years later – snapped up by collectors.

Top speed:	125 mph (200 km/h)
0–60 mph (0–95 km/h):	9.6 sec
Engine type:	V6
Displacement:	174 ci (2,850 cc)
Transmission	5-speed manual
Max power:	145 bhp (108 kW) @ 5,500 rpm
Max torque:	162 lb ft (219 Nm) @ 2,750 rpm
Weight:	2,840 lb (1,290 kg)
Economy:	16.8 mpg (5.9 km/l)

Dodge Challenger R/T SE

With the muscle-car era at its height in the late 1960s, Dodge finally got its own pony car in 1970. Aptly named the Challenger, it came with a huge list of options, including 12 engines. In Dodge tradition, the R/T (Street/Track) package was the high-performance model. The base engine option was a 335bhp (250kW) 383ci (6.3-litre) V8, but the car could be ordered with the mighty 426ci (7-litre) Street Hemi or 440ci (7.2-litre) V8s, which gave out 425bhp (316kW) and 375bhp (279kW) respectively. It was built on Chrysler's new E-body platform, sharing its firewall and front subframe with the bigger B-body cars like the Charger. The new model also used Chrysler's proven torsion bar front suspension with beefed up anti-roll bar, though the rear had leaf springs on a live axle, the latter requiring the Sure-Grip limited-slip differential option to put all the torque to the ground.

Top speed:	128 mph (205 km/h)
0–60 mph (0–95 km/h):	7.2 sec
Engine type:	V8
Displacement:	440 ci (7,210 cc)
Transmission	4-speed manual
Max power:	390 bhp (449 kW) @ 4,700 rpm
Max torque:	490 lb ft (663 Nm) @ 3,200 rpm
Weight:	3,437 lb (1,562 kg)
Economy:	9 mpg (3.2 km/l)

Dodge Charger Daytona

Debuted in 1969, the Dodge Charger Daytonas started NASCAR by impressing everyone with lap speeds just under 200mph (322km/h). A Charger won that debut race and through the season Daytonas won another 21 times. The following year, the Daytonas were joined by their similar stablemates, the Plymouth Superbirds, but 1971 was to be both their last year, as a ruling on their rear spoiler meant a reduction of engine size by a quarter, hence they couldn't be competitive. The NASCARs from this era were still relatively stock, hence the Dayonta used torsion bar front and leaf spring rear suspension, all uprated. However, the doors were welded shut to increase body stiffness, and inside a full roll cage was added for safety. The legendary Hemi engines under the hood were raised in compression to 13.3:1 and used single plane racing manifolds with a single carburettor.

Top speed:	200 mph (320 km/h)
0–60 mph (0–95 km/h):	4.3 sec
Engine type:	V8
Displacement:	426 ci (6,980 cc)
Transmission	4-speed manual
Max power:	556 bhp (415 kW) @ 6,000 rpm
Max torque:	497 lb ft (673 Nm) @ 5,400 rpm
Weight:	3,100 lb (1,409 kg)
Economy:	N/A

Dodge Coronet R/T 1970

Dodge introduced its Coronet to the public in 1967 and with sales of over 10,000, people appreciated its complete high-performance package. By 1970 the Coronet R/T (Road and Track) was not so popular, but it remained a good combination for the street or strip-racing enthusiast. In base form it used the 440ci (7.2-litre) Wedge engine, so called because of the shape of the combustion chambers. This was a more reliable and easier to maintain engine than the famed 'Hemi' which was optional. Even in base form, the 440ci had 375bhp (279kW) with a single carb, or 390bhp (291kW) with the 'Six Pack' carb option. A torsion bar front and live axle rear, as per most in the Chrysler group, kept it smooth. In 1970 the car was barely afloat in a sea of beautiful and powerful cars (ironically, many from the Chrysler stable), and its sales dropped to 2,615. Of those only 13 had the Hemi.

Top speed:	123 mph (197 km/h)
0–60 mph (0–95 km/h):	6.6 sec
Engine type:	V8
Displacement:	440 ci (7,210 cc)
Transmission	3-speed auto
Max power:	375 bhp (279 kW) @ 4,600 rpm
Max torque:	480 lb ft (650 Nm) @ 3,200 rpm
Weight:	3,546 lb (1,612kg)
Economy:	10.6 mpg (3.8 km/l)

DODGE

Dodge Durango

Although based on the Dakota truck chassis, the 1997 Durango didn't display truck-like handling. The frame was stiffened before being put into duty under the four-wheel drive, but kept the Dakota-style suspension with double wishbones acting on a torsion bar spring up front and a live axle rear hanging on leaf springs. The 4x4 intentions were obvious through the ride height, and while a driver had low or high ratio full-time 4WD available, they could select rear drive only to save fuel while on the highway. Three engine options were available, the 238ci (3.9-litre) V6, the better 318ci (5.2-litre) V8, or the top-of-the-range 360ci (5.9-litre) which gave exceptional performance for the big and heavy Sport Utility Vehicle. Vented 11-inch (279mm) discs could handle the pace, cruising high speed across country, or descending a 3:1incline. Inside it could seat eight comfortably.

Top speed:	115 mph (184 km/h)
0–60 mph (0–95 km/h):	8.7 sec
Engine type:	V8
Displacement:	360 ci (5,898 cc)
Transmission	4-speed auto
Max power:	250 bhp (186 kW) @ 4,000 rpm
Max torque:	335 lb ft (454 Nm) @ 3,200 rpm
Weight:	5,050 lb (2,295 kg)
Economy:	15 mpg (5.3 km/l)

Dodge Hurst Hemi Dart

Manufacturers used drag racing to display their products in the 1960s. The 1968 Hurst Hemi Dart was very successful in the NHRA Super Stock class, with no vehicle coming close. Hurst Performance and Chrysler built the 72 cars as stripped-out racers. They had the radio, heater, rear seats, sound-deadening and windows winders removed, had the battery mounted in the trunk and came in flat grey primer ready for racing paint schemes. The front fenders and hood were glass-fibre, while the steel doors and fenders were acid-dipped to thin them, and thus lose more weight. Bigger rear arches were fitted to cater for the large slick tyres and a Dana axle was fitted with 4.88:1 race gears. With 12.5:1 compression, a forged crank, solid lifter cam and twin Holley four-barrel carbs, the engine was highly tuned and was eventually rated at a more truthful 500bhp (373kW) by the NHRA.

Top speed:	140 mph (224 km/h)
0–60 mph (0–95 km/h):	3.6 sec
Engine type:	V8
Displacement:	426 ci (6,980 cc)
Transmission	4-speed manual
Max power:	425 bhp (317 kW) @ 6,000 rpm
Max torque:	480 lb ft (650 Nm) @ 4,600 rpm
Weight:	3,000 lb (1,361kg)
Economy:	6 mpg (2.1 km/l)

Dodge Ram

The new Ram from Dodge came along in 1994 and made the outgoing model look very dated. The new truck's bold styling with raised hood and low-down headlights was popular; it also became the look for Dodge's later Sport Utility Vehicle, the Dakota. The range-topping Ram used a cast-iron version of the Dodge Viper's V10 engine, and it's the biggest motor available in a production pick-up. With a relatively low 8.6:1 compression ratio it has been designed to be more of a torquey low rpm unit, though still runs the sequential fuel injection. The truck used a ladder-type chassis separate to the body and the standard suspension consists of double wishbones at the front plus a live axle rear on leaf springs, which was basic but very functional and heavy duty. Four-wheel drive was an option, and with the tremendous torque, there was little the V10 Ram couldn't do.

Top speed:	113 mph (180 km/h)
0–60 mph (0–95 km/h):	7.5 sec
Engine type:	V10
Displacement:	488 ci (7,996 cc)
Transmission:	4-speed auto
Max power:	300 bhp (224 kW) @ 4,000 rpm
Max torque:	440 lb ft (595 Nm) @ 2,800 rpm
Weight:	5,383 lb (2,446 kg)
Economy:	13.6 mpg (4.8 km/l)

Dodge Stealth R/T Turbo

Although badged a Dodge, the 1990 Stealth was a re-bodied Mitsubishi 3000GT, though was a superb driver's machine. It was built on the same assembly line in Japan and uses the same chassis, engine, transmission and suspension. The latter is MacPherson struts all around with trailing arms at the rear and anti-roll bars at each end. The engine had a iron block with extra ribs for strength, while the dual-overhead cam 24v heads were aluminium alloy. In base form the engine had 164bhp (122kW), while in R/T guise it managed 222bhp (165kW). The best was the R/T Turbo, which had twin Mitsubishi TD04 turbos with intercoolers to add 10psi boost for 300bhp (223kW). Hi-tech additions were four-wheel drive and four-wheel steer, a front spoiler which lowered at 50mph (80km/h) to re-direct airflow around the car, and a rear spoiler to increase downforce.

Top speed:	151 mph (243 km/h)
0–60 mph (0–95 km/h):	5.3 sec
Engine type:	V6
Displacement:	181 ci (2,966 cc)
Transmission	5-speed manual
Max power:	300 bhp (224 kW) @ 6,000 rpm
Max torque:	307 lb ft (415 Nm) @ 2,500 rpm
Weight:	3,803 lb (1,729 kg)
Economy:	18 mpg (6.4 km/l)

DODGE

Dodge Super Bee 1969

Chrysler wanted to stay ahead in the muscle-car wars, and that prompted the creation of the Super Bee in 1969. Basically a bare-bones Coronet, the new Dodge was achieved by stuffing their 440ci (7.2 litres) into the lightest intermediate bodyshell available. The power came through additions such as a free-flow dual exhaust, but mostly it was down to the 'Six Pack' carburettor system. This consisted of three two-barrel Holley carbs, on which the centre one would work at part throttle, then all three at full throttle, feeding more fuel in and unleashing the full power which could propel the car down the quarter-mile in under 14 seconds. The car also handled reasonably well, thanks to heavy-duty torsion bar front suspension. The Super Bee came with a tough Dana axle with 4.1:1 gearing as standard, plus black steel wheels to show its bare-bones nature.

Top speed:	130 mph (208 km/h)
0–60 mph (0–95 km/h):	6.0 sec
Engine type:	V8
Displacement:	440 ci (7,210 cc)
Transmission:	4-speed manual
Max power:	390 bhp (291 kW) @ 4,700 rpm
Max torque:	490 lb ft (663 Nm) @ 3,200 rpm
Weight:	4,100 lb (1,863 kg)
Economy:	7 mpg (2.5 km/l)

Dodge Viper R/T 1992

Shown as a concept at the Detroit international Auto Show in 1989, the Viper received such an overwhelming response from the public that it couldn't fail to go into production. It was designed as a modern-day version of the 1960's 427 Cobra, with remarkably similar traits. The engine was up front and was full of torque, being the biggest production engine in the world. It sat in a tubular steel chassis which also housed independent wishbone suspension front and back. The car used rear-wheel drive, and torque was sent back via a specially designed Borg Warner gearbox, which had a lockout shift mechanism to go from first gear straight to fourth at light throttle. The motor could even pull from as little as 500rpm, or 35 mph (56 km/h) in sixth gear. The body was reinforced glass-fibre to help lightweight and the brakes were 13-inch (330mm) Brembo discs and calipers, giving immense stopping power.

Top speed:	162 mph (260 km/h)
0–60 mph (0–95 km/h):	5.4 sec
Engine type:	V10
Displacement:	488 ci (7,998 cc)
Transmission	6–speed manual
Max power:	400 bhp (298 kW) @ 4,600 rpm
Max torque:	488 lb ft (662 Nm) @ 3,600 rpm
Weight:	3,477 lb (1,580 kg)
Economy:	12 mpg (4.2 km/l)

Dodge Viper GTS

Chrysler debuted the first concept Viper in 1989 at the Detroit Motor Show. It was very well received. Two years later a production Viper RT/10 paced the Indy 500 and by 1992 the car was on sale, with buyers lining up. A year later, Chrysler did the same again by debuting a coupe concept of the Viper, and again it hit the spot with potential buyers. The first GTS coupe appeared in 1996 and addressed some of the roadster's shortcomings. It had a roof for a start, and every body panel was new. Virtually new was the engine, with so many components changed for the GTS. Power was up, naturally, but cleverly the weight was down by over 40lb (18kg) due to composite bodywork and all-aluminium suspension. It was surprisingly practical, thanks to the rear hatch/window and generous trunk space. Massive 335/35x17 radials helped put down the enormous torque through rear-wheel drive.

Top speed:	179 mph (286 km/h)
0–60 mph (0–95 km/h):	4.7 sec
Engine type:	V10
Displacement:	488 ci (7,996 cc)
Transmission	6-speed manual
Max power:	450 bhp (336 kW) @ 5,200 rpm
Max torque:	490 lb ft (663 Nm) @ 3,700 rpm
Weight:	3,384 lb (1,538 kg)
Economy:	24 mpg (8.5 km/l)

Dodge Viper GTS-R

It was logical for Chrysler to turn the GTS into a race machine and they debuted the GTS-R in 1995. In 1997 two cars entered the GT2 class in World Sportscar Racing and came first and second at the Le Mans 24 Hours in France. The GTS-R even took the World GT2 Championship overall, a first for an American production model. Despite looking very similar to the road car, the R version had many changes. The engine sat further back to aid weight-distribution and was full balanced and given 12:1 compression along with stronger forged steel connecting rods for high rpm use. A dry sump oiling system helped maintain oil pressure under hard cornering. The chassis was strengthened and fitted with spherical joints on the suspension to ensure maximum response. Panels were swapped for lightweight carbon-fibre versions, and the low bodywork was deepened to aid air flow.

Top speed:	203 mph (324.8 km/h)
0–60 mph (0–95 km/h):	3.1 sec
Engine type:	V10
Displacement:	488 ci (7,996 cc)
Transmission	6-speed manual
Max power:	650 bhp (484 kW) @ 6,000 rpm
Max torque:	650 lb ft (880 Nm) @ 5,000 rpm
Weight:	2,750 lb (1,250 kg)
Economy:	N/A

Ferrari 250 GT SWB

The 1959 250 GT SWB was a shorter version of the 250 GT, the SWB standing for Short Wheelbase Berniletta. This was to improve the car's agility for racing, and it worked. A year after its launch, British driver Stirling Moss took a SWB to victory at the Tourist Trophy race at Goodwood, England, and another SWB won the Tour of France. The car used a tubular steel chassis and, unusually, a live axle instead of de Dion rear. In conjunction with the double wishbone front with anti-roll bar, the set-up was very effective. To save weight there were plastic side windows and all-alloy panels for the racing cars, with the Lusso street versions having less use of alloy. Disc brakes were another first for Ferrari and vents in the nose section kept them cool. The engine had its spark plugs moved so the mechanics could access them easier, plus many eventually used six twin choke carbs.

Top speed:	140 mph (224 km/h)
0–60 mph (0–95 km/h):	6.7 sec
Engine type:	V12
Displacement:	180 ci (2,953 cc)
Transmission	4-speed manual
Max power:	280 bhp (209 kW) @ 7,000 rpm
Max torque:	203 lb ft (275 Nm) @ 5,500 rpm
Weight:	2,805 lb (1,275 kg)
Economy:	13.8 mpg (4.9 km/l)

Ferrari 275 GTB

Launched at the Paris Motor Show, France, in 1964, the 275 GTB was the most advanced Ferrari of the time. Underneath it used the traditional tubular chassis design, but instead of a live axle of de Dion rear, as used in previous Ferraris, it had double wishbones and coil springs at the rear, making it a fully independent suspension car. Also out back was a five-speed transaxle, which evened out weight-distribution very well, making the car beautifully balanced and better, many reckon, than the mighty Daytona. The front-mounted V12 was a development of the 1947 Ferrari 166 engine, but by this time it was using four camshafts and six twin-choke carburettors on the 275 GTB/4, as pictured here. Four wheel disc brakes were standard and the wheels were Campagnolo alloys, though the ultra-rare 275 GTB/C (competizione) wore Borrani wire wheels.

Top speed:	165 mph (264 km/h)
0–60 mph (0–95 km/h):	7.0 sec
Engine type:	V12
Displacement:	200 ci (3,286 cc)
Transmission:	5-speed manual
Max power:	300 bhp (224 kW) @ 8,000 rpm
Max torque:	202 lb ft (274 Nm) @ 5,500 rpm
Weight:	2,426 lb (1,102 kg)
Economy:	14.7 mpg (5.2 km/l)

Ferrari 308

Probably one of the most famous Ferraris due to the amount produced (over 6,000), the 308 was also one of the most stylish from the Modena, Italy, factory. Launched in 1975 and designed to replace the V6 Dino, the 308 was to continue on the small-engined theme but it ended up a V8 and mid-engined, with the motor transversely mounted. It used the same Dino suspension and this made it a real purist's Ferrari, with plenty of potential in acceleration, deceleration and handling. The quad-cam V8 (with belt driven cams against previous Ferraris' chain drive) all-alloy and initially using multi carburettors, changed to fuel injection in 1981. Basic square-section chassis was as per Ferrari tradition, as was the double wishbone suspension which made for very nimble handling. The body was initially made in glass-fibre but this changed in 1977, when all panels became steel.

Top speed:	145 mph (232 km/h)
0–60 mph (0–95 km/h):	7.3 sec
Engine type:	V8
Displacement:	178 ci (2,927 cc)
Transmission	5-speed manual
Max power:	205 bhp (153 kW) @ 7,000 rpm
Max torque:	181 lb ft (245 Nm) @ 5,000 rpm
Weight:	3,305 lb (1,502 kg)
Economy:	16.8 mpg (5.9 km/l)

Ferrari 308 GT4

This was the first car from Ferrari which tried the 2+2 seating arrangement and it was unusual aside from this as Bertone styled it, instead of mainstay Pininfarina. The sharp-edged lines and out-of-proportion roof because of the extra seating required made it unconventional and disliked by many Ferrari purists. The other first was the use of a V8 which Ferrari mid-mounted for the handling benefits. Cleverly they also managed to package the gearbox below the engine to make the drive train short and therefore give extra room for the rear passengers. The chassis was a carry-over from the Dino, being fully independent with wishbones and using four-wheel vented disc brakes. The V8 was a close relative of the 268ci (4.4-litre) V12 which powered the 365 GTB, sharing its stroke and bore. Its block and heads were aluminium and it had quad cams and Weber carburettors.

Top speed:	154 mph (246 km/h)
0–60 mph (0–95 km/h):	6.9 sec
Engine type:	V8
Displacement:	178 ci (2,926 cc)
Transmission:	5-speed manual
Max power:	250 bhp (186 kW) @ 7,700 rpm
Max torque:	210 lb ft (284 Nm) @ 5,000 rpm
Weight:	3,235 lb (1,470 kg)
Economy:	20 mpg (7.1 km/l)

FERRARI

Ferrari 355

Ferrari replaced the 348 with the 355 and created such a beautiful supercar that customers all but stopped buying their 12-cylinder Testarossa. The 355 was easier than any Ferrari before to drive and had such creature comforts as the latest in in-car entertainment plus air-conditioning as standard. Further developed than the previous 348 was the engine, which used five valves per cylinder and from a comparably small output of just under 213ci (3.5 litres) managed to put out 375bhp (279kW) at over 8,000rpm. The 355 used a similar chassis to the 348, being sheet and tubular steel forming a central stress-bearing unit with subframe at either end for the double wishbone suspension. It was far more dynamic to drive than the 348, however, and had an aerodynamically designed undertray to eliminate lift at high speed. Magnesium alloy wheels kept the weight under 3,000lb (1,360kg).

Top speed:	183 mph (293 km/h)
0–60 mph (0–95 km/h):	4.7 sec
Engine type:	V8
Displacement:	213 ci (3,496 cc)
Transmission:	6-speed manual
Max power:	375 bhp (279 kW) @ 8,250 rpm
Max torque:	268 lb ft (363 Nm) @ 6,000 rpm
Weight:	2,977 lb (1,353 kg)
Economy:	18.1 mpg (6.4 km/l)

Ferrari 360 Modena

As a replacement for the 355, the new 360 Modena not only had to look exquisite, it had to be quicker and more nimble in the handling. Pininfarina styled the body and through thousands of hours wind-tunnel testing came up with a shape that instantly shouted 'Ferrari'. But it was clever too, in that without a spoiler front or rear, it had more downforce at 70mph (113km/h) than the previous 355 had at top speed. The functional undertray helped this immensely. The 360 was the first Ferrari of all-aluminium construction, making it 131lb (59kg) lighter than the 355. Through adaptive damping, the ride quality was kept very good too, despite a set-up biased towards handling. The V8 engine was all new, with 40 valves, titanium con-rods and two cams per bank. It had one of the world's highest specific outputs of 111bhp (82kW) per litre.

Top speed:	185 mph (296 km/h)
0–60 mph (0–95 km/h):	4.5 sec
Engine type:	V8
Displacement:	219 ci (3,586 cc)
Transmission:	6-speed semi-automatic
Max power:	394 bhp (294 kW) @ 8,500 rpm
Max torque:	275 lb ft (372 Nm) @ 4,750 rpm
Weight:	3,065 lb (1,393 kg)
Economy:	16 mpg (5.7 km/l)

Ferrari 512 BB Le Mans

When Ferrari withdrew from its sportscar racing programme in the early 1970s to concentrate on Formula One, it left a huge gap. To compensate, the North American Racing Team developed its own competition machine, based on the 512 BB (Berlinetta Boxer). They changed the front bodywork and incorporated more powerful lights for night racing, plus used hood vents to cool the radiator and side vents to air the rear-mounted 12-cylinder horizontally opposed engine. The chassis was very similar to the street car as required by racing regs, being tubular and using double wishbones front and rear, but using much bigger brake discs to cope with the endurance racing. The all-alloy flat 12 engine was based on the 183ci (3-litre) F1 engine from 1970, but strengthened and fitted with dry sump lubrication and mechanical fuel injection, which could be tuned up to 600bhp (804kW).

Top speed:	203 mph (324.8 km/h)
0–60 mph (0–95 km/h):	3.6 sec
Engine type:	Flat 12
Displacement:	302 ci (4,942 cc)
Transmission	5-speed manual
Max power:	480 bhp (358 kW) @ 7,400 rpm
Max torque:	N/A
Weight:	2,161 lb (982 kg)
Economy:	N/A

Ferrari 550 Marenello

The 550 Marenello, named after Ferrari's home town, was another stunning Pininfarina styling job. Launched in 1996, it replaced the ageing 512 TR, itself little more than a re-styled Testarossa. Unusually, Ferrari put a front-mounted V12 in the 550, the first time since the Daytona of 1974. Although an all-new car, the Maranello had roots in the 1992 456GT and shared the same layout of double wishbones all around. To distribute the weight evenly, the gearbox was at the rear, while the engine and heads were aluminium to help reduce weight. It featured four camshafts, four-valves-per-cylinder and variable geometry intake and exhaust systems to make the most of power throughout the rev range. Incredibly, it met all emissions standards worldwide, though some felt it was over-silenced in order to meet noise regulations, hence that Ferrari wail was muted.

Top speed:	199 mph (318 km/h)
0–60 mph (0–95 km/h):	4.4 sec
Engine type:	V12
Displacement:	334 ci (5,474 cc)
Transmission	6-speed manual
Max power:	485 bhp (362 kW) @ 7,000 rpm
Max torque:	398 lb ft (539 Nm) @ 5,000 rpm
Weight:	3,726 lb (1,697 kg)
Economy:	11.8 mpg (4.2 km/l)

Ferrari Boxer

The 1973 Boxer was the result of direct competition from Lamborghini with their V12 Miura and the soon-to-be-debuted Countach. Ferrari used all their knowledge from Formula One to mount their horizontally opposed 12-cylinder engine behind the driver, and the result was one of the all-time Ferrari greats. The car used a hefty steel frame with twin wishbones and anti-roll bars front and rear, plus coil-over-shocks units all around but doubled up at the rear because of the extra weight. The brakes were 11-inch (279mm) discs sat behind magnesium alloy rims. Because of the length of the flat 12 engine, the gearbox had to be mounted underneath, which meant the motor was rather higher than ideal. Ferrari kept it light as possible by using Silumin alloy for the block. It also had two camshafts per side and four Weber carbs, replaced in 1981 by Bosch fuel injection.

Top speed:	165 mph (264 km/h)
0–60 mph (0–95 km/h):	6.4 sec
Engine type:	Flat 12
Displacement:	302 ci (4,942 cc)
Transmission:	5-speed manual
Max power:	360 bhp (268 kW) @ 6,200 rpm
Max torque:	333 lb ft (451 Nm) @ 4,600 rpm
Weight:	3,427 lb (1,558 kg)
Economy:	13 mpg (4.6 km/l)

Ferrari Daytona

This was the last and greatest of all the front-engined, rear-wheel drive two-seater Ferrari's and some purists regard it as one of the best Ferraris of all time. The Daytona, model name 365GTB/4, oozed style with its Pininfarina body with long hood that hid a quad-cam V12 fed by six Weber carburettors. To balance out the huge engine, the gearbox was mounted at the rear in the transaxle, giving near perfect 52:48 weight distribution. As with many Ferraris of the era, the Daytona used double wishbone suspension and anti-roll bars both ends, and had vented discs to cope with the enormous speed it was capable of. The chassis was a multi-tube affair hidden by a steel body but with alloy doors, hood and trunk lid. For 1970 this was the fastest car in the world; in fact, it remained that way for years, because 100mph (160km/h) could arrive in under 13 seconds.

Top speed:	174 mph (278 km/h)
0–60 mph (0–95 km/h):	5.6 sec
Engine type:	V12
Displacement:	268 ci (4,390 cc)
Transmission:	5-speed manual
Max power:	352 bhp (262 kW) @ 7,500 rpm
Max torque:	330 lb ft (447 Nm) @ 5,500 rpm
Weight:	3,530 lb (1,604 kg)
Economy:	11.8 mpg (4.2 km/l)

Ferrari Dino 246 GT

Though the earlier 1967–1968 Dino 206 styled by Pininfarina (never badged a Ferrari) had all the right ingredients of a howling V6, 5-speed gearbox and fully independent suspension, it didn't have its bugs ironed out, so the 1969 Ferrari 246GT was a better car. The Dino was advanced in that it ran the V6 mid-mounted and transverse, and because it was the first switch by Ferrari to rack and pinion steering. It used a tubular chassis with double wishbones all around, but while the first Dino had an alloy body, the 246 GT used steel so was slightly heavier. Early cars had just 121ci (1,998cc) displacement in the all-alloy engine derived from Ferrari's 97ci (1.6-litre) F2 motor, but in 1969 the blocks were made in cast iron by Fiat and given a longer stroke and larger bore. Brilliant handling and an engine which would rev past its 7,800rpm redline ensured the Dino became a collector's car.

Top speed:	148 mph (237 km/h)
0–60 mph (0–95 km/h):	7.3 sec
Engine type:	V6
Displacement:	148 ci (2,418 cc)
Transmission	5-speed manual
Max power:	195 bhp (145 kW) @ 5,000 rpm
Max torque:	166 lb ft (224 Nm) @ 5,500 rpm
Weight:	2,611 lb (1,187 kg)
Economy:	22 mpg (7.8 km/l)

Ferrari F40

The F40 stole the limelight for Ferrari in 1987, the 40th anniversary of Enzo Ferrari's first car. It re-established their stand as top exotic car producer and gave the new models an edge which earlier 1980s cars had lacked. It was a race car for the street and indeed was developed on the track using a GTO Evoluzione as a testbed. The bonded composite panels were made of woven carbon-fibre and either Kevlar or Nomex, all of which were glued into place to save weight. As an example, each door weighed less than 3.5lb (1.6kg). Underneath the body there was a tubular steel spaceframe to which the engine was attached. The mid-mounted V8 for each F40 was handbuilt by Ferrari craftsmen, and twin turbos upped power. A transaxle provided drive and at each corner double wishbones and coilover shocks made the race car suspension very firm around town, but perfect over 100mph (160km/h).

Top speed:	201 mph (322 km/h)
0–60 mph (0–95 km/h):	4.2 sec
Engine type:	V8
Displacement:	179 ci (2,936 cc)
Transmission:	5-speed manual
Max power:	478 bhp (356 kW) @ 7,000 rpm
Max torque:	423 lb ft (572 Nm) @ 4,000 rpm
Weight:	2,425 lb (1,102 kg)
Economy:	24 mpg (8.5 km/l)

Ferrari F50

Celebrating their 50th anniversary, Ferrari produced the F50 in 1997. The idea was to make it like a Formula One car for the street, even though it would be far more civilized. Built with such items as a progressive clutch to ensure you didn't stall pulling away from a standstill, plus a precise gearchange and handling slightly biased towards understeer, it was very user-friendly. A strictly functional interior plus carbon-fibre monocoque chassis kept weight to a minimum. Double wishbones and inboard pushrod-operated springs took care of the suspension, and there was also adaptive damping to suit varying conditions. The engine was an F1 unit stroked to increase displacement, though remaining rev-happy to 8,700rpm. Race engine extras included dry sump lubrication, titanium connecting rods and five valves per cylinder operated by four camshafts.

Top speed:	202 mph (323 km/h)
0–60 mph (0–95 km/h):	3.7 sec
Engine type:	V12
Displacement:	287 ci (4,698 cc)
Transmission	6-speed manual
Max power:	513 bhp (382 kW) @ 8,000 rpm
Max torque:	347 lb ft (470 Nm) @ 6,500 rpm
Weight:	3,080 lb (1,400 kg)
Economy:	12 mpg (4.2 km/l)

Ferrari Testarossa

Meaning 'redhead' because of its red-coloured valve covers on the Flat 12, the Testarossa was Ferrari's supercar for the 1980s. It was launched at the 1984 Paris Motor Show to mixed reviews because of the ostentatious side vents and massively wide rear just shy of 6.5ft (2m). The vents led to fan-assisted radiators either side, while the width was needed to house the engine, which was a progression of the 512 Berniletta Boxer engine from the 1970s. The Testarossa used a tubular steel frame with double wishbones front and rear, all covered in aluminium body panels. The transmission was mounted under the engine which meant more interior space. As Ferrari put it, 'The cockpit: a living room at 190 mph.' Testers said while the Testarossa was tricky to get into, once there, it exuded Ferrari and always seemed to have more power to offer.

Top speed:	170 mph (272 km/h)
0–60 mph (0–95 km/h):	5.4 sec
Engine type:	Flat 12
Displacement:	302 ci (4,942 cc)
Transmission:	5-speed manual
Max power:	390 bhp (291 kW) @ 6,300 rpm
Max torque:	360 lb ft (487 Nm) @ 4,500 rpm
Weight:	3,675 lb (1,670 kg)
Economy:	14 mpg (5 km/l)

Fiat 124 Spider Abarth

The Abarth tuning company was in financial trouble in 1971, so Fiat stepped in and took them over as part of their return to rallying. The 124 was soon conceived as the car with which that return would be made, and between the two companies a very capable machine was created in the Abarth Rallye. While the chassis remained the same, a switch from live axle to fully independent rear, with MacPherson struts and trailing arms, was made which vastly improved the car in corners. Also helping was a spherical joint front anti-roll bar which resisted body roll better. The 107ci (1,756cc) four-cylinder engine was taken from the Fiat 132 and had few changes, though each was balanced and blueprinted to ensure maximum output and reliability. Twin Weber carburettors and high compression pistons helped output, which was 200bhp (149kW) for competition versions.

Top speed:	118 mph (189 km/h)
0–60 mph (0–95 km/h):	7.5 sec
Engine type:	In-line four
Displacement:	107 ci (1,756 cc)
Transmission	5-speed manual
Max power:	128 bhp (95 kW) @ 6,200 rpm
Max torque:	117 lb ft (158 Nm) @ 5,200 rpm
Weight:	2,070 lb (941 kg)
Economy:	27 mpg (9.6 km/l)

Fiat Dino

The Dino was a well-produced joint effort by Ferrari, who needed a large company to produce its Formula 2 V6 engine and Fiat, who wanted an open-top sportscar with real credibility. The result was excellent, a high performance car with independent suspension for a great handling. The Pininfarina-styled convertible appeared first at the Turin Motor Show, Italy in 1964, while the Bertone-designed coupe came three years later. Fiat's Dino shared the Ferrari Dino's engine and gearbox, and early versions used a live rear axle, though this was changed in 1969 to an independent suspension with struts and semi-trailing arms. However, the convertible was 12 inches (305mm) shorter than the later coupe, which made it more nimble, despite the rear end handicap. While the Dino was never available in the USA, all were left-hand drive, so many have since found their way there.

Top speed:	130 mph (208 km/h)
0–60 mph (0–95 km/h):	7.7 sec
Engine type:	V6
Displacement:	147 ci (2,418 cc)
Transmission:	5-speed manual
Max power:	180 bhp (134 kW) @ 6,600 rpm
Max torque:	159 lb ft (215 Nm) @ 4,600 rpm
Weight:	2,579 lb (1,172 kg)
Economy:	18 mpg (6.4 km/l)

Ford Coupe 1934

The 1934 Ford was one of the first from the blue oval company to get away from the overly square look which had dated cars back to the look of a horse-drawn carriage. The shapely, swept-back grille and flowing fenders quickly gained many fans and because all 1934 models came with a V8, the cars were also popular to tune up and thus came into the world of hot rodders. Like all cars of the era, the 1934 used a separate steel chassis and these still figure in many hot rodders' re-builds today. This car in fact retains the beam front axle too, though with telescopic dampers. At the rear it's much more high-tech with the use of a Corvette independent suspension. This hot rod has a very period appearance with many accessories of the era attached to the body. It goes like a modern supercar, however, thanks to a tuned small-block Chevy which has been bored out to 358ci (5,866cc).

Top speed:	127 mph (203 km/h)
0-60 mph (0–95 km/h):	8.7 sec
Engine type:	V8
Displacement:	358 ci (5,866 cc)
Transmission	4-speed manual
Max power:	330 bhp (264 kW) @ 5,500 rpm
Max torque:	339 lb ft (459 Nm) @ 3,400 rpm
Weight:	2,403 lb (1,092 kg)
Economy:	13.8 mpg (4.9 km/l)

Ford Coupe 1940

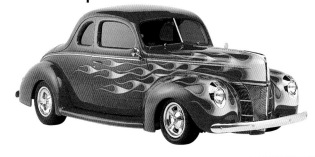

While still using the separate fender design which had evolved from the 1920s and 1930s, the 1940 Ford coupe had rounded lines which dictated how cars were to appear in the next decade. The car, while once proving affordable and simple transportation for many Americans, went on to be a hot rodders' favourite, as its Flathead V8 could be easily tuned. As V8 engines developed and more became available cheaply, so hot rodders fitted older cars with increasingly powerful engines, the small-block Chevy being a favourite. This car uses the basic rails strengthened to take Mustang II front suspension and a 9-inch (229mm) Ford live rear axle on leaf springs. The small-block has been treated to a high-lift camshaft, re-worked heads, a dual plane intake manifold plus Holley four-barrel carb, so it can run the quarter in 14 seconds while giving cruising comfort for four.

Top speed:	123 mph (197 km/h)
0–60 mph (0–95 km/h):	6.4 sec
Engine type:	V8
Displacement:	350 ci (5,735 cc)
Transmission:	3-speed auto
Max power:	345 bhp (257 kW) @ 5,600 rpm
Max torque:	360 lb ft (487 Nm) @ 4,000 rpm
Weight:	2,769 lb (1,259 kg)
Economy:	15 mpg (5.3 km/l)

Ford Escort RS1600

Looking like one of the ordinary Escorts, the RS1600 certainly didn't shout about its potential the way modern rally winners do, though it was very successful. Ford had used the 1968 Escort Twin Cam to replace the Lotus Cortinas and a competition version of the car won the Finland 1000 Lakes Rally that year and the following two seasons. In 1970 Ford homologated a Cosworth-engined, 16-valve version of the regular Escort, using the Twin Cam's reinforced bodyshell, negative camber plates on the strut front suspension, plus lowered and uprated rear leaf springs. Larger 5.5x13-inch (139x330mm) steel rims were fitted, though many were changed for Minilite magnesium rims. The engine was based on the cast-iron Cortina block, but with alloy head, twin camshafts, 16 valves and 10:1 compression. Twin Weber carbs and an oil cooler re-located the battery in the trunk.

Top speed:	114 mph (182 km/h)
0–60 mph (0–95 km/h):	8.3 sec
Engine type:	In-line four
Displacement:	98 ci (1,601 cc)
Transmission	4-speed manual
Max power:	120 bhp (89 kW) @ 6,500 rpm
Max torque:	112 lb ft (152 Nm) @ 4,000 rpm
Weight:	1,965 lb (893 kg)
Economy:	20 mpg (7.1 km/l)

Ford Escort RS Cosworth

Ford planned the Escort to take over from the Sierra in rallying as early as 1988, as they needed a smaller car to win the World Rally Championship (WRC). They gave the job of development to SVE (Special Vehicle Engineering) and Cosworth, who shortened the Sierra Cosworth 4WD sedan's floorpan and put it under the Escort shell, giving it wider arches to maintain the standard track width. Viscous couplings split the power 34:66 front /rear, giving a bias towards rear-wheel drive which proved very effective. The four-cylinder Cosworth engine was fitted with a hybrid Garrett T3/TO4B turbocharger and two stage intercooler, and to help reduce turbo lag, a Weber-Marelli multi-point electronic fuel injection system tuned the turbo to overboost slightly. While successful in various races, it took until the car's last season, 1997, for Spanish driver Carlos Sainz to bring home the WRC for Ford.

Top speed:	137 mph (219 km/h)
0-60 mph (0–95 km/h):	5.8 sec
Engine type:	In-line four
Displacement:	122 ci (1,993 cc)
Transmission:	5-speed manual
Max power:	227 bhp (169 kW) @ 6,250 rpm
Max torque:	224 lb ft (303 Nm) @ 3,500 rpm
Weight:	2,811 lb (1,278 kg)
Economy:	25 mpg (8.9 km/l)

Ford Escort RS2000

Ford was famous for its rally cars of the 1970s, and its RS2000 was the most prominent and successful European rally car of the era, and soon became a performance road car. It shared the basic mechanicals of other MkII Escorts, with MacPherson struts at the front and a live axle rear on leaf springs. Although lowered and uprated, little else was done to the suspension. Externally it was a different matter, with a small trunk spoiler, matt black fenders and grille, a sloping nose cone with spoiler and quad lights, and the classic Ford RS four-spoke alloys. The engine was a derivative of the American 'Pinto' unit, and was called such. Although used in other Fords, the RS got a slightly increased compression ratio and free-flowing exhaust so was more powerful. Inside it used Recaro seats with fishnet headrests and had a short-throw shifter which made gear-changing a blast.

Top speed:	108 mph (173 km/h)
0–60 mph (0–95 km/h):	8.7 sec
Engine type:	In-line four
Displacement:	122 ci (1,993 cc)
Transmission	4-speed manual
Max power:	110 bhp (74 kW) @ 5,500 rpm
Max torque:	119 lb ft (161 Nm) @ 4,000 rpm
Weight:	2,035 lb (925 kg)
Economy:	25 mpg (8.9 km/l)

Ford Fairlane 427

It was right in the middle of the fierce muscle-car wars that Ford launched the Fairlane 427. They widened the shock towers in the engine bay and fitted larger front coil springs in order to cope with both the size and weight of the 427, which basically was a de-tuned race engine. The output was a 'mere' 410bhp (305kW) with single carburettor, but on the Fairlane most came with twin carbs and, therefore, 425bhp (317kW). The body and chassis were unitary and the car could be ordered with a handling package which consisted of longer leaf springs on the live rear axle, front disc brakes and larger 15-inch (381mm) wheels fitted with blackwall tyres. Only one gearbox, Borg-Warner's 'Top Loader' T10, could handle the engine's torque, so every Fairlane 427 got one. Being a thinly disguised race car meant potential purchasers had to be carefully screened by dealers.

Top speed:	121 mph (194 km/h)
0-60 mph (0–95 km/h):	6.0 sec
Engine type:	V8
Displacement:	427 ci (6,997 cc)
Transmission	4-speed manual
Max power:	425 bhp (317 kW) @ 6,000 rpm
Max torque:	480 lb ft (650 Nm) @ 3,700 rpm
Weight:	4,100 lb (1,863 kg)
Economy:	16 mpg (5.7 km/l)

Ford Falcon GT (racer)

The successful start of the Falcon in 1960 led Ford to develop the car further in the following years. Although over 410,000 cars had sold the previous year, in 1961 they produced a Falcon Sprint model with a V8, then in 1962 they sent race-prepared cars to Europe for use in rallying events. In 1964 the car was re-styled with squarer, neater lines, though it faced tough competition from in-house with the new Mustang which, ironically, was a Falcon underneath. This race Falcon is today used in historic circuit competition. It uses lowered and stiffened suspension and in order to lose weight, its hood, trunk, and front fenders have been moulded in glass-fibre. The engine is a High Performance V8, which means it has a slightly increase compression ratio, higher-lift camshaft and free-flowing exhaust. It works through the brutally strong Borg Warner T10 'Top Loader' gearbox.

Top speed:	135 mph (216 km/h)
0–60 mph (0–95 km/h):	6.4 sec
Engine type:	V8
Displacement:	289 ci (4,735 cc)
Transmission	4-speed manual
Max power:	271 bhp (202 kW) @ 6,000 rpm
Max torque:	312 lb ft (422 Nm) @ 3,400 rpm
Weight:	2,811 lb (1,278 kg)
Economy:	12.4 mpg (4.4 km/l)

Ford Falcon GT HO Phase III

The Australian Ford Falcon came out in 1967. It was based on the XR four-door sedan, but out went the straight-six in favour of a 289ci (4.7-litre) V8, and in went buckets seats and a four-speed manual. By 1971 the car reached its high-point with the 351ci (5.8-litre), 300bhp (231kW) XT-sedan based Falcon GT HO, the latter letter standing for 'Handling Option'. The Phase II was born to win Australia's famous 'Bathurst 500' race, so had front and rear anti-roll bars, stiffened springs, front discs, enlarged rear drum brake and a lower ride height. Under the hood there was the famous Cleveland 351ci (5.75-litre) engine which had more performance through better balancing, free-flowing heads, a solid-lifter camshaft and 780cfm carburettor. In this lightweight car it made the performance shattering. The Falcon GTs were known as 'Super Roos' and had logos on each front wing.

Top speed:	144 mph (230 km/h)
0–60 mph (0–95 km/h):	5.7 sec
Engine type:	V8
Displacement:	351 ci (5,751 cc)
Transmission:	4-speed manual
Max power:	300 bhp (223 kW) @ 5,400 rpm
Max torque:	380 lb ft (314 Nm) @ 3,400 rpm
Weight:	2,748 lb (1,249 kg)
Economy:	14 mpg (5 km/l)

FORD

Ford F-150 Lightning

The F-150 Ford had been providing transport for many Americans since the 1960s. It had always used V8s but none had a performance edge. When, in 1992, the F-series truck was given a facelift, it became a best-seller for Ford, so to further enhance it they had their Special Vehicle Team (SVT) produce a hot rod version, the Lightning. SVT wanted it to drive and perform like a supercar so they re-valved the steering for better response, added lowered and stiffened springs then put 17-inch (431mm) wheels at each corner with wide, low-profile tyres. The team chose the 351ci (5.8-litre) Windsor small-block V8 and added GT40 heads, new manifolds, a Lightning-specific cam, and a custom computer from the Mustang GT. The fenders and grille were colour-coded to distinguish it and the interior fitted with buckets seats, completing it as a real driver's truck.

Top speed:	120 mph (192 km/h)
0–60 mph (0–95 km/h):	7.5 sec
Engine type:	V8
Displacement:	351 ci (5,751 cc)
Transmission	4-speed auto
Max power:	240 bhp (179 kW) @ 4,200 rpm
Max torque:	340 lb ft (460 Nm) @ 3,200 rpm
Weight:	4,378 lb (1,990 kg)
Economy:	17 mpg (6 km/l)

Ford Galaxie 500

Like many muscle cars, the 1966 Galaxie 500 used the simple formula of a massive engine up front driving the rear wheels. It had stacked headlamps, all new suspension and the emphasis was more on comfort, despite obviously being a muscle machine. The A-arm suspension was very good and went on to be used in NASCAR competition, while at the rear coil springs and control arms replaced the former leaf spring set-up. It all added up to a refined ride but the big-block up front could soon change that. Up to 1965 the biggest engine in the Galaxie had been the 427ci (6.9 litres), but the 428ci (7-litre), also part of the FE range of big-block Fords, was built mainly to produce torque. It was a more streetable engine than the 427 engine, but still had plenty of power and incredible torque at low rpm. Inside, being a top-of-the-range car, the 500 featured leather seats and wood trim.

Top speed:	105 mph (168 km/h)
0–60 mph (0–95 km/h):	8.2 sec
Engine type:	V8
Displacement:	428 ci (7,013 cc)
Transmission	3-speed auto
Max power:	345 bhp (257 KW) @ 4,600 rpm
Max torque:	462 lb ft (626 Nm) @ 2,800 rpm
Weight:	4,059 lb (1,845 kg)
Economy:	9 mpg (3.2 km/l)

FORD

Ford GT40

Ford attempted to buy Ferrari in 1963, and when they failed, it was all-out war on the race track. Ford joined with Lola to turn the Lola GT into the prototype Ford GT, then in 1964 came out with the GT40, so called because it stood just 40 inches (1016mm) high. They weren't very successful and failed to finish in any races. But with huge resources the programme continued with Carroll Shelby at the helm, and in 1965 production of the road-going GT40 started for homologation plus a GT40 won its first race. In 1966 three GT40s fitted with 427 big-block engines took Le Mans with a 1-2-3 win, beating Ferrari. After this the cars used the smaller 289ci (4.7-litre) V8s, but were just as successful. They had a sheet steel semi-monocoque with separate subframes for the rear engine and gearbox, and very deep sills (where the fuel cells were housed) meant the whole structure was extremely stiff.

Top speed:	165 mph (264 km/h)
0–60 mph (0–95 km/h):	5.5 sec
Engine type:	V8
Displacement:	289 ci (4,735 cc)
Transmission	4-speed manual
Max power:	306 bhp (229 kW) @ 6,000 rpm
Max torque:	328 lb ft (444 Nm) @ 4,200 rpm
Weight:	2,200 lb (1,000 kg)
Economy:	14.7 mpg (5.2 km/l)

Ford Hi-Boy 1932 Roadster

The term 'hot rod', to many people involved with such cars, can mean only one car: the 1932 Ford roadster. These cars have been the backbone of the rodding scene for over 60 years, the trend for them beginning as early as the late 1930s. Back then, young guys were picking them up very cheaply, stripping everything but the essentials off of them, then racing their cars on the street or, in the case of Southern California where the movement began, on the dry lake beds which were both flat and vast. While the hot-rod movement has grown to incorporate all manner of cars, the 1932 roadster remains. This one is typical of the cars built in the 1960s, with split wishbone front radius arms, a beam front axle, live axle rear and a small-block up front, though in this case it's Ford. Period touches include the wide steel rims and fenderless body which saved weight.

Top speed:	120 mph (192 km/h)
0-60 mph (0–95 km/h):	6.0 sec
Engine type:	V8
Displacement:	302 ci (4,948 cc)
Transmission	3-speed manual
Max power:	250 bhp (186 kW) @ 4,500 rpm
Max torque:	275 lb ft (372 Nm) @ 3,000 rpm
Weight:	2,250 lb (1,022 kg)
Economy:	15 mpg (5.3 km/l)

Ford Lotus Cortina

It was Ford's Walter Hayes who in 1963 persuaded Lotus boss Colin Chapman to produce a limited run of Cortinas with Lotus engines. The intention was to produce 1,000 cars, but its popularity saw three times that amount made. In 1964 Jim Clark won the British Saloon Car Championship and in 1965 Sir John Whitmore won the European Saloon Car Championship. Looking fairly plain externally apart from the green stripes, the Lotus Cortinas sat lower and the front MacPherson struts had new uprated springs and shocks, while at the rear the leaf springs were removed and replaced by an A-frame arrangement plus radius arms and coil-over-shock units. The standard 1500 Ford bottom end was used along with a twin-cam head and twin Webers. A great car to drive fast, the Lotus Cortinas now command high prices and are still used in historic racing.

Top speed:	106 mph (170 km/h)
0–60 mph (0–95 km/h):	9.9 sec
Engine type:	In-line four
Displacement:	95 ci (1,558 cc)
Transmission:	4-speed manual
Max power:	105 bhp (78 kW) @ 5,500 rpm
Max torque:	108 lb ft (146 Nm) @ 4,000 rpm
Weight:	2,038 lb (926 kg)
Economy:	28 mpg (9.9 km/l)

Ford Mustang GT 1965

With massive sales in its first year, Ford pushed the Mustang further by bringing out the performance GT 2+2 in 1965. It used a fastback roofline to gain extra rear space, and had sporty touches such as the louvers on the rear pillars. As costs had to be kept down, little was done to the stock chassis which had a double wishbone front and leaf spring rear. A special handling package did come with the GT however, which included heavy duty springs and shocks plus quicker 22:1 ratio steering, Standard for the GT also were fade-resistant front disc brakes. Although three transmissions were available, the one to have was the four-speed Borg Warner 'Top Loader', while the engine to order was the 'K-code' which had 10.5:1 compression, four-barrel carb, solid lifter camshaft and high-flow air filter. Testers christened the K-code car 'a four-passenger Cobra'.

Top speed:	123 mph (197 km/h)
0–60 mph (0–95 km/h):	7.3 sec
Engine type:	V8
Displacement:	289 ci (4,735 cc)
Transmission:	4-speed manual
Max power:	271 bhp (202 kW) @ 6,000 rpm
Max torque:	312 lb ft (422 Nm) @ 3,400 rpm
Weight:	3,100 lb (1,409 kg)
Economy:	15 mpg (5.3 km/l)

Ford Mustang Boss 302

While Ford lead the sales war of the 1960s with the Mustang, Chevrolet won on the street with the Camaro Z28. Ford needed an answer and it came in 1969 with the Boss 302. They mated the larger 351ci (5.7-litre) Cleveland heads to the smaller Windsor 302ci (5.0-litre) block, then increased the compression ratio and fitted a larger carb plus high-lift camshaft. The resulting high-rpm V8, though rated at 290bhp (216kW), was closer to 350bhp (261kW). Stylist Larry Shinoda used his aerodynamics expertise and created the functional front and rear spoilers, plus a set of rear window slats. To cope with the power, the car used a Borg Warner T10 'Toploader' gearbox. All the Boss 302s used a Hurst shifter with T-handle, and this added more driveability to the car. The Boss 302 carried on production into 1970, and that year it won the Trans-Am manufacturers' title, thus creating a legend.

Top speed:	128 mph (205 km/h)
0–60 mph (0–95 km/h):	6.5 sec
Engine type:	V8
Displacement:	302 ci (4,948 cc)
Transmission	4-speed manual
Max power:	290 bhp (216 kW) @ 5,800 rpm
Max torque:	290 lb ft (392 Nm) @ 4,300 rpm
Weight:	3,227 lb (1,467 kg)
Economy:	14 mpg (5 km/l)

Ford Mustang Boss 429

When Ford wanted to use a new engine in NASCAR, to qualify it was required to build 500 production cars. Instead of putting their new 429ci (7.2-litre) into the mid-sized Torinos which they were racing, they decided to shoehorn it into the Mustang. The 429 motor was unlike any other Ford motor, being much wider in the cylinder head, thanks to its semi-'Hemi' combustion chamber design. It meant the Mustang strut towers had to be widened and the battery moved to the trunk. The Boss used a the 'Top Loader' close-ratio, four-speed manual transmission because the autos couldn't handle the power. Modified suspension comprised uprated springs, anti-roll bar and re-valved shocks. The Boss 429 was the most expensive non-Shelby Mustang ever to be produced, but nonetheless the 428 Cobra Jet version was the fun on the street.

Top speed:	118 mph (189 km/h)
0–60 mph (0–95 km/h):	6.8 sec
Engine type:	V8
Displacement:	429 ci (7,030 cc)
Transmission	4-speed manual
Max power:	375 bhp (279 kW) @ 5,200 rpm
Max torque:	450 lb ft (609 Nm) @ 3,400 rpm
Weight:	3,870 lb (1,760 kg)
Economy:	13.8 mpg (4.9 km/l)

Ford Mustang 1980s

With the arrival of the 'Fox' Mustang in 1979, Ford had built themselves a winner and sold over a million cars up to 1993. Because of sheer amount of 1979–1993 cars, a massive aftermarket worth billions of dollars was established, and modifications go from the likes of a high-flow air filter to blown 700bhp (522kW) road cars which can cover the quarter-mile in under 10 seconds. This particular car is a wild road machine, fitted with fender extensions to fit the 10-inch (254mm) and 13-inch (330mm) wide wheels, a new nose section, huge rear wing to aid downforce and some good engine mods to boost the powerful V8. A larger throttle body to allow more air in, plus a high lift camshaft and free-flow exhaust help this car to run in 13.4 seconds on the quarter-mile. Saleen Racecraft suspension has been fitted also, both lowering and uprating the handling.

Top speed:	150 mph (240 km/h)
0–60 mph (0–95 km/h):	5.2 sec
Engine type:	V8
Displacement:	306 ci (5,014 cc)
Transmission	5-speed manual
Max power:	370 bhp (276 kW)@ 4,800 rpm
Max torque:	300 lb ft (406 Nm) @ 3,000 rpm
Weight:	3,560 lb (1,618 kg)
Economy:	17 mpg (6 km/l)

Ford Mustang Cobra 1993

The Series 3 Mustang had been in production since 1979, so by 1993 was well overdue for replacement. To bow out with a bang, the Ford engineers came up with the best version of all: the Cobra. Using the 215bhp (160kW) GT as a base, a new grille, sill panel mouldings, rear valance and spoiler were made, plus the car was given 17-inch (432mm) wheels and low-profile tyres. Lowered suspension, interestingly with softer rate springs, gave the car better handling and a more civilized ride. Power was up to 235bhp (175kW) thanks to GT40 heads, a special intake, bigger throttle body, larger injectors and a revised roller camshaft. Disc brakes all around improved the braking over the standard GT, but aside from this, the car was similar. The most radical was the Cobra R, a race-only version which had luxuries removed – such as the air-con, radio, and rear seats – to save weight.

Top speed:	151 mph (242 km/h)
0–60 mph (0–95 km/h):	5.8 sec
Engine type:	V8
Displacement:	302 ci (4,948 cc)
Transmission:	5-speed manual
Max power:	235 bhp (175 kW) @ 5,000 rpm
Max torque:	285 lb ft (386 Nm) @ 4,000 rpm
Weight:	3,225 lb (1,465 kg)
Economy:	21 mpg (7.4 km/l)

Ford Mustang Cobra R 1995

Up until the introduction of the 2000 Cobra R, the 1995 model was the fastest Mustang ever. The 'R' stood for race and the Special Vehicle Team (SVT) at Ford made sure owners weren't going to lose any. Inside the car the sound-deadening was deleted, as was the radio, rear seats, rear window defrost, electric windows and air-conditioning, in an effort to save weight. The Cobra R even came with basic velour seats, as Ford realized most people would change these for race buckets. Eibach progressive rate springs and Koni adjustable shocks were fitted, and the front anti-roll bar was fattened. The engine was that from the Ford Lightning, a 351ci (5.8-litre) V8 with GT40 heads, special Cobra intake, SVO camshaft and bigger mass air meter. It put out so much torque that Ford had to fit a stronger gearbox so chose the Tremec 3550. This car ran 12-second quarter-mile times.

Top speed:	150 mph (240 km/h)
0–60 mph (0–95 km/h):	5.5 sec
Engine type:	V8
Displacement:	351 ci (5,751 cc)
Transmission	5-speed manual
Max power:	300 bhp (224 kW) @ 4,800 rpm
Max torque:	365 lb ft (494 Nm) @ 3,750 rpm
Weight:	3,325 lb (1,511 kg)
Economy:	17 mpg (6 km/l)

Ford Mustang GT 1998

The 1998 Mustang GT was a progression of the body style which appeared in 1994, taking over from the much-loved but dated Series 3 'Fox' Mustang. Though heavier than the Series 3 due to extra stiffening in the shell structure, the car felt more solid to drive and handled far better. The real change was when the 5.0L V8 engine was replaced by the all-new 281ci (4.6-litre) 'Modular' V8 in 1996, which offered an increase in refinement at the cost of torque. By 1998 the GT was putting out 225bhp (167kW) and 285lb ft (386Nm) torque and the engine was a keen revver. It used a live axle with four locating bars and separate coil springs and shocks at the rear, while at the front MacPherson struts with lower wishbones gave a good ride and handling. To satisfy Mustang lovers, Ford added scoops on the side bodywork and vertically segmented rear lights, plus a running horse in the grille.

Top speed:	141 mph (226 km/h)
0–60 mph (0–95 km/h):	6.3 sec
Engine type:	V8
Displacement:	281 ci (4,604 cc)
Transmission	5-speed manual
Max power:	225 bhp (167 KW) @ 4,400 rpm
Max torque:	285 lb ft (386 Nm) @ 3,500 rpm
Weight:	3,462 lb (1,573 kg)
Economy:	20 mpg (7.1 km/l)

Ford Mustang 5.0 LX

Few cars can claim to have made such an impact on the United States during the 1980s as the 1987–1993 5.0L Mustang. For a cheap price it gave enthusiasts a powerful V8 engine, enough luxury and good handling, and because of this was a big hit. In base 'LX' form, the car came without the range-topping GT's bodykit, hence it weighed less and was quicker. Various magazines testing the car in the USA had the Borg Warner T5 manual five-speed versions running low-14-second quarter-miles, surpassing many higher powered muscle cars of the 1960s and early 1970s. Certainly it was vastly superior in handling, thanks to progressive rate springs and a 'Quadra-shock' horizontal shocks at either side of the axle to prevent wheel hop and increase traction. The LX was so quick in standard form that even the US police chose it for high-speed patrol work.

Top speed:	138 mph (221 km/h)
0–60 mph (0–95 km/h):	6.2 sec
Engine type:	V8
Displacement:	302 ci (4,948 cc)
Transmission	5-speed manual
Max power:	225 bhp (167 KW) @ 4,400 rpm
Max torque:	300 lb ft (406 Nm) @ 3,000 rpm
Weight:	3,145 lb (1,429 kg)
Economy:	22 mpg (7.8 km/l)

Ford Mustang Mach 1

The 1973 Mach 1 was the biggest of all Mustangs, and a long way from the sporty car intention of the early Mustang design. Not only was it larger (due to complaints about cramped passenger space in the early cars), it was also heavier and plusher, though it handled well, due to the competition suspension which included heavy-duty front and rear springs, front and rear anti-roll bars and re-valved shocks. Coming in 1973, the car was strangled by emissions and as such the 302ci (5-litre) engine offered a fraction of the performance available in 1969 with the very first Mach 1. But you could opt for the 351ci (5.8-litre) engine with a four-barrel carburettor if you wanted to hot things up a little. The 1973 Mach 1's stylish fastback lines and comfortable ride made it a hit, and over 35,000 cars were produced, which was good, considering the fuel crisis hitting gas-guzzler sales.

Top speed:	110 mph (176 km/h)
0–60 mph (0–95 km/h):	10.4 sec
Engine type:	V8
Displacement:	302 ci (4,948 cc)
Transmission	3-speed auto
Max power:	136 bhp (101 kW) @ 4,200 rpm
Max torque:	232 lb ft (314 Nm) @ 2,200 rpm
Weight:	3,090 lb (1,404 kg)
Economy:	14 mpg (5 km/l)

Ford Mustang SVO

Putting a four-cylinder engine and pushing it as a high-performance model gave Ford a hard time in 1984. They were just reacting to higher fuel prices and the demand for smaller-engined cars, using the 'Fox' platform from regular Mustangs and fitting an uprated version of their 140ci (2.3-litre) engine. The four-cylinder came in 88bhp (65kW) form as standard, but the addition of a turbo gave it 143bhp (107kW). This wasn't enough to ensure good sales, however, so power was upped for 1985 1/2 cars onwards to 175bhp (130kW) with 15psi boost. In 1986 it was the best for power and handling, thanks to the lightweight engine. A stiffer front anti-roll bar, rear anti-roll bar, uprated springs, and adjustable Koni shocks made cornering very rapid, while four-wheel disc brakes brought the stopping power up to scratch. Cheaper fuel brought the V8 back, and the SVO was no more after 1986.

Top speed:	140 mph (224 km/h)
0–60 mph (0–95 km/h):	6.7 sec
Engine type:	In-line four
Displacement:	140 ci (2,294 cc)
Transmission	5-speed manual
Max power:	205 bhp (153 kW) @ 5,000 rpm
Max torque:	240 lb ft (325 Nm) @ 3,000 rpm
Weight:	3,036 lb (1,380 kg)
Economy:	25 mpg (8.9 km/l)

Ford RS200

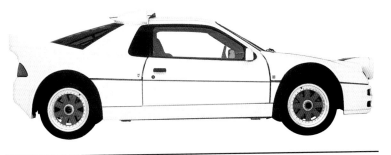

Amidst the fury of 600bhp (447kW) Group B rally cars, Ford needed a serious competitor, so launched the 1984 RS200, 'RS' standing for Rallye Sport, while the number simply meant the amount produced. A year later, the factory's RS won the first rally event it entered, then came third in the World Rally Championship. In 1986, following horrific crashes in Portugese Rally in which spectators were killed, Group B rally cars were banned, but the RS200s continued to be used in motorsport and on the road. The RS used a mid-mounted four-cylinder with the transmission in the front axle. It used a built-in roll cage tied into large tubular subframes. The engine was the ultimate development of Cosworth's BD (belt-driven camshaft) all-alloy motor, with Garrett turbocharger, four valves per cylinder and dry sump lubrication. Road versions had 250bhp (185kW), competition 700bhp (522kW).

Top speed:	140 mph (224 km/h)
0–60 mph (0–95 km/h):	6.1 sec
Engine type:	In-line four
Displacement:	110 ci (1,803 cc)
Transmission:	5-speed manual
Max power:	250 bhp (185 kW) @ 6,500 rpm
Max torque:	215 lb ft (291 Nm) @ 4,000 rpm
Weight:	2,607 lb (1,185 kg)
Economy:	16 mpg (5.7 km/l)

Ford Sierra Cosworth RS 500

When Ford debuted its new jelly mould Sierra in 1982, it was a radical design, a long way from the boxy Cortina it'd replaced. Yet few people envisaged it being a high-performance machine capable of taking on supercars. Ford did produce the V6-equipped XR4i in 1983 and even though it showed potential in the Sierra chassis, it wasn't radically quick. The 1985 RS Cosworth was, however, very fast, and Ford wanted to race it so needed to homologate the car. They produced the RS500, made exactly 500 and added many performance extras. A large rear spoiler with extra raised lip increased downforce at speed, while the rear end driveshafts and bearings were uprated to cope and the four vented discs given an anti-lock system. The engine used a thicker casting block, forged internal parts and a larger turbo which gave out 9psi as stock but 22psi in competition for 570bhp (425kW).

Top speed:	154 mph (246 km/h)
0–60 mph (0–95 km/h):	6.1 sec
Engine type:	In-line four
Displacement:	122 ci (1,993 cc)
Transmission:	5-speed manual
Max power:	224 bhp (167 kW) @ 6,000 rpm
Max torque:	205 lb ft (277 Nm) @ 3,500 rpm
Weight:	2,734 lb (1,243 kg)
Economy:	20 mpg (7.1 km/l)

Ford Thunderbird 1955

The Thunderbird appeared a year after the Corvette and was direct competition. Ford's new two-seater had the same layout of a separate chassis with live rear axle on leaf springs, but with one important difference: it had a V8. The 265ci (4.3-litre) engine gave the performance people expected and a year later, a larger, 312ci (5.1-litre) unit was available. The T-bird had other advanced features such as power brakes and steering, making it a better car to drive. The car came with a glass-fibre bolt-on hardtop, but had the option of a folding convertible roof for an extra $290. At first the T-Bird carried its spare wheel above the rear fender, but Ford extended the rear for 1957, which meant it could be carried in the trunk. The extra weight put into the rear of the car also helped ride quality. Most desirable is the rare 300bhp (225kW) supercharged 1957 F-Bird, of which just 211 were made.

Top speed:	122 mph (195 km/h)
0–60 mph (0–95 km/h):	9.5 sec
Engine type:	V8
Displacement:	292 ci (4,785 cc)
Transmission:	3-speed manual
Max power:	212 bhp (158 kW) @ 4,400 rpm
Max torque:	297 lb ft (402 Nm) @ 2,700 rpm
Weight:	3,050 lb (1,386 kg)
Economy:	13 mpg (4.6 km/l)

Ford Torino Talladega

In 1969 NASCAR Ford and Chrysler battled it out. In response to the dominating Dodge Charger 500, Ford came up with the Torino Talladega which cleaned up in its first year with 30 victories. Based on the Fairlane Torino which had appeared in 1968, the Talladega had the same monocoque chassis. The suspension used a double wishbone front and a leaf spring rear, though the back had staggered shocks to counter wheel hop. All Talladegas came with the 428ci (7-litre) Cobra Jet big-block V8 engine, rated at 335bhp (250kW); for insurance output was closer to 450bhp (335kW). It had 10.6:1 compression, a steel crank, stronger con rods and a 735cfm Holley carb. The suspension used stiffer springs and shocks plus a thicker anti-roll bar up front. At the rear a Traction Lok diff and 3.25:1 gears were stock. For better aerodynamics a tapered nose was stretched by 5 inches (127mm).

Top speed:	130 mph (208 km/h)
0–60 mph (0–95 km/h):	5.8 sec
Engine type:	V8
Displacement:	428 ci (7,013 cc)
Transmission:	3-speed auto
Max power:	335 bhp (250 kW) @ 5,200 rpm
Max torque:	440 lb ft (595 Nm) @ 3,400 rpm
Weight:	3,536 lb (1,607 kg)
Economy:	14 mpg (5 km/l)

Ford Woody

Woodys were always regarded as the family station wagon with a country feel, until surfers found them useful for their long boards. They became firm favourites with both surfers and hot rodders, who had lifestyles that were very alike with a disregard to conforming to the norm. Most surf wagons were kept stock mechanically but just lowered and sometimes fitted with custom wheels. This 1950 Ford has taken the Woody to another level with late-model Mustang independent front suspension and a narrowed 9-inch (228mm) Ford axle located on a four-bar set-up. The power comes via a supercharged small-block Chevy with massive torque, and to put the power down the owner has fitted 13-inch (330mm) wide Mickey Thompson Pro Street Radials at the rear. The rear seat has been removed, but the interior features air-conditioning and a multi-speaker sound system.

Top speed:	147 mph (235 km/h)
0–60 mph (0–95 km/h):	4.7 sec
Engine type:	V8
Displacement:	406 ci (6,653 cc)
Transmission:	4-speed auto
Max power:	410 bhp (305 kW) @ 5,100 rpm
Max torque:	450 lb ft (609 Nm) @ 3,100 rpm
Weight:	3,402 lb (1,546 kg)
Economy:	16.7 mpg (5.9 km/l)

Ginetta G4

The Walklett brothers – Ivor, Bob, Douglas and Trevor – made their first production car in 1958, and during the 1960s their cars were successful club racers. Their first G4 was sold in 1964 and was remarkably similar to this 1998 version. That first G4 used very lightweight design with a tubular space frame and independent front suspension but a live rear axle, and power came from a 92ci (1,500cc) Ford engine which could get it to 60mph (95km/h) in less than 7 sec. The modern car retained the same chassis layout and independent wishbone front, but with an independent rear wishbone set-up too. Adjustable Spax coil-over-shocks provided good tuneability at each corner. The new G4 also used a Ford engine, this time the ultra modern Zetec unit as fitted in the Focus. Available with either fuel injection or twin Weber carbs, the latter produced the quickest car.

Top speed:	130 mph (208 km/h)
0–60 mph (0–95 km/h):	5.0 sec
Engine type:	In-line four
Displacement:	110 ci (1,796 cc)
Transmission:	5-speed manual
Max power:	150 bhp (113 kW) @ 6,250 rpm
Max torque:	130 lb ft (176 Nm) @ 3,700 rpm
Weight:	1,256 lb (571 kg)
Economy:	27 mpg (9.6 km/l)

GMC Syclone

The Syclone was based on GMC's Sonoma truck, and while it didn't have a great deal of load space, it was exceptionally quick with a 4.9 second 0–60mph (0–95 km/h) time, which then was faster than a Ferrari 348 and even the mighty Corvette ZR-1. But it wasn't all straight-line performance for the pick-up, because with its four-wheel drive system it was also incredibly good through the bends too. GMC kept the bias towards rear-wheel drive with a 35:65 front/rear torque split, adding a limited-slip differential in the live rear axle to ensure maximum traction. They also gave the pick-up both lowered and uprated springs and shocks to further enhance the pick-up's sporting feel. The Syclone quickly built up a strong following in the USA, and while as standard they could run the quarter-mile in 14 seconds, the current record for a road Syclone stands in the 10s.

Top speed:	125 mph (km/h)
0–60 mph (0–95 km/h):	5.2 sec
Engine type:	V6
Displacement:	262 ci (4,293 cc)
Transmission:	4-speed auto
Max power:	280 bhp (208 kW) @ 4,400 rpm
Max torque:	350 lb ft (474 Nm) @ 3,600 rpm
Weight:	3,422 lb (1,555 kg)
Economy:	25 mpg (8.8 km/l)

GMC Typhoon

Part of GMC's plans to move its image into the performance market started with creating the ultimate pick-up, the GMC Syclone. But a year later, with the continuing popularity of Sport Utility Vehicles, GMC followed that with the Typhoon which had room enough for five adults plus their luggage space. The Typhoon used the same underpinnings at the Syclone with a separate chassis, live rear axle and 11-inch (279mm) ABS-assisted and vented discs. The engine was from the GMC Jimmy, all cast-iron but uprated from the stock 165bhp (123kW) thanks to an intercooled turbo and re-calibrated engine management. The torque was split 35:65 front/rear with a mechanical centre differential and viscous coupling, though the live rear axle also used a limited-slip differential. A four-speed auto just about handled the torque but a strict warning sticker not to tow with the vehicle had to be put inside.

Top speed:	124 mph (198 km/h)
0–60 mph (0–95 km/h):	5.4 sec
Engine type:	V6
Displacement:	262 ci (4,293 cc)
Transmission	4-speed auto
Max power:	280 bhp (209 kW) @ 4,400 rpm
Max torque:	350 lb ft (474 Nm) @ 3,600 rpm
Weight:	3,822 lb (1,737 kg)
Economy:	25 mpg (8.8 km/l)

Honda Accord Type R

Up until the 1990s Honda had been known for sensible family cars, but that all changed with the development of their V-Tech models which demonstrated a new performance side of the company. The 1997 Accord was re-designed as more roomy and was available with a V6 engine, but it wasn't until the following year that the fireworks really started with the launch of the Type R. This used an Accord sedan platform, but with a much stiffer body and uprated and lowered suspension on the all-round double wishbone set-up. Power came through a 134ci (2.2-litre) twin-cam 16v four-cylinder using the latest development of Honda's V-Tech system. With 11:1 compression, low friction pistons and sequential fuel injection it would rev through to 8,500rpm, and thanks to a limited-slip differential could put the power down, making it one of the best-handling front-wheel drive sedans.

Top speed:	140 mph (224 km/h)
0–60 mph (0–95 km/h):	7.1 sec
Engine type:	In-line four
Displacement:	132 ci (2,157 cc)
Transmission	5-speed manual
Max power:	209 bhp (156 kW) @ 7,200 rpm
Max torque:	158 lb ft (214 Nm) @ 6,700 rpm
Weight:	3,098 lb (1,408 kg)
Economy:	25 mpg (8.8 km/l)

Honda Civic CRX

Looking like a small hatchback, the CRX had more in common with the two-seater sports coupes of the 1980s. It started with a 92ci (1.5-litre) three-valve per cylinder unit which produced an impressive 100bhp (74kW), but the car was re-designed in 1986 and packed a fearsome punch with its new twin-cam 16v engine which coaxed 125bhp (93kW) from just 98ci (1.6 litres). The new CRX benefited from a new suspension design with double wishbones all around and anti-roll bars, though it still handled on the firm side and many regarded it as a street-legal go-kart. Being strictly a front-engined, front-wheel drive two-seater meant that the car was nose heavy, so it needed the rear spoiler to provide downforce. Even so, the car's handling and steering was extremely precise and with the engine buzzing around the 6,000rpm power peak, it was a formidable opponent cross-country.

Top speed:	121 mph (194 km/h)
0–60 mph (0–95 km/h):	8.6 sec
Engine type:	In-line four
Displacement:	97 ci (1,590 cc)
Transmission	5-speed manual
Max power:	125 bhp (93 kW) @ 6,000 rpm
Max torque:	100 lb ft (135 Nm) @ 5,000 rpm
Weight:	2,086 lb (948 kg)
Economy:	30 mpg (10.7 km/l)

Honda NSX

A iming to build the perfect sportscar and Honda racing experience and put it all into one of the most dynamic shapes ever from Japan, the NSX challenged Ferrari for looks and Porsche for build quality but conquered all in the ease of driving. The car was very simple to use and drive very quickly. Aluminium alloys were used exclusively throughout the car, from suspension arms through the entire engine to the body. Twin wishbones front and back made the car's handling exceptional, while electric power-steering reduced the assistance as speed increased, down to nothing at high speed. The V6 engine was another marvel of Honda's V-Tech engineering with quad cams, the intake of which activated a more aggressive cam profile beyond 5,800rpm, thus not sacrificing torque. To cheat wind the underside was flat and the rear shape of the car helped reduce lift at speed.

Top speed:	162 mph (259 km/h)
0–60 mph (0–95 km/h):	5.4 sec
Engine type:	V6
Displacement:	182 ci (2,977 cc)
Transmission	5-speed manual
Max power:	274 bhp (204 kW) @ 7,000 rpm
Max torque:	210 lb ft (284 Nm) @ 5,300 rpm
Weight:	3,021 lb (1,373 kg)
Economy:	16.2 mpg (5.7 km/l)

Honda NSX Type-R

The NSX was an easy supercar to drive quickly, but what Honda wanted with its 1992 Type-R version was a more suitable track car, hence the 'R' for 'racing'. Unlike other Type-Rs, this one really was for smooth surfaces only. While little could be done to save weight on the alloy chassis and suspension components, Honda manage to lose 268lb (121kg) from the car by scrapping the air-con, underseal, stereo, and spare wheel, and replacing the stock seats and removing other non-essential items. The body had few items which hadn't already been given lightweight consideration, but Honda did change the plastic-covered steel fenders for alloy items, thus helping the car's diet. The only other change was the wheels, which were lighter, forged units, rather than cast. Engine power barely changed, though the unit was fully balanced and blueprinted to withstand racing use.

Top speed:	169 mph (270 km/h)
0–60 mph (0–95 km/h):	5.1 sec
Engine type:	V6
Displacement:	183 ci (2,997 cc)
Transmission	5-speed manual
Max power:	280 bhp (209 kW) @ 7,300 rpm
Max torque:	209 lb ft (283 Nm) @ 5,400 rpm
Weight:	2,712 lb (1,233 kg)
Economy:	18 mpg (6.4 km/l)

Honda Prelude VTi

Honda's sporty Prelude appeared in 1992 but was replaced by the sharp version here in 1996 and output was up by 7bhp (5kW) in the VTi. In Honda's racing tradition, it used double wishbone suspension all-around and managed to combine very little body roll in corners with a surprisingly supple ride. The car used electronics to give four-wheel steering which first saw light on the early Preludes; at low speed the rear wheels would turn one way to make parking easier, while at high speed the wheels turn to improve the handling and cornering. Massive ABS-assisted discs at each corner give the Prelude VTi the finest brakes in the sports coupe market. But the car wasn't all about sporty pretensions, because inside it was jam-packed with luxuries such as power sunroof, heated seats, air-conditioning, a leather wheel, cruise control and a high-power audio system.

Top speed:	142 mph (227 km/h)
0–60 mph (0–95 km/h):	6.6 sec
Engine type:	In-line four
Displacement:	132 ci (2,157 cc)
Transmission:	5-speed manual
Max power:	197 bhp (147 kW) @ 7,100 rpm
Max torque:	156 lb ft (211 Nm) @ 5,250 rpm
Weight:	2,908 lb (1,322 kg)
Economy:	28 mpg (9.9 km/l)

Jaguar D-Type

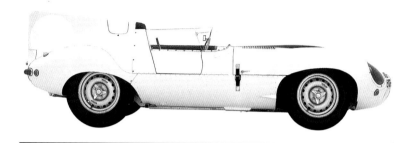

The D-Type was built with one race in mind: Le Mans, in France. But it wasn't as if Jaguar had been without success, as their XK 120C MkII, otherwise known as the C-Type, had been successful in the early 1950s and had been clocked doing 180mph (289km/h) on a closed Belgian highway. To make it as light and advanced as possible, the D-Type used a centre monocoque section with separate front subframe, where most cars were using ladder frames. There was still a live axle at the rear, but up front were double wishbones and longitudinal torsion bar springs. The engine was a version of Jaguar's famous XK unit, featuring an iron block and ally head with twin high-lift camshafts, bigger inlet valves and three twin Weber carbs. It used dry sump lubrication to remain reliable in racing. Later, fuel injection gave 304bhp (227kW). The rear fin was for high-speed stability.

Top speed:	162 mph (259 km/h)
0–60 mph (0–95 km/h):	5.4 sec
Engine type:	In-line six
Displacement:	210 ci (3,442 cc)
Transmission	4-speed manual
Max power:	250 bhp (186 kW) @ 6,000 rpm
Max torque:	242 lb ft (327 Nm) @ 4,000 rpm
Weight:	2,460 lb (1,118 kg)
Economy:	20 mpg (7.1 km/l)

Jaguar E-Type

When the E-Type was displayed at the Geneva Motor Show, Switzerland, in 1961, orders flooded into Jaguar because nothing else at the time could match it for looks, pace and performance at the $3,400 price. It used a monocoque similar to the one developed in the racing D-Type Jags, with separate steel subframes, the front carrying double wishbones and torsion bar springs, while the rear rubber mounted unit held an excellent lower wishbone/upper driveshaft arrangement with large inboard discs and two coil-cover-shocks units per side. The engine was again a development of the previously used XK straight-six, with triple SU carbs giving a very smooth and torquey power delivery that was well suited to the four-speed and long-geared final-drive gears. Testing on Britain's famous M1 motorway proved these cars were very capable of their quoted 150mph (241km/h) top speed.

Top speed:	150 mph (240 km/h)
0–60 mph (0–95 km/h):	7.3 sec
Engine type:	In-line six
Displacement:	231 ci (3,781 cc)
Transmission	4-speed manual
Max power:	265 bhp (197 kW) @ 5,500 rpm
Max torque:	260 lb ft (352 Nm) @ 4,000 rpm
Weight:	2,463 lb (1,119 kg)
Economy:	14.5 mpg (5.1 km/l)

Jaguar E-Type Lightweight

While the E-Type was based on a similar chassis to the racing D-Type, and used an even more advanced independent rear suspension, it was never designed to be a race car. However, it had encouraging results in the hands of private racers, which persuaded Jaguar to make a limited number of very special 'Lightweight' cars. The body was made in aluminium and the fenders were removed completely while other omissions included badges, trim and most of the interior. The car was based on the E-Type roadster, but used a fixed hardtop which helped with rigidity. Suspension was uprated with stiffer torsion bars and a fatter anti-roll bar up front. At the rear it had modified wishbones, lightened hub carriers and stiffer shocks. Power was upped with Lucas fuel injection and a cast-alloy block. Just 12 cars were produced, and most are still about, having a great racing history.

Top speed:	157 mph (251 km/h)
0-60 mph (0–95 km/h):	5.0 sec
Engine type:	In-line six
Displacement:	230.5 ci (3,781 cc)
Transmission	5-speed manual
Max power:	344 bhp (255 kW) @ 6,500 rpm
Max torque:	314 lb ft (424 Nm) @ 4,750 rpm
Weight:	2,220 lb (1,009 kg)
Economy:	15 mpg (5.3 km/l)

Jaguar XJ220

It was top Jaguar engineer Jim Randle who came up with the idea for a 542 bhp (403 kW) supercar. A Concept was built for the British Motor Show in 1988, but it wasn't until Ford took over Jaguar the following year that the go ahead for production was given. Jaguar with a V12 and four-wheel drive, the car eventually debuted at the track with a twin-turbo V6 and two-wheel drive, plus it was 9.8 inches (250mm) shorter than the concept. The Sport got the job of building it and while the concept was shown, debut car crushed the track record at the famous 14–mile (22-km) Nurburgring circuit, Germany, and reached test speeds of 213 mph (340 km/h). This resulted in a final model in 1992 which went into production, taking 12 days to make each one of the 275 built. Each one cost $400,000 and, at the time, it was the fastest production car ever.

Top speed:	218 mph (349 km/h)
0-60 mph (0–95 km/h):	3.8 sec
Engine type:	V6
Displacement:	213.5 ci (3,498 cc)
Transmission	5-speed manual
Max power:	542 bhp (403 kW) @ 7,000 rpm
Max torque:	N/A
Weight:	3,250 lb (1,477 kg)
Economy:	10 mpg (3.5 km/l)

Jaguar XJR-9LM

With a history of racing that hadn't been pushed properly in 30 years, Jaguar decided to get serious about endurance racing after the USA 'Group 44' team took a Jaguar back to Le Mans in 1986. Jaguar put motorsport guru Tom Walkinshaw in charge of their World Championship campaign and the following year they ran the XJR-8, winning eight rounds to take the FIA Prototype Championship with almost twice as many points as their nearest rival. In 1988 the new and agile XJR-9 debuted and won three races before entering the Le Mans 24-hour, France, in which one of the three entered won outright. The XJR-9's monocoque chassis was made in carbon-fibre and Kevlar composite and used double wishbones plus 13-inch (330mm) disc brakes all around. Part of the car's success, the mid-mounted all-alloy V12, was very reliable in competition.

Top speed:	236 mph (377 km/h)
0–60 mph (0–95 km/h):	N/A
Engine type:	V12
Displacement:	426 ci (6,995 cc)
Transmission:	5-speed manual
Max power:	745 bhp (556 kW) @ 7,250 rpm
Max torque:	610 lb ft (826 Nm) @ 5,500 rpm
Weight:	2,315 lb (1,052 kg)
Economy:	N/A

Jaguar XJR-S

Being associated with luxury cars that floated along, Jaguar needed outside help when it came to pumping up their ageing XJS in 1988. They turned to Tom Walkinshaw, in charge of running Jaguar Sport. Walkinshaw set about making important tweaks here and there to put the flabby-handling XJS back on track. In the suspension revised spring pressures, re-valved shocks and new bushes made it much more taut in corners. Wider wheels and tyres took care of the rest of the driver feedback, and the steering also had its assistance reduced to improve the feel. The all-alloy V12 was pushed out to 366ci (5,997cc) in displacement from the standard 323ci (5,337) unit by increasing the stroke of the crankshaft, then in 1991 the XJR-S got a new look and a race-derived engine management system, along with revisions to the intake and exhaust. Production ended in 1995.

Top speed:	155 mph (248 km/h)
0–60 mph (0–95 km/h):	6.5 sec
Engine type:	V12
Displacement:	366 ci (5,993 cc)
Transmission:	3-speed auto
Max power:	333 bhp (248 kW) @ 5,250 rpm
Max torque:	365 lb ft (494 Nm) @ 3,650 rpm
Weight:	4,023 lb (1,828 kg)
Economy:	14 mpg (5 km/l)

Jaguar XKR

The all-new XK8 appeared at the Geneva Motor Show, Switzerland, in 1996, with both the coupe and convertible versions powered by the new lightweight alloy AJ-V8 244ci (4-litre) engine. In 1997 came Jag's new sedan, the XJR which used a supercharger on the same V8 for incredible performance, which overshadowed the more sporting XK8. So, for 1998 the blown V8 was installed in the coupe and called the XKR. While running the same chassis as the XK8, the XKR had re-calibrated suspension with computer-adjustable damping. The quad-cam V8 was all-alloy and the lightest V8 in its class, plus it was high-tech with variable camshaft timing. The Eaton M112 supercharger gave 28 percent more power, and to cope the XKR had 12-inch (305mm) vented discs all around with high-friction pads. The gearbox was from a Mercedes Benz to handle the increased torque.

Top speed:	155 mph (248 km/h)
0–60 mph (0–95 km/h):	5.1 sec
Engine type:	V8
Displacement:	244 ci (3,996 cc)
Transmission	5-speed auto
Max power:	370 bhp (275 kW) @ 6,150 rpm
Max torque:	387 lb ft (524 Nm) @ 3,600 rpm
Weight:	3,850 lb (1,750 kg)
Economy:	14 mpg (5 km/l)

Jaguar XK120

When launched in 1948, the XK120 was an incredibly fast machine. Its six-cylinder engine was very smooth and the power almost unending, but the car remained easy to drive, thanks to a large steering wheel and progressive handling. Its styling was also very modern, with the swoopy curves and aerodynamic shape inspired by the early 1940s BMW 328 Mille Miglia racer. The 120 used wishbone front suspension with torsion bar springs, while at the rear a live axle remained on leaf springs. It was effective enough, especially on the C-Type race car, which was based on the XK120. Inside it had Jaguar comfort with full Connolly leather seats and door trims, plus a well laid-out dash with large gauges. The twin-cam straight-six was an extremely robust unit which was used up until the 1960s in XJ sedans. In the 120 it had twin SU carbs and a torque-biased power delivery.

Top speed:	121 mph (194 km/h)
0–60 mph (0–95 km/h):	11.3 sec
Engine type:	In-line six
Displacement:	210 ci (3,442 cc)
Transmission	4-speed manual
Max power:	180 bhp (134 kW) @ 5,300 rpm
Max torque:	203 lb ft (275 Nm) @ 4,000 rpm
Weight:	3,039 lb (1,381 kg)
Economy:	13.8 mpg (4.9 km/l)

Jeep Grand Cherokee

The success and heritage of the Jeep name was something Chrysler wanted to capitalize on when they launched the Jeep Grand Cherokee in 1993. It boasted Chrysler's Uni-frame structure which was a monocoque crafted in steel and using Quadra-Coil suspension on live front and rear axles with anti-roll bars and gas-filled shocks. The Quadra-Trac 4WD was very useful, being an on-demand system with a viscous coupling centre differential with the torque split between front and rear axles, depending on surface conditions. The body was more rounded than previous Cherokees and in fact it had one of the most aerodynamic shape of any Sport Utility Vehicle. It also had short overhangs and could approach a hill of 37 degrees or leave one of 30 degrees. Best of all was the 360ci (5.9-litre) V8 which gave the Grand Cherokee more supercar-like performance on the road.

Top speed:	124 mph (198 km/h)
0–60 mph (0–95 km/h):	8.2 sec
Engine type:	V8
Displacement:	360 ci (5,899 cc)
Transmission	4-speed auto
Max power:	237 bhp (176 kW) @ 4,050 rpm
Max torque:	345 lb ft (467 Nm) @ 3,050 rpm
Weight:	4,218 lb (1,917 kg)
Economy:	13 mpg (4.6 km/l)

Jensen CV8

Richard and Alan Jensen began as coachbuilders, producing attractive bodies on various chassis available from British manufacturers, but went into production of their own cars in 1935. Their 1940s and 1950s cars were large and used some of the biggest British engines of the time, typically Austin straight-six 244ci (4-litre) units. Their range turned more sporty from 1952 with the 541, very similar in looks to this CV8 which appeared 10 years later. The slanted headlights provoked love 'em or hate 'em reactions, but what won many fans was the use of a new 360ci (5.9-litre) V8 engine from Chrysler. With the CV8 having a lightweight glass-fibre body, the motor gave tremendous performance. The chassis comprised two main large tubes which ran front to rear, with Austin-derived front wishbones and a limited-slip differential equipped live axle which hung on leaf springs.

Top speed:	136 mph (218 km/h)
0–60 mph (0–95 km/h):	6.7 sec
Engine type:	V8
Displacement:	383 ci (6,276 cc)
Transmission:	3-speed auto
Max power:	330 bhp (246 kW) @ 4,800 rpm
Max torque:	425 lb ft (575 Nm) @ 3,000 rpm
Weight:	3,600 lb (1,636 kg)
Economy:	13 mpg (4.6 km/l)

Jensen Interceptor

Replacing the controversially styled CV8 in 1966, just four years after it'd been launched, the Interceptor was virtually the same car underneath. It used a steel tube chassis, four-wheel disc brakes, double wishbone front and leaf spring rear suspension, plus a Panhard rod and live rear axle. What made the difference to buyers was the Vignale-styled steel body, though it did have a downside as it was prone to bad rusting. The Chrysler powerplants remained, options being a 383ci (6.2-litre) or, from 1971 on, a 440ci (7.2-litre) which even came with the legendary Six pack triple carb set-up. Although the car went through various updates from 1969 to 1971, Jensen went out of business through loss of sales in 1976. However, a MkIV version did make it out in 1983, built by new company Jensen Parts & Service. The late 1990s also saw a revival in the Jensen name and new models.

Top speed:	137 mph (219 km/h)
0–60 mph (0–95 km/h):	6.4 sec
Engine type:	V8
Displacement:	383 ci (6,276 cc)
Transmission	3-speed auto
Max power:	330 bhp (246 kW) @ 4,600 rpm
Max torque:	450 lb ft (609 Nm) @ 2,800 rpm
Weight:	3,696 lb (1,680 kg)
Economy:	10.7 mpg (3.8 km/l)

Lamborghini Countach

The Bertone-styled Lamborghini Countach stunned everyone when it was launched in 1971 at the Geneva Motor Show, Switzerland. It went into production three years later and, incredibly, could reach speeds of up to 190mph (305km/h). Through the 1980s it was developed, particularly with the engine which went to four camshafts with the 'Quattrovalvole' version, for a mighty 455bhp (339kW). Though many supercars were using fuel injection by 1990, the Countach shunned this in favour of six Weber downdraught carburettors, and sounded all the better for it. Double wishbones at the front and trailing arms plus wishbones at the rear kept the cornering very flat, while massive discs with cooling ducts from the bodywork kept braking highly efficient, no matter what the speed. This is a design icon which lasted 20 years prior to the equally stunning Diablo taking over.

Top speed:	178 mph (285 km/h)
0–60 mph (0–95 km/h):	5.2 sec
Engine type:	V12
Displacement:	315 ci (5,167 cc)
Transmission	5-speed manual
Max power:	455 bhp (339 kW) @ 7,000 rpm
Max torque:	369 lb ft (499 Nm) @ 5,200 rpm
Weight:	3,188 lb (1,449 kg)
Economy:	11.8 mpg (4.2 km/l)

Lamborghini Diablo

With the Countach looking very dated by the late 1980s, Lamborghini needed an answer to take them into the next decade. The company created a super Countach in order to evaluate parts for its new sportscar. At first the car came out with just rear-wheel drive, but in 1991 it was decided that in order to harness the full power quota which the car was to put out, it would need 4WD, so the VT version was launched. This was still heavily biased to rear-wheel drive, however, with just 27 per cent going to the front. The engine used was the same throughout, being a 60-degree V12 which was based on a design from Lamborghini's first V12 in 1963. It was all-alloy in construction and use short stroke to allow very high revving. Handling was nothing short of amazing, with double wishbones all around and a very wide track.

Top speed:	205 mph (328 km/h)
0–60 mph (0–95 km/h):	4.3 sec
Engine type:	V12
Displacement:	350 ci (5,729 cc)
Transmission	5-speed manual
Max power:	492 bhp (366 kW) @ 7,000 rpm
Max torque:	428 lb ft (579 Nm) @ 5,200 rpm
Weight:	3,475 lb (1,579 kg)
Economy:	13.1 mpg (4.6 km/l)

Lamborghini LM002

In 1977 Lamborghini hoped to be part of a US military project and produced the rear-engined Cheetah concept for the 1977 Geneva Motor Show, Switzerland. By the early 1980s, though, American company AM had won the Army contract with their cheaper Humvee. Despite this, Lamborghini pressed on with the LM002 and it was available from 1985. It used a brutally strong and complex steel spaceframe chassis with bonded aluminium panels. Independent self-levelling suspension was fitted and Kevlar-reinforced tyres were specially developed. The engine came straight from the Countach supercar, virtually unchanged except for a waterproof air intake and fuel injection. A more powerful LM004 model with Lamborghini's marine V12 put out 434lb ft (587Nm) torque. The interior was fully loaded with leather trim, air-con and power everything as standard.

Top speed:	126 mph (202 km/h)
0–60 mph (0–95 km/h):	8.5 sec
Engine type:	V12
Displacement:	315 ci (5,167 cc)
Transmission	5-speed manual
Max power:	450 bhp (336 kW) @ 6,800 rpm
Max torque:	369 lb ft (536 Nm) @ 4,500 rpm
Weight:	5,954 lb (2,706 kg)
Economy:	10.2 mpg (3.6 km/l)

Lamborghini Miura

This was the stunning machine that, in 1966, started the mid-engined trend in supercars, making Ferraris appear out of date both in technology and looks. The Miura was also the first supercar with a quad-cam V12 engine. The sensation of the Geneva Motor Show, Switzerland in 1966, the Bertone low-slung design was almost space-age in concept, and firmly put an identity on future supercars. Its massive side sills were an indication of the new chassis design, using a steel monocoque with big sills and a large centre tunnel. The engine was held in a stamped steel frame behind the occupants and featured an alloy block and heads, with classic hemispherical combustion chambers borrowed from an American design, and four camshafts even though it had only two valves per cylinder. The later, SV version had more power with 385bhp (287kW) in 1971, but the fuel crisis saw the end of the car in 1973.

Top speed:	172 mph (275 km/h)
0–60 mph (0–95 km/h):	6.9 sec
Engine type:	V12
Displacement:	240 ci (3,929 cc)
Transmission	5-speed manual
Max power:	370 bhp (276 kW) @ 7,700 rpm
Max torque:	286 lb ft (387 Nm) @ 5,500 rpm
Weight:	2,851 lb (1,296 kg)
Economy:	11.2 mpg (4 km/l)

Lancia Delta Integrale

Originally conceived as a homologation special for rallying, this car was first launched as the Delta HF Turbo 4x4 in 1987, but within months was badged the Integrale. It grew wide arches for fatter alloys, but retained four doors and remained practical. The road car echoed the rally car, using a permanent 4WD system with epicyclic centre differential and viscous coupling, plus Torsen limited-slip differentials. Suspension was similar front and rear with MacPherson struts and anti-roll bars. The car used a development of the 122ci (2-litre) four-cylinder engine from the Thema sedan, with a cast-iron block and alloy head. Multi-point injection and a turbo were standard, and from 1989 it was also 16v. As a combination of handling, balance and power, few cars could beat the Intergrale, and it lasted until 1994, remaining as good as many of the upcoming road/rally cars.

Top speed:	137 mph (219 km/h)
0–60 mph (0–95 km/h):	5.7 sec
Engine type:	In-line four
Displacement:	122 ci (1,997 cc)
Transmission	5-speed manual
Max power:	210 bhp (157 kW) @ 5,750 rpm
Max torque:	227 lb ft (307 Nm) @ 2,500 rpm
Weight:	2,954 lb (1,342 kg)
Economy:	22 mpg (7.8 km/l)

Lancia Stratos

Italian coachbuilder Bertone can take credit for the Stratos, as it debuted the concept at the 1970 Turin Motor Show, Italy. Inspired by the first car, the Stratos HF appeared a year later at the same show, using a Ferrari V6 engine. Lancia had taken note of the car, and when in 1973 they needed 500 cars built for rally homologation they commissioned Bertone to do the work. Later that year the Stratos took its first win at the Spanish Firestone Rally, but the real results came the following year when the homologation production was completed and the Stratos won the first of three consecutive World Rally Championships. Its success is down to how well it was built. It had a centre steel cage with rear frame holding the engine and strut suspension while the front end had wishbones. Lancia continued using the quad-cam Dino engine, with three Weber twin-choke carbs in road form.

Top speed:	140 mph (224 km/h)
0–60 mph (0–95 km/h):	7.0 sec
Engine type:	V6
Displacement:	147 ci (2,418 cc)
Transmission	5-speed manual
Max power:	190 bhp (141 kW) @ 7,000 rpm
Max torque:	166 lb ft (224 Nm) @ 5,500 rpm
Weight:	2,161 lb (982 kg)
Economy:	16.8 mpg (6 km/l)

Lexus LS400

For a Japanese firm to challenge the likes of BMW and Mercedes for top honours in the executive class might have seemed too big a mountain to climb, but Lexus was on the ball straight away when it launched the LS400 in 1990. It might not have had the badge, but thanks to a quad-cam 250bhp (186kW) 244ci (4-litre) V8 and masses of equipment for a bargain price, it quickly gained fans. Double wishbone suspension made it an agile car given its size too, while rack and pinion steering kept it precise in corners, and an intelligent five-speed transmission gave the driver the best of both worlds, depending on their mood. Massive brake discs of 12-inches (304mm) all around with, naturally, ABS, were reassuring given the speeds the LS400 was capable of and inside the luxury of satellite navigation, a CD-Rom, sound system, leather and wood made it a very comfortable grand tourer.

Top speed:	155 mph (248 km/h)
0–60 mph (0–95 km/h):	6.3 sec
Engine type:	V8
Displacement:	242 ci (3,969 cc)
Transmission	5-speed auto
Max power:	290 bhp (216 kW) @ 6,000 rpm
Max torque:	300 lb ft (406 Nm) @ 4,000 rpm
Weight:	3,886 lb (1,766 kg)
Economy:	17 mpg (6 km/l)

Light Car Co. Rocket

With project accomplishments such as the McLaren MP4/4 F1 car and the road-going McLaren F1, designer Gordon Murray knew what a good road/race car needed. Hence, when he formed the Light Car Company with Chris Craft in 1991, the two-seater Rocket used all his ideas. Being lightweight was imperative and to achieve this the car used a multi-tube spaceframe chassis with thin but strong double A-arms at either end and coilover shock units. The engine is straight from a Yamaha FZR 1000 motorbike and sits in the rear as a stressed member, giving the chassis yet more strength. The standard sequential gearbox provides drive to twin speed axle, which makes cruising more relaxed, plus provides a reverse which isn't available on the bike gearbox. The engine used a roller bearing crank, five valves per cylinder and four Mikuni carbs, plus an 11,000rpm redline.

Top speed:	130 mph (208 km/h)
0–60 mph (0–95 km/h):	4.8 sec
Engine type:	In-line four
Displacement:	61 ci (1,002 cc)
Transmission	5-speed sequential
Max power:	143 bhp (107 kW) @ 10,500 rpm
Max torque:	77 lb ft (104 Nm) @ 8,500 rpm
Weight:	882 lb (401 kg)
Economy:	20 mpg (7.1 km/l)

Lincoln MkVIII

Being Ford USA's premium brand, Lincoln has always had the bias towards luxury, but the MkVIII took it to a new level. Carrying on developments made in the MkVII, the 1993 model became superior and had radically modern looks in order to take on the influx of European and Japanese cars. The new swoopy lines won many fans, as did the new all-alloy 32-valve V8 Modular engine later used in the Mustang Cobra. Coupled to the new 4R70W automatic overdrive transmission, the drive train made the MkVIII a capable performer, which could also be laid-back. Handling was very good too, the car feeling agile whilst remaining supple, thanks to air springs at each corner. To get in you had to punch in a code before the door handle would operate, but once inside you were treated to a very modern and ergonomic dash, with a full complement of toys.

Top speed:	123 mph (197 km/h)
0–60 mph (0–95 km/h):	7.0 sec
Engine type:	V8
Displacement:	281 ci (4,601 cc)
Transmission	4-speed auto
Max power:	290 bhp (216 kW) @ 5,750 rpm
Max torque:	285 lb ft (386 Nm) @ 4,500 rpm
Weight:	3,765 lb (1,711 kg)
Economy:	22 mpg (7.8 km/l)

Lincoln Navigator

The Sport Utility vehicle market has become bigger than ever in the USA in the past decade, and at the top in terms of prestige and capabilities is the Lincoln Navigator. It hit the market in 1998 and used the floorpan and running gear of the Ford Expedition, which itself could be traced back to the F-150 pick-up. However, for both comfort and adjustability, the Navigator used air springs which work in conjunction with the automatic load-levelling facility, and when off-road, the car lifts by an inch for extra clearance. Though the live axle might have seemed dated, it was well located with upper and lower trailing arms plus a Panhard rod. The engine was a larger version of the modular unit used in other Fords, called the 'Triton'. It used a single cam per bank and sequential fuel injection and was highly reliable, not needing servicing for 100,000 miles (160,000km).

Top speed:	109 mph (174 km/h)
0–60 mph (0–95 km/h):	11.4 sec
Engine type:	V8
Displacement:	330 ci (5,400 cc)
Transmission:	4-speed auto
Max power:	230 bhp (171 kW) @ 4,250 rpm
Max torque:	325 lb ft (440 Nm) @ 3,000 rpm
Weight:	5,557 lb (2,526 kg)
Economy:	14.7 mpg (5.2 km/l)

Lister Storm

L ister were involved with Jaguar racing cars back in the 1950s, but in 1983 they were commissioned to build racing versions of the Jaguar XJS V12, which was the first step to producing its own Lister Le Mans and MkIII race cars. Company founder Laurence Pearce wanted to realize a dream of making a supercar for the road, and by 1991 enough capital had been raised to start on the Storm. The car was more function over form, with an alloy honeycomb structure forming the monocoque and carbon-fibre making up the bodywork. The engine it used was still an enlarged Jaguar V12 unit, but with twin superchargers running at 9psi boost. Pulling it down from the huge speed were 14.5 (368mm) and 12.5-inch (317mm) vented Brembo discs with alloy four-pot callipers. The suspension with tubular A-arms at front and a multi-link rear was stiff, but ideal for fast road and track use.

Top speed:	200 mph (320 km/h)
0–60 mph (0–95 km/h):	4.1 sec
Engine type:	V12
Displacement:	427 ci (6,996 cc)
Transmission	6-speed manual
Max power:	594 bhp (443 kW) @ 6,100 rpm
Max torque:	580 lb ft (785 Nm) @ 3,450 rpm
Weight:	3,169 lb (1,440 kg)
Economy:	12 mpg (4.2 km/l)

Lotus Elan 1971

The flyweight Lotus Elan is regarded as one of the best-handling cars ever made which is some tribute, given it was designed in the 1960s. Created by Lotus founder Colin Chapman, it used a simple backbone chassis and fitted Triumph Herald independent front suspension with Chapman's own patented struts on the independent rear. The car was supposed to use a glass-fibre monocoque, but in order to test prototypes quickly, they had a separate steel chassis. It worked so well that the Elan went into production like this, with a glass-fibre body. The engine was from the Lotus Cortinas of the time, starting out as a 85ci (1.4-litre) unit but later changing to 95ci (1.5-litre). The power was exceptional but it was the car's 1515lb (687kg) that made it so lively. In corners it didn't under- or oversteer, but tracked on a line around bends and gave huge levels of grip even on 6.4-inch (165mm) tyres.

Top speed:	118 mph (189 km/h)
0–60 mph (0–95 km/h):	7.0 sec
Engine type:	In-line four
Displacement:	95 ci (1,558 cc)
Transmission	4-speed manual
Max power:	126 bhp (94 kW) @ 6,500 rpm
Max torque:	113 lb ft (153 Nm) @ 5,500 rpm
Weight:	1,515 lb (688 kg)
Economy:	26 mpg (9.2 km/l)

Lotus Elan 1989

Although the concept was a sound one, the new Elan came at a bad time for Lotus. Launched in 1989 with a worldwide recession looming, the car had been built using an Isuzu drive train to help reduce costs, but people weren't convinced enough by the front-wheel drive car to let it live far beyond the lean times. Lotus had used a version of its own backbone-style chassis adapted for the new powerplant and it all worked very well. The car had amazing grip and the 98ci (1.6-litre) fuel injected engine revved freely and gave plenty of torque thanks to a water-cooled turbocharger. The body was made via Vacuum-Assisted Resin Injection using a form of glass-fibre, so was very light. A specially designed front suspension wishbone arrangement kept torque steer down to a minimum while at the rear lower wishbones and upper transverse links kept the car very flat in cornering.

Top speed:	136 mph (218 km/h)
0–60 mph (0–95 km/h):	6.5 sec
Engine type:	In-line four
Displacement:	97 ci (1,588 cc)
Transmission:	5-speed manual
Max power:	165 bhp (123 kW) @ 6,600 rpm
Max torque:	148 lb ft (200 Nm) @ 4,200 rpm
Weight:	2,254 lb (1,024 kg)
Economy:	19.6 mpg (7 km/l)

Lotus Elise

Few people in the early 1990s expected the floundering UK-based Lotus to come up with such a impressive car. The company wowed everyone with the debut of the handsome Elise at the Frankfurt Motor Show, Germany in 1995, the theory behind the design being pure Lotus, in that it had to be lightweight with an emphasis on handling and performance. The stark nature of the interior helped get the Elise down to an incredibly low 1600lb (725kg). It also stayed slim by utilizing aluminium alloys wherever possible, including brake discs and uprights. The Elise team were clever in other areas too, using an extruded aluminium chassis made in sections and bonded together, as opposed to welding. Power came from Rover's compact K-series engine, again all-alloy and with remarkable output, particularly torque, from its 110ci (1.8 litres).

Top speed:	124 mph (198 km/h)
0–60 mph (0–95 km/h):	5.5 sec
Engine type:	In-line four
Displacement:	109 ci (1,796 cc)
Transmission:	5-speed manual
Max power:	118 bhp (88 kW) @ 5,500 rpm
Max torque:	122 lb ft (165 Nm) @ 3,000 rpm
Weight:	1,594 lb (724 kg)
Economy:	29.4 mpg (10.5 km/l)

Lotus Esprit Turbo

The Esprit remains one of the longest production run supercars ever. Launched in 1980, it is still being made in the 21st century, albeit in a much revised high-performance machine. Yet it is unique among supercars because it uses just four cylinders, aided by a Garrett T3 intercooled turbo. In typical Lotus fashion the Esprit used a steel backbone chassis into which the engine is mounted longitudinally directly behind the driver. Independent suspension featured throughout with double wishbones at the front and a twin transverse link at the rear. The engine was all-alloy with 16 valves and a special overboost facility to harness a full 300bhp (224kW) in short bursts. In 1996 the four-cylinder 134ci (2.2-litre) S4 was replaced by a V8 version to satisfy stringent American emissions regulations, later supplemented with a 240bhp (179kW), 122ci (2-litre) Esprit GT3.

Top speed:	162 mph (259 km/h)
0–60 mph (0–95 km/h):	4.7 sec
Engine type:	In-line four
Displacement:	133 ci (2,174 cc)
Transmission	5-speed manual
Max power:	264 bhp (197 kW) @ 6,500 rpm
Max torque:	264 lb ft (357 Nm) @ 3,900 rpm
Weight:	2,649 lb (1,204 kg)
Economy:	21 mpg (7.5 km/l)

Lotus Carlton/Omega

Mixing one of the world's top sportscar names with a mass-production manufacturer resulted in one of the most striking and fastest sedans with the 1990 Lotus Carlton. Using a standard Vauxhall Carlton GSi 3000 bodyshell, Lotus took it and re-designed the running gear, putting in a multi-link rear axle, twin tube shocks and some of the biggest brakes ever seen on a production sedan with 13-inch (330mm) and 11.8-inch (299mm) discs. For power Lotus started with the 183ci (3-litre) twin-cam straight six and fitted a longer stroke crank to produce 220ci (3.6 litres), plus new pistons for a lower compression to allow the fitting of twin Garret T25 turbos. The turbos were intercooled and helped propel the car to just shy of 180mph (290km/h), with an acceleration that left most exotic machines behind. Just 950 were produced; 510 were left-hand drive, called Lotus Omegas.

Top speed:	176 mph (282 km/h)
0–60 mph (0–95 km/h):	5.1 sec
Engine type:	In–line six
Displacement:	221 ci (3,615 cc)
Transmission	6–speed manual
Max power:	377 bhp (281 kW) @ 5,200 rpm
Max torque:	419 lb ft (567 Nm) @ 4,200 rpm
Weight:	3,640 lb (1,655 kg)
Economy:	20 mpg (7.1 km/l)

Marcos Mantis

Like many small car manufacturers in the early 1970s, Marcos went out of business but was revived in 1981 when founder Jem Marsh made a comeback with updated versions of his sporty coupes. Although the cars started out with four-cylinder engines, by the mid-1980s a Rover V8 was being used. As the Rover went out of production in the mid-1990s, Marcos turned to Ford for their modular V8 and the Mantis was born. The wild glass-fibre bodywork hid a strong, separate tubular steel backbone, with MacPherson struts up front and wishbones at the rear. The wheels were 17-inch (432mm) up front while the rears were taller and wider. All Mantis cars with seven-spoke alloys ran a Vortech supercharger on the Ford 32-valve modular engine which gave 450bhp (336kW). The massive hood bulge both made room for the motor and extracted hot air via vents.

Top speed:	161 mph (258 km/h)
0–60 mph (0–95 km/h):	4.8 sec
Engine type:	V8
Displacement:	281 ci (4,601 cc)
Transmission:	5–speed manual
Max power:	352 bhp (262 kW) @ 6,000 rpm
Max torque:	300 lb ft (406 Nm) @ 4,800 rpm
Weight:	2,620 lb (1,191 kg)
Economy:	21 mpg (7.4 km/l)

Maserati 3500GT

An Italian muscle car, the 3500GT combined stylish lines with a highly strung and powerful straight-six engine. The car was more to be enjoyed as a grand tourer than a circuit machine for the street, as its steering wasn't very communicative. It used a tubular steel chassis consisting of two main members running the length of the car with outriggers along the sills. To the front sat a double wishbone arrangement and at the rear, leaf springs were highest tech option at the time. The engine was a twin-cam design made in alloy and was ahead of its time by using twin spark plugs fired by twin coil, plus mechanical fuel injection by Lucas. For 1958 the 3500GT was one very quick car in a straight line, beating both the Aston DB4 and Ferrari 250 Lusso. For that reason it's a highly sought after classic worth many times more than its original sale price.

Top speed:	129 mph (206 km/h)
0–60 mph (0–95 km/h):	7.5 sec
Engine type:	In-line six
Displacement:	213 ci (3,485 cc)
Transmission	4-speed manual
Max power:	230 bhp (171 kW) @ 5,500 rpm
Max torque:	224 lb ft (303 Nm) @ 4,500 rpm
Weight:	3,180 lb (1,445 kg)
Economy:	17 mpg (6 km/l)

Maserati Biturbo

A s a former producer of supercars which had folded in 1975 and been brought out by Alejandro de Tomaso, Maserati needed a big revival come the early 1980s. It needed a mainstream car so they chose to mimic the 3-Series BMW with a new compact sedan that would have power, refinement and driver involvement. The 1981 Biturbo was the result. It used a MacPherson strut front and Chapman strut rear, and had performance extras such as a Sensi-tork limited-slip differential and four-wheel disc brakes. The aluminium V6 engine started out with 122ci (2-litre) displacement but had grown to 170ci (2.8-litres) by 1988. The twin turbos suffered from lag to start with, but this was all but gone in later models, though the oversteer was still very evident, especially in the wet. One of the car's best attributes was the steering, which was widely praised by critics.

Top speed:	128 mph (205 km/h)
0–60 mph (0–95 km/h):	7.2 sec
Engine type:	V6
Displacement:	152 ci (2,491 cc)
Transmission	5-speed manual
Max power:	185 bhp (138 kW) @ 5,500 rpm
Max torque:	208 lb ft (282 Nm) @ 3,000 rpm
Weight:	2,394 lb (1,088 kg)
Economy:	17 mpg (6 km/l)

Maserati Bora

Through financial backing from Citroen, who became the major shareholder in 1968, Maserati agreed to produce two mid-engined cars, the V6 Marek and V8 Bora. The Bora was Maserati's first to use mid-engine mounting and it created a supercar to rival the likes of Ferrari and Lamborghini. It had a semi-monocoque design with folded sheet steel front and cabin sections, while the rear had a subframe in which both the engine, gearbox and suspension were mounted. The 287ci (4.7-litre) V8 had been designed in the 1950s and used four overhead camshafts, an aluminium block and heads, and hemispherical combustion chambers for increased power. The body was steel and, despite no wind-tunnel testing, managed a drag coefficient of just 0.30, which wasn't equalled in years of car production. A long production run of 9 years saw 570 cars made.

Top speed:	160 mph (256 km/h)
0–60 mph (0–95 km/h):	6.5 sec
Engine type:	V8
Displacement:	288 ci (4,719 cc)
Transmission	5-speed manual
Max power:	310 bhp (231 kW) @ 6,000 rpm
Max torque:	325 lb ft (440 Nm) @ 4,200 rpm
Weight:	3,570 lb (1,623 kg)
Economy:	10 mpg (3.5 km/l)

Maserati Ghibli

Although it never achieved massive success, the 1992 Ghibli was a stunning machine. Its main competition being the BMW 3-series, it used a similar layout with a two-door coupe monocoque body and front-engined/rear-wheel drive package. MacPherson struts and semi-trailing arm rear combined with four position shocks, all thoroughly developed through Maserati's race experience, made the ride and handling inspiring. Steering through the rack and pinion was equally razor-sharp. What further enhanced the experience was an all-alloy, four-valve per cylinder short-stroke 171ci (2.8-litre) V6 which liked to be revved. Coupled with twin turbos, the Ghibli's powerplant produced stunning torque, easily enough to rival BMW's M3. This is an Italian thoroughbred from a company which has successfully produced supercars alongside sedans.

Top speed:	153 mph (245 km/h)
0–60 mph (0–95 km/h):	5.6 sec
Engine type:	V6
Displacement:	170 ci (2,790 cc)
Transmission:	5-speed manual
Max power:	280 bhp (209 kW) @ 5,500 rpm
Max torque:	317 lb ft (429 Nm) @ 3,750 rpm
Weight:	2,998 lb (1,363 kg)
Economy:	24 mpg (8.5 km/l)

Mazda Miata

Looking like the Lotus Elan from the 1960s, the Mazda Miata (MX5 in UK) re-ignited the sportscar market single-handedly in 1989. Like the Elan, it used a very simple formula of front-engine, rear-wheel drive with tight suspension, all in a lightweight package. The car started with just 97ci (1.5 litres) and 116bhp (86kW) thanks to 16 valves and a slightly increased redline over the Mazda 323 model it came from. Underneath was a steel monocoque with engine/transmission plus rear axle subframes, and double wishbones front and rear. The rack and pinion steering was made high-geared so drivers could adjust the car's line very quickly in corners, though it needed a lot of provocation to go off line as the handling was well-balanced and neutral. The car was easy for a convertible, too, requiring just two buttons to be pressed and two levers to be folded before the roof would go down.

Top speed:	121 mph (194 km/h)
0–60 mph (0–95 km/h):	9.1 sec
Engine type:	In-line four
Displacement:	97 ci (1,598 cc)
Transmission:	5-speed manual
Max power:	116 bhp (86 kW) @ 6,500 rpm
Max torque:	100 lb ft (136 Nm) @ 5,500 rpm
Weight:	2,073 lb (942 kg)
Economy:	24.8 mpg (8.8 km/l)

Mazda RX-7

After a successful Le Mans in 1991, in which Mazda came first with its 700bhp, (522kW) high-revving R26B rotary-powered car, the new RX-7 made its debut. It immediately jumped from sportscar to supercar, thanks to a design brief which stated the car had to be as light and fast as possible. While the shell was steel, the advanced double wishbone suspension was all-alloy, and components were directly bolted to the chassis without bushings for more precise handling. Alloy cross braces were used within the body, making a very stiff structure. The engine was based on the original twin rotor Wankel design, and having few moving parts meant it could rev very quickly. The key was the twin-turbo set-up, one of which started the lag-free performance, the other joining in at 4,500rpm, whereupon it would rapidly rev to its redline.

Top speed:	156 mph (250 km/h)
0–60 mph (0–95 km/h):	5.3 sec
Engine type:	Twin rotor Wankel
Displacement:	158 ci (2,616 cc)
Transmission	5-speed manual
Max power:	255 bhp (190 kW) @ 6,500 rpm
Max torque:	217 lb ft (294 Nm) @ 5,000 rpm
Weight:	2,800 lb (1,273 kg)
Economy:	13.8 mpg (4.9 km/l)

McLaren F1

Every McLaren F1 made lost money, such was the attention to detail and over-meticulous design from the UK-based F1 team. Just 100 were produced, going to specialist collectors around the world and having standard extras such as a complete tool kit (a 6ft/1.8m high chest), gold-plated engine bay, custom-fit McLaren F1 luggage, and full McLaren engine diagnostics anywhere in the world. The F1 was made from carbon composites with honeycomb crossbeams for an immensely strong structure. It needed every bit of strength with power that could accelerate the car to 150mph (241km/h) in 12 seconds. The undertray used venturi tunnels to create a drop in pressure, thus pulling the car towards the ground. A central driving position was ideal and the car easy to drive. At around $1,130,000 when debuted, it was the most expensive road car ever to buy new.

Top speed:	231 mph (370 km/h)
0–60 mph (0–95 km/h):	3.2 sec
Engine type:	V12
Displacement:	370 ci (6,064 cc)
Transmission	6-speed manual
Max power:	627 bhp (468 kW) @ 7,300 rpm
Max torque:	479 lb ft (649 Nm) @ 4,000 rpm
Weight:	2,245 lb (1,020 kg)
Economy:	12.4 mpg (4.4 km/l)

Mercedes 300SL

The infamous 'Gullwing' first saw light in 1952 as a race car. It used a spaceframe chassis with a network of small tubes and hence was lightweight, though the high chassis sides meant fitting conventional doors was out of the question, hence the 'Gullwing' design, which just about provided enough room to get in. While strong, the chassis was let down by the suspension fitted to it, in particular the rear which used as swing axle set-up that made for tricky handling, and the brakes which were all drums and not very efficient. The SL used a sedan engine, but with dry sump lubrication and mechanical fuel injection, which required a bulge in the hood, the other bulge being simply to balance the design. The 1957 Roadster was much better, with improved rear suspension, power disc brakes, and a less cramped interior.

Top speed:	165 mph (265 km/h)
0–60 mph (0–95 km/h):	9.0 sec
Engine type:	In-line six
Displacement:	183 ci (2,996 cc)
Transmission:	4-speed manual
Max power:	240 bhp (197 kW) @ 6,100 rpm
Max torque:	216 lb ft (292 Nm) @ 4,800 rpm
Weight:	2,850 lb (1,295 kg)
Economy:	18 mpg (6.4 km/l)

Mercedes Benz 560 SEC

This was the final guise of the W126 S-Class coupes, and Mercedes decided on using the biggest engine option available as their main rival, BMW, was rumoured to be bringing out a V12 luxury car. It was the first time the 338ci (5.6-litre) V8 had been used in anything but the flagship S-class four-door sedan, but it suited the intended luxury sport nature of the coupe very well, making it a very quick car. While the coupe ran the same suspension and drive train, its wheelbase was shortened, which made it a more nimble handler, but it retained some luxury on the rear with an optional self-levelling rear. The engine was one of Mercedes' energy concept V8s which had appeared in S-Class sedans in 1979. It featured air-swirl injection for optimum fuel atomization, fuel cut-off on the over-run, and a very low idle speed, yet in Europe could still muster 300bhp (224kW).

Top speed:	145 mph (232 km/h)
0–60 mph (0–95 km/h):	7.0 sec
Engine type:	V8
Displacement:	338 ci (5,547 cc)
Transmission	4-speed auto
Max power:	238 bhp (177 kW) @ 5,200 rpm
Max torque:	287 lb ft (388 Nm) @ 3,500 rpm
Weight:	3,858 lb (1,753 kg)
Economy:	20 mpg (7.1 km/l)

Mercedes Benz S600

Replacing the 560SEL as Mercedes' flagship model, the S600 set new standards in big sedan production. While its luxury was something many people had come to expect from the Stuttgart, Germany company, the car still had a few surprises. Items such as rain-sensitive windscreen wipers, electronic everything, including front and rear seats, sun shades and steering wheel adjustment, showed that Mercedes were at the forefront of limousine-like quality. But the S600 was marketed as being more than just a gadget machine, with adverts showing it as a performance car with a lot of driver involvement. Thanks to double wishbones at the front and a self-levelling multi-link rear, it handled very well. The brand new all-alloy 48v V12 engine was insisted on by Mercedes' marketing department, and it had massive torque through the rev range. For safety it used ASR to prevent tailslides during loss of traction.

Top speed:	155 mph (248 km/h)
0–60 mph (0–95 km/h):	6.6 sec
Engine type:	V12
Displacement:	365 ci (5,987 cc)
Transmission	5-speed auto
Max power:	389 bhp (290 kW) @ 5,300 rpm
Max torque:	420 lb ft (569 Nm) @ 3,800 rpm
Weight:	4,960 lb (2,254 kg)
Economy:	17 mpg (6 km/l)

Mercedes Benz 190E 2.5-16 Evo II

Mercedes put out a Cosworth tuned 190E in 1983, but in 1988 it needed to homologate a car for Group A racing and the 225bhp (167kW) 190E 2.5-16 Evo was the result. Just a year later, the Evo II came with an extra 10bhp (7kW) and this was the ultimate 190E. At the front the car used a MacPherson strut set-up, while the rear had a multi-link. The springs were lowered and the shocks uprated, but they also incorporated full adjustability and self-levelling with a sophisticated system. The bodywork was styled on the European touring cars, with extended arches covering new 8x17-inch (203x431mm) alloys. The spoilers front and rear had function, being adjustable to increase downforce. Cosworth again worked their magic on the four-cylinder 150ci (2.4-litre) engine, balancing the rotating assembly and giving it more aggressive cam timing to achieve the power.

Top speed:	156 mph (250 km/h)
0–60 mph (0–95 km/h):	6.8 sec
Engine type:	In-line four
Displacement:	150 ci (2,463 cc)
Transmission	5-speed manual
Max power:	232 bhp (173 kW) @ 7,200 rpm
Max torque:	181 lb ft (245 Nm) @ 5,000 rpm
Weight:	2,955 lb (1,343 kg)
Economy:	20 mpg (7.1 km/l)

Mercedes Benz 500SL

The SL line started in 1952 with the 'Gullwing', but even with the launch of the fourth-generation model in 1989, the car remained a comfortable grand tourer with a quick turn of speed. The V8 500SL was the top of the line in 1989 and mixed high-tech with luxury. It used a very strong monocoque structure with MacPherson struts and a multi-link rear allied to electronically controlled shocks which had four different settings, depending on the driver's mood. If the worst happened and the car tipped over, hydraulic rams would spring a roll bar into place in one-third of a second. The power top could fold away in 30 sec, the five-way adjustable seats had the belts mounted on them, and the gearbox had standard or sport mode settings. High-tech continued in the engine, with electronic variable valve timing, which changed depending on load and speed, all the time remaining immensely smooth.

Top speed:	155 mph (248 km/h)
0–60 mph (0–95 km/h):	6.1 sec
Engine type:	V8
Displacement:	303 ci (4,973 cc)
Transmission	4-speed auto
Max power:	326 bhp (243 kW) @ 5,500 rpm
Max torque:	332 lb ft (449 Nm) @ 4,000 rpm
Weight:	4,167 lb (1,894 kg)
Economy:	13.4 mpg (4.7 km/l)

Mercedes Benz C36 AMG

Like its big brother, the awesome E55, the C36 was equally devastating. With a launch of the C-Class in 1993 to replace the 190 model, it wasn't long before Mercedes-Benz's tuning arm, AMG, got their hands on the sedan. The company started with the very popular 195ci (3.2-litre) in-line six powering the bigger E-Class and S-Class cars. AMG increased the displacement to 220ci (3.6 litres) before installing it, thus making it the largest six-cylinder produced by Mercedes-Benz at the time. Four other areas were also modified, these being the wheels which comprised wide 17-inch (432mm) alloys and low-profile tyres, the suspension which used lowered coil springs and adjustable shocks, the discs which were increased in size and the transmission which featured sporting tweaks. The body was subtle with tell-tale wheels and twin square exhaust pipes unique to the model.

Top speed:	152 mph (243 km/h)
0–60 mph (0–95 km/h):	6.0 sec
Engine type:	In-line six
Displacement:	220 ci (3,606 cc)
Transmission	4-speed auto
Max power:	268 bhp (199 kW) @ 5,750 rpm
Max torque:	280 lb ft (379 Nm) @ 4,000 rpm
Weight:	3,458 lb (1,571 kg)
Economy:	20 mpg (7.1 km/l)

Mercedes Benz SLK

Mercedes had never built a small, affordable sportscar prior to the 1996 SLK, but in creating the car, took on the likes of Porsche, BMW, Alfa and MG in what was fast becoming a very popular new market. The car therefore needed to be lightweight, handle well and offer a style-conscious appearance. Mercedes kept the car rigid, strong yet light by using magnesium and high-strength steel in the unitary construction. Suspension was multi-link rear and double-wishbone front, while the roof was an engineering masterpiece. In 25 seconds the handsome fixed top would turn into a complex folding arrangement that went into the trunk. With the roof down there was little wind buffeting due to excellent aerodynamics and a rear wind deflector. The 140ci (2.3-litre) four-cylinder engine received a supercharger which livened up the car, making the most of its superb chassis.

Top speed:	143 mph (229 km/h)
0–60 mph (0–95 km/h):	7.5 sec
Engine type:	In-line four
Displacement:	140 ci (2,295 cc)
Transmission:	5-speed manual
Max power:	193 bhp (144 kW) @ 5,300 rpm
Max torque:	200 lb ft (271 Nm) @ 2,500 rpm
Weight:	2,922 lb (1,328 kg)
Economy:	17.3 mpg (6.1 km/l)

Mercedes C43 AMG

The formula for the C43 AMG seemed so simple: drop a big engine into small wagon, add sports suspension and one practical high-speed hauler was produced. But the conversion was by no means quickly carried out, and much thought went into the fitting of the V8. Being all-alloy meant the new motor was actually lighter than the cast-iron straight-six, creating a better balanced car. AMG added stiffer springs, shocks and anti-roll bars, plus 17-inch (432mm) alloys, slighter wider at the rear, to make the handling superb. Mercedes' own ESP (Electronic Stability Program) kept the traction and also had reigns on the yaw to prevent sideways slippage. AMG revised the camshafts on the engine, an oil cooler and free-flowing intake to extract a further 27bhp (20kW) and 7 lb ft (9.4Nm), making an awesome package, reaching 100mph (160km/h) in just over 15 seconds.

Top speed:	155 mph (248 km/h)
0–60 mph (0–95 km/h):	5.9 sec
Engine type:	V8
Displacement:	260 ci (4,266 cc)
Transmission	5-speed auto
Max power:	302 bhp (225 kW) @ 5,850 rpm
Max torque:	302 lb ft (409 Nm) @ 3,250 rpm
Weight:	3,448 lb (1,567 kg)
Economy:	24 mpg (8.5 km/l)

Mercedes Benz E55 AMG

Few are as subtle about their performance as the AMG Mercedes sedans. The E55 looked barely different from the regular car, but massive 18-inch (457mm) rims, reduced body height and low-profile tyres meant much to those in the know. It was based on the E-Class sedan with power from a re-worked version of the 262ci (4.3-litre) V8. The car featured an advanced multi-link rear suspension with double wishbones at the front, all uprated and with lower springs. Another aid was ESP, Electronic Stability Protection, which kept the car stable in all conditions via ABS and traction control. The engine was bored and stroked for its 329ci (5,391cc) displacement and the fourth valve in each cylinder was sacrificed for an extra spark plug, ignited just after the first for compete combustion. A variable length intake manifold widened the torque curve on the V8, making it a true highway stormer.

Top speed:	155 mph (248 km/h)
0–60 mph (0–95 km/h):	5.4 sec
Engine type:	V8
Displacement:	332 ci (5,439 cc)
Transmission	5-speed auto
Max power:	354 bhp (264 kW) @ 5,500 rpm
Max torque:	391 lb ft (529 Nm) @ 3,000 rpm
Weight:	3,600 lb (1,636 kg)
Economy:	15 mpg (5.3 km/l)

Mercedes Benz ML320

The ML was Mercedes' first proper 4WD, as the former G-Wagon was really just a development of the van and hence drove like one. The ML, on the other hand, was like a Mercedes saloon, thanks to a well-designed independent suspension system using coil springs all around. The 4WD set-up used Mercedes ETS with two differentials and if the system detected a loss of traction to a wheel, it would apply brake pressure and force more traction to the other three wheels. It made the car very capable off road, whilst retaining very civilized on-road ride quality. Underneath was well protected, with nothing lower than 8.5 inches (216mm) and the fuel tank, exhaust and differential protected by crossmembers on the ladder frame chassis. The V6 engine used three valves and twin spark plugs per cylinder, ensuring maximum combustion and low emissions, essential for sales in California.

Top speed:	112 mph (179 km/h)
0–60 mph (0–95 km/h):	8.9 sec
Engine type:	V6
Displacement:	195 ci (3,199 cc)
Transmission	5-speed auto
Max power:	215 bhp (160 kW) @ 5,500 rpm
Max torque:	233 lb ft (315 Nm) @ 3,000 rpm
Weight:	4,200 lb (1,909 kg)
Economy:	15.7 mpg (5.6 km/l)

Mercury Cougar Eliminator

Mercury launched their own pony car two years after the Mustang. Called the Cougar, it was essentially a stretched Mustang. The Eliminator came in 1969 and had an independent front with double wishbones and coils springs and a live axle rear on leaf springs, with staggered shocks to limit wheel hop under acceleration. And it could accelerate hard, no matter which engine option you had, either the Boss 302 or 428 Cobra Jet. The smaller of the two pumped out 290bhp (216kW) while the latter was conservatively rated at 335bhp (250kW) to fool the insurance companies, though it was more like 410bhp (305kW). The 428 could also be ordered with a ram air system and if the owner specified the 'Drag Pak', the car would receive an oil cooler and 4.3:1 axle gears. Owners got over-the-counter help: quadruple Weber carbs, two four-barrel carbs and race exhaust headers.

Top speed:	106 mph (170 km/h)
0–60 mph (0–95 km/h):	5.6 sec
Engine type:	V8
Displacement:	428 ci (7,013 cc)
Transmission	3-speed auto
Max power:	335 bhp (250 kW) @ 5,200 rpm
Max torque:	440 lb ft (595 Nm) @ 3,400 rpm
Weight:	3,780 lb (1,718 kg)
Economy:	6.2 mpg (2.2 km/l)

Mercury Lead Sled

In the 1950s as hot rodding took over America, both the racing side and the street side developed. Styles started to fracture and some guys turned to improving their cars for show, more than go, hence customs became popular. The new-in-1949 Mercury was a very radical design, aerodynamic and flowing and looking almost ready-chopped with its low roof line. Within a few years it was available cheaply and hot rodders began using the Merc body so much that it quickly became synonymous with customizing. The car is referred to as lead sled because in the days before plastic bodyfiller, car re-finishers used molten lead to fill seams or trim holes, which was then shaped with body files. This particular car is typical of the late 1950s/early 1960s, with custom wheel caps, flame paint, 1954 De Soto toothed grille and rear fenders skirts. It runs a small-block Chevy for power.

Top speed:	120 mph (192 km/h)
0–60 mph (0–95 km/h):	7.8 sec
Engine type:	V8
Displacement:	350 ci (5,735 cc)
Transmission	3-speed auto
Max power:	380 bhp (283 kW) @ 5,100 rpm
Max torque:	380 lb ft (514 Nm) @ 3,200 rpm
Weight:	3,374 lb (1,533 kg)
Economy:	9 mpg (3.2 km/l)

MG Maestro Turbo

When Austin Rover launched the Maestro in 1983, it hardly won people's hearts. It looked dowdy and dated, but it was cheap and offered a wide range of models plus a 98ci (1.6-litre) MG version. A year on, through criticism about a lack of power considering it was a sporting brand, the MG Maestro got a 122ci (2.0-litre) engine and 115bhp (86kW), which helped sales considerably, though critics were still sceptical about the MG branding on this slightly warm hatchback. The big difference came when the Maestro Turbo was launched at the British Motor Show in 1988. With a 10psi Garrett T3 turbo bolted to the new O-Series engine, it was the quickest MG ever, remaining so until well into the 1990s. Uprated and lowered suspension, bigger brake discs and 15-inch (381mm) alloys meant it handled very well too. Just 505 cars were built, making it a collectable in the UK.

Top speed:	135 mph (216 km/h)
0–60 mph (0–95 km/h):	6.4 sec
Engine type:	In-line four
Displacement:	122 ci (1,994 cc)
Transmission:	5-speed manual
Max power:	150 bhp (112 kW) @ 5,100 rpm
Max torque:	169 lb ft (229 Nm) @ 3,500 rpm
Weight:	2,460 lb (1,118 kg)
Economy:	25 mpg (8.9 km/l)

MG Metro 6R4

Just like Ford with its RS200, Austin Rover wanted the ultimate Group B World Rally Championship machine, but had to homologate 200 road-going models. The project was given to Williams Grand Prix Engineering in 1981 and by the end of 1982 they had their first mid-engined Metro with a V6 that was simply a Rover V8 minus two cylinders. Later production cars used a bespoke V6, dubbed the V6 4V because of the four valves per cylinder. While the car looked like an Austin Metro on steroids, it only used that car's body, strengthened by an integral roll cage and using MacPherson struts at each corner of the tubular chassis. The car had a full length undertray which hid three torque-splitting differentials on the four-wheel drive system. Road going cars had 250bhp (186kW), but later Evo models were up to 410bhp (335kW) while full rallycross cars could produce 600bhp (487kW).

Top speed:	140 mph (224 km/h)
0–60 mph (0–95 km/h):	4.5 sec
Engine type:	V6
Displacement:	182 ci (2,991 cc)
Transmission	5-speed manual
Max power:	250 bhp (186 kW) @ 7,000 rpm
Max torque:	225 lb ft (305 Nm) @ 6,500 rpm
Weight:	2,266 lb (1,030 kg)
Economy:	20 mpg (7.1 km/l)

MGB GT V8

Fitting a V8 into the MGB had been tried prior to the launch of the official car by British Leyland (BL) in 1973. Many specialist tuners had completed the conversion and the ideal engine was within the BL stable, that being the Rover V8, the design of which had been bought from Buick in the 1960s. The Rover displaced just 214ci (3,499cc) and, being all-aluminium, weighed barely more than the MGB's cast-iron four-cylinder engine. This kept the MGB V8's handling very balanced, though it was obvious the set-up leaned more towards a grand tourer than out-and-out sports car. Up front the car used double wishbones with coil springs and lever arm shocks, while the rear had leaf springs on a live axle. A brake servo helped the disc front and drum rear cope with the extra speed available. All MGB GT V8s came in fastback form, and not until the 1992 MG RV8 was there a V8 in a roadster.

Top speed:	125 mph (200 km/h)
0–60 mph (0–95 km/h):	8.5 sec
Engine type:	V8
Displacement:	215 ci (3,528 cc)
Transmission:	4-speed manual
Max power:	137 bhp (102 kW) @ 5,000 rpm
Max torque:	193 lb ft (261 Nm) @ 2,900 rpm
Weight:	2,387 lb (1,085 kg)
Economy:	24 mpg (8.5 km/l)

MG

MGF

The MG name was kept alive by Rover during the 1980s with cars like the MG Metro and MG Maestro, though purists disregarded these as 'badge cars'. In order to keep the MG spirit alive properly, the 1992 MG RV8 was launched, but what MG really needed in the 1990s was a high-production, modern roadster and it came about with the launch of the MGF in 1995. The car used a revolutionary hydro-gas independent suspension system with gas-filled 'springs' interconnected front and rear, and on wishbones. This gave it an amazing ride and unrivalled ride quality. The engine, too, was advanced, being Rover's ultra light 110ci (1.8-litre) K-series unit, with Rover's Variable Valve Control (VVC) that continuously varied the intake cam timing. Mounting the motor midships gave the MGF incredible balance and turned it into an enthusiast driver's car, true to the MG spirit.

Top speed:	131 mph (210 km/h)
0–60 mph (0–95 km/h):	7.8 sec
Engine type:	In-line four
Displacement:	110 ci (1,796 cc)
Transmission	5-speed manual
Max power:	143 bhp (107 kW) @ 7,000 rpm
Max torque:	128 lb ft (173 Nm) @ 4,500 rpm
Weight:	2,471 lb (1,123 kg)
Economy:	23 mpg (8.2 km/l)

MG RV8

The 1992 MG RV8 was an attempt to re-create a classic as a celebration of the 30th anniversary of the first MGB. The bodywork looked distinctly MG, but with rounded edges, blended-in fenders and lights, which echoed all the original touches. In fact, the doors and trunk lid were identical to the old car's, as was the underneath. Still there was the front wishbone suspension and live axle suspension on leaf springs, but with Koni telescopic shocks. What brought the car alive was its 244ci (4-litre) V8 engine, taken from the Range Rover but being a development of the old Buick all-aluminium V8. The unit gave excellent torque at low rpm but couldn't keep up with other British sportscars from the likes of TVR or Marcos. Inside the RV8, again it looked familiar, but the theme was luxury with a full walnut-veneer dashboard and leather seats/panels.

Top speed:	136 mph (218 km/h)
0–60 mph (0–95 km/h):	7.0 sec
Engine type:	V8
Displacement:	240 ci (3,946 cc)
Transmission:	5-speed manual
Max power:	190 bhp (142 kW) @ 4,750 rpm
Max torque:	234 lb ft (137 Nm) @ 3,200 rpm
Weight:	2,425 lb (1,102 kg)
Economy:	22 mpg (7.8 km/l)

Austin Mini (modified)

In the UK the Mini has been the most popular car to modify for the past 40 years. Its combination of cute looks, great handling and pure simplicity has put it in the top five of British people's most loved car, and its long production run from 1959 to 2000 proves this. During its time, many modified versions have come from the factory but it's the home tuners who have pushed the little car's limits the most. Because of this, a huge aftermarket has grown around the car. This roadster version is perhaps one of the most extreme both in looks and performance. Its roof has been cut off and the body reduced by 3 inches (76mm) in height, as well as being made into a two-seater. The car features a highly tuned engine which, due to the light weight of the car, can get it down the quarter-mile faster than most American muscle car models.

Top speed:	136 mph (218 km/h)
0–60 mph (0–95 km/h):	5.4 sec
Engine type:	In-line four
Displacement:	85 ci (1,400 cc)
Transmission	4-speed manual
Max power:	125 bhp (93 kW) @ 6,500 rpm
Max torque:	95 lb ft (128 Nm) @ 4,000 rpm
Weight:	1,300 lb (591 kg)
Economy:	18 mpg (6.4 km/l)

Mitsubishi 3000GT

The 1991 3000GT was loaded with gadgets. Underneath, the chassis was a rigid steel monocoque with MacPherson struts up front and a double wishbone rear with trailing arms, and electronically adjustable shocks. There was a four-wheel steering system which could increase steering angles up to 1.5 degrees according to speed, steering wheel input and surface friction. Then there was the 4WD with viscous coupling between the front and rear wheels which incorporated a torque split transfer system to prevent loss of grip. Inside it was fully loaded, with a digital screen to control temperature. The engine was state-of-the-art, with quad cams, twin intercooled turbochargers and multi-point fuel injection. Externally, front and rear spoilers lowered and raised at 50mph (80km/h) to help aerodynamics. The only hindrance was the car's weight because of all the equipment.

Top speed:	152 mph (243 km/h)
0–60 mph (0–95 km/h):	6.0 sec
Engine type:	V6
Displacement:	181 ci (2,972 cc)
Transmission:	5-speed manual
Max power:	281 bhp (209 kW) @ 6,000 rpm
Max torque:	300 lb ft (406 Nm) @ 3,000 rpm
Weight:	3,990 lb (1,814 kg)
Economy:	21 mpg (7.4 km/l)

Mitsubishi Pajero Evo

The Paris-Dakar Rally runs each year from France to Africa, across deserts and extreme rough terrain. Cars built for it need to have a rugged 4WD, loads of space for supplies, but most of all they have to be fast and reliable. Mitsubishi launched their Pajero Evo in 1997 to compete in the rally and immediately scored a 1-2-3 win, proving it wasn't a fluke by doing the same in 1998. The Pajero uses a very strong ladder frame chassis with thick crossmembers, and up front features a double wishbones independent, while at the rear a live axle sits on coil springs. The 4WD system can switch to 2WD at speeds up to 60mph (96km/h). The 215ci (3.5-litre) all-alloy engine has four valves per cylinder and uses Mitsubishi's MIVEC system which electronically changes the valve timing. The huge fenders came from the rally-winning machine and covered 10-inch (254mm) wide tyres.

Top speed:	125 mph (200 km/h)
0–60 mph (0–95 km/h):	8.0 sec
Engine type:	V6
Displacement:	213 ci (3,497 cc)
Transmission	5-speed semi-auto
Max power:	280 bhp (209 kW) @ 6,500 rpm
Max torque:	256 lb ft (347 Nm) @ 3,500 rpm
Weight:	4,370 lb (1,986 kg)
Economy:	19 mpg (6.7 km/l)

Mitsubishi Eclipse Spyder GS-T

Initially only available in coupe form when it was launched in 1989, the Eclipse was built in Illinois and not Japan. It was based on the Galant running gear and featured front-wheel drive in the top GS-T model, but an outstanding 4WD system in the other range-topping model, the GSX, which was virtually unstickable in corners. It wasn't until 1996 that the roadster version became available, and without a roof it needed much strengthening. Mitsubishi did this by including a new rear deck and seat panel, thicker sills, re-designed inner arches and a reinforced windshield frame. The suspension remained, being effective from the start, thanks to a wishbone front and multi-link rear system. The engine featured an alloy head with twin overhead camshafts, four valves per cylinder, multi-point electronic fuel injection and a Garrett turbo which ran 1.0 bar (14.5 psi) boost.

Top speed:	130 mph (208 km/h)
0–60 mph (0–95 km/h):	6.4 sec
Engine type:	In-line four
Displacement:	122 ci (1,997 cc)
Transmission	5-speed manual
Max power:	210 bhp (157 kW) @ 6,000 rpm
Max torque:	214 lb ft (289 Nm) @ 3,000 rpm
Weight:	3,053 lb (1,382 kg)
Economy:	21.4 mpg (7.6 km/l)

Mitsubishi FTO

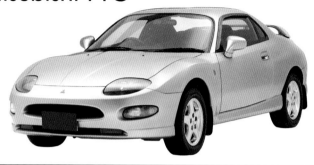

The 1995 FTO was only produced for Japan, but due to public demand and the growth of importers around the world, it was in many other countries soon after. It had an excellent combination of a revvy engine, brilliant front-wheel drive handling and a luxurious interior in a shapely coupe. The front suspension had MacPherson struts and lower wishbones while the rear was more complex with transverse upper and lower links, longitudinal links and an anti-roll bar. The brakes were very effective, being discs all around which required very little effort to pull the car's speed down rapidly. Though it came with a 110ci (1.8-litre) four-cylinder in base form, the real performer was the MIVEC (Mitsubishi Induction Valve Electronic Control) 122ci (2-litre) V6, which beyond 5,600rpm would use a more radical camshaft profile for more power up to the 8,200rpm redline.

Top speed:	140 mph (224 km/h)
0–60 mph (0–95 km/h):	7.5 sec
Engine type:	V6
Displacement:	122 ci (1,998 cc)
Transmission:	5-speed manual
Max power:	200 bhp (149 kW) @ 7,500 rpm
Max torque:	148 lb ft (200 Nm) @ 4,800 rpm
Weight:	2,534 lb (1,152 kg)
Economy:	28 mpg (9.9 km/l)

Mitsubishi Galant VR4

The Galant which was launched in 1987 didn't look like a performance car, with its dull, boxy shape. However, in VR-4 form it was a formidable rally car, with Pentti Arikkala driving the car to victory in the British Lombard-RAC Rally. The car was packed with high-tech gadgetry in a way only Mitsubishi knew how. Its Active Four system had 4WD, four-wheel steer which would alter the rear wheel angle by up to 1.5 degrees under 32mph (51km/h), plus anti-lock brakes and all-round independent suspension with MacPherson struts up front and double wishbones at the rear. Also fitted was electronically controlled suspension, with the world's first active ride in a production car, and it used electronic valves in the shocks to limit roll in corners and pitch during acceleration or braking. The multi-valve, twin-cam engine used an intercooled turbo which in rally form could hit 290bhp (216kW).

Top speed:	135 mph (216 km/h)
0–60 mph (0–95 km/h):	6.4 sec
Engine type:	In-line four
Displacement:	122 ci (1,997 cc)
Transmission:	5-speed manual
Max power:	195 bhp (145 kW) @ 6,000 rpm
Max torque:	203 lb ft (275 Nm) @ 3,000 rpm
Weight:	3,250 lb (1,477 kg)
Economy:	28 mpg (9.9 km/l)

Mitsubishi Lancer Evo 5

A rally car for the street was how to describe Mitsubishi's Evo 5. It was in fact a very easy car to drive very quickly cross-country, no matter what the weather. This is did with a permanent four-wheel drive biased slightly towards the rear wheels, and an Active Yaw Control to prevent sideways slippage. Excess speed was easily dealt with thanks to 12-inch (305mm) vented discs and powerful four-pot Brembo callipers at each corner. The 16-valve 122ci (2-litre) four-cylinder engine was a development of previous Evo models and featured contra-rotating balance shafts to keep the engine smooth up to the 6,500rpm redline. The turbo's massive intercooler mounted in the front grille ensured a dense supply of air, which aided the enormous power output and hit of torque. The car was good enough to give make Tommy Makinen World Rally Championship Champion three times.

Top speed:	147 mph (235 km/h)
0–60 mph (0–95 km/h):	4.7 sec
Engine type:	In-line four
Displacement:	122 ci (1,997 cc)
Transmission	5-speed manual
Max power:	276 bhp (206 kW) @ 6,500 rpm
Max torque:	274 lb ft (371 Nm) @ 3,000 rpm
Weight:	3,160 lb (1,436 kg)
Economy:	26 mpg (9.2 km/l)

Mitsubishi Starion

The Starion was one of the first Japanese sports cars to use a turbocharger, being launched in 1982 with a 170bhp (126kW) engine. That car suffered from turbo lag, but it got better in later models and by 1989 it was all-but gone, though by then the engine had increased to 158ci (2.6 litres) in size and peak power had actually gone down, thanks to a catalytic converter being required. Even with the power drop, the 1989 model was the best Starion there had been. It also looked more aggressive, with widened arches. The neutral handling was mostly due to the good balance of 53:47 front/rear weight distribution. The car used MacPherson struts front and rear and the spring rates were set hard, so body was minimal but at the cost of a very firm ride. Out back two things helped to down power, one being wider tyres than the front with 225/50x16s, the other being a limited-slip differential.

Top speed:	135 mph (216 km/h)
0–60 mph (0–95 km/h):	8.3 sec
Engine type:	In-line four
Displacement:	156 ci (2,555 cc)
Transmission:	5-speed manual
Max power:	168 bhp (125 kW) @ 5,000 rpm
Max torque:	215 lb ft (291 Nm) @ 2,500 rpm
Weight:	3,050 lb (1,386 kg)
Economy:	22 mpg (7.8 km/l)

Morris Minor

The Morris Minor, Britain's dearly loved small car, had a production span of 23 years. Revolutionary when it came out, thanks to the independent torsion bar front suspension and spacious interior, it became the cheap practical motor for thousands of families and remains a popular car in the UK today. This example was built from one of the Traveller woody-type two-door estates and has kept a very stock look, though cleverly it has a 2-inch (50mm) roof chop and widened rear arches to house the bigger tyres needed. Under the hood, where there used to be a 50ci (830cc) four-cylinder, there's now a supercharged 241ci (3.9-litre) Rover all-aluminium V8, which can get the car down the quarter-mile in under 14 seconds. Inside, the car is very stock too, featuring a full original interior with just the enlarged transmission tunnel giving evidence of any change.

Top speed:	125 mph (200 km/h)
0–60 mph (0–95 km/h):	5.1 sec
Engine type:	V8
Displacement:	241 ci (3,950 cc)
Transmission	3-speed auto
Max power:	300 bhp (224 kW) @ 5,750 rpm
Max torque:	325 lb ft (440 Nm) @ 4,300 rpm
Weight:	2,400 lb (1,090 kg)
Economy:	16 mpg (5.7 km/l)

Nissan 200SX

With the 300ZX about to end production in 1995, Nissan needed to fill the gap. The 200SX had been in production since 1988 and had steadily been growing in popularity, so they took that car and complete re-vamped it for 1994, adding more performance and improving areas where the old car had been criticized. Formerly a fastback inspired by the Porsche 944, the new car had a coupe body and was also re-styled inside to look more European. The engine was increased in size from 110 to 122ci (1.8 to 2 litres) and featured twin overhead cams, variable intake timing to increase torque at low rpm and a low-pressure turbocharger with intercooler. A MacPherson front and multi-link rear suspension set-up gave fantastic handling, more biased to driver involvement because it used rear-wheel drive. Due to low sales, the car was re-styled with a more aggressive front for 1996.

Top speed:	146 mph (234 km/h)
0–60 mph (0–95 km/h):	7.5 sec
Engine type:	In-line four
Displacement:	122 ci (1,998 cc)
Transmission	5-speed manual
Max power:	197 bhp (147 kW) @ 5,600 rpm
Max torque:	195 lb ft (264 Nm) @ 4,800 rpm
Weight:	2,789 lb (1,268 kg)
Economy:	26 mpg (9.2 km/l)

Nissan 300ZX Turbo

When the 300ZX's ancestor, the 240Z, was launched in 1969 it established itself as a diver's machine with plenty of torque, good handling and handsome coupe styling. Over the years that car turned into the early 1980s bloated 300ZX, which even in turbocharged form wasn't a great car. So when Nissan wanted to produce a replacement 300ZX, it started with a clean sheet. The 1990 hi-tech car had a stiffened bodyshell, double wishbone and multi-link rear suspension complemented by four-wheel steering. The engine was state-of-the-art with 24 valves, quad camshafts, variable valve-timing on the inlet cams, sequential fuel injection and direct ignition with a coil for each cylinder. Hybrid Garret T2/T25 twin turbos blew through twin intercoolers for the massive power output. The car wasn't as pure as the original 240Z, but it did provide as much driver involvement.

Top speed:	155 mph (248 km/h)
0–60 mph (0–95 km/h):	5.8 sec
Engine type:	V6
Displacement:	180 ci (2,960 cc)
Transmission	5-speed manual
Max power:	300 bhp (223 kW) @ 6,400 rpm
Max torque:	273 lb ft (369 Nm) @ 3,600 rpm
Weight:	3,485 lb (1,584 kg)
Economy:	14 mpg (5 km/l)

Nissan Silvia Turbo

In the mid-1980s Nissan needed to re-create some of the magic of the 240Z, so set to work designing a compact coupe shape with plenty of punch. The Silvia Turbo was the result, and while it didn't convince many in the looks, it certainly had the power and handling. Sensibly, they kept the car rear-wheel drive which meant the engine was mounted longitudinally up front at a time when most manufacturers were switching to transverse engines and front-wheel drive applications. The independent suspension was kept simple with MacPherson struts up front and semi-trailing arms rear, with fat anti-roll bars both ends along with disc brakes, which were also vented up front. As a turbo was used, Nissan felt it unnecessary to have 16 valves, so stuck with a basic 8-valve engine which was both effective and lightweight, though it did need revving to make the power.

Top speed:	124 mph (198 km/h)
0–60 mph (0–95 km/h):	8.3 sec
Engine type:	In-line four
Displacement:	110 ci (1,809 cc)
Transmission	5-speed manual
Max power:	137 bhp (102 kW) @ 6,000 rpm
Max torque:	191 lb ft (258 Nm) @ 4,000 rpm
Weight:	2,580 lb (1,173 kg)
Economy:	23 mpg (8.1 km/l)

Nissan Skyline GT-R

The Skyline name goes back to 1955, but it wasn't until the launch of the first GT-R in 1989, by then the eighth-generation model, that it was noticed. By 1994 the car had developed into a street racer and used many high-tech gadgets. It had Super HICAS four-wheel steering which detected steering input, turning rate, the car's speed, the YAW rate and lateral G-forces for the best grip. The four-wheel drive system was computer-controlled for optimum traction, with sensors and a multi-plate clutch at each wheel so no wheelspin occurred. The brakes consisted of 12.8-inch (325mm) and 11.8-inch (299mm) vented discs, all ABS assisted. The engine was equally high-tech with throttle bodies for each cylinder and twin turbos. It could put out far more than was advertised and held the Nurburgring production car lap record for years, taking 8 minutes to cover 14 miles (22 km).

Top speed:	155 mph (248 km/h)
0–60 mph (0–95 km/h):	5.6 sec
Engine type:	In-line six
Displacement:	157 ci (2,568 cc)
Transmission:	5-speed manual
Max power:	277 bhp (207 kW) @ 6,800 rpm
Max torque:	271 lb ft (367 Nm) @ 4,400 rpm
Weight:	3,530 lb (1,604 kg)
Economy:	15.7 mpg (5.6 km/l)

Nissan Sunny GTi-R

The 1980s Sunny was a typical small hatchback, so when Nissan decided they wanted to go rallying with it later that decade, it had to go through severe changes. The monocoque was strengthened to cope and Nissan gave the car a sophisticated 4WD system with a central viscous coupling and limited-slip differentials for remarkable grip. Independent MacPherson strut suspension was fitted all around with a slightly lowered ride height but only understated 14-inch (335mm) alloys. With the body also restrained (just a rear spoiler and hood vent), the GTi-R was a stealthy machine. The all-aluminium engine had twin cams, 16 valves, Bosch electronic multi-point fuel injection and an air-to-air intercooled turbo which was free of lag and gave tremendous torque. The car lasted from 1990 to 19'94 and was more a spectacular road car than successful rally car.

Top speed:	134 mph (214 km/h)
0–60 mph (0–95 km/h):	6.1 sec
Engine type:	In-line four
Displacement:	122 ci (1,998 cc)
Transmission:	5-speed manual
Max power:	220 bhp (164 kW) @ 6,400 rpm
Max torque:	197 lb ft (267 Nm) @ 4,800 rpm
Weight:	2,750 lb (1,250 kg)
Economy:	21 mpg (7.4 km/l)

Oldsmobile Cutlass Rallye 350

Back in the 1960s, insurance was turning into a headache on big-block muscle cars, so manufacturers offered alternatives with small-block engines. The Oldsmobile Rallye 350 was one of the best but was offered only in 1970. It was regular in engineering terms as it was based on the Cutlass, featuring wishbones front and coil-sprung live axle rear with upper and lower control arms. However, front and rear anti-roll bars, heavy duty springs and shocks meant good handling, and more balance, too, with less weight up front than the big-block cars. Also good was performance, with the 350ci (5.7-litre) engine producing plenty of power and impressive torque. All the Rallyes came in Sebring Yellow and featured the functional cold-air intake hood from the W30 big-block model. For 1971 the Rallye was dropped and power on the small-block Cutlass went down to 260bhp (194kW).

Top speed:	122 mph (195 km/h)
0–60 mph (0–95 km/h):	7.0 sec
Engine type:	V8
Displacement:	350 ci (5,735 cc)
Transmission:	3-speed auto
Max power:	310 bhp (231 kW) @ 4,600 rpm
Max torque:	390 lb ft (528 Nm) @ 3,200 rpm
Weight:	3,574 lb (1,624 kg)
Economy:	14 mpg (5 km/l)

Oldsmobile Hurst/Olds

In the 1960s George Hurst owned a speed shop and in 1968 one of his engineers, Jack 'Doc' Watson, built him a special Oldsmobile 4-4-2. George was so taken by the car he approached Oldsmobile with the idea of building hopped-up cars for them. The result was the Hurst/Olds, and by 1972 the cars were so revered that a convertible was chosen to pace the 56th Indy 500. The pace car was based on the W30 model which was fitted with the 455ci (7.4-litre) big-block engine. This had as much as 500lb ft (677Nm) torque in previous tune, though emissions regulations kept it down for 1972, even with the hood's functional cold-air scoops. A special Hurst shifter sat on the TurboHydramatic three-speed gearbox, which kept it lively. Uprated springs and shocks, with front and rear anti-roll bars, gave the Hurst/Olds well-balanced handling. In typical luxury, the hood was power operated.

Top speed:	132 mph (211 km/h)
0–60 mph (0–95 km/h):	6.8 sec
Engine type:	V8
Displacement:	455 ci (7,456 cc)
Transmission	3-speed auto
Max power:	300 bhp (223 kW) @ 4,700 rpm
Max torque:	410 lb ft (555 Nm) @ 3,200 rpm
Weight:	3,844 lb (1,747 kg)
Economy:	8 mpg (2.8 km/l)

Panoz Roadster

Likened to a Shelby Cobra of modern times, the Panoz Roadster used a similar build and borrowed many components from Ford's Mustang. Head of the company Danny Panoz took over the Irish motorsports company in 1994 to create a car which offered pure thrills for driving enthusiasts. The Roadster debuted that same year. Two years later the car had developed further into the AIV (aluminium-intensive vehicle) Roadster, so called as it used aluminium in the chassis, engine and body. The original frame was conceived by racing-car engineer Frank Costin (the 'cos' in Marcos) and consisted of large-bore aluminium tubes with backbone. Race A-arm suspension came in either standard or sport form, while the 13-inch (330mm) ABS disc brakes were straight from the Mustang Cobra and provided the Panoz with astonishing braking power. The engine was Ford's 32-valve unit.

Top speed:	131 mph (210 km/h)
0–60 mph (0–95 km/h):	4.5 sec
Engine type:	V8
Displacement:	281 ci (4,604 cc)
Transmission	5-speed manual
Max power:	305 bhp (227 kW) @ 5,800 rpm
Max torque:	300 lb ft (406 Nm) @ 4,800 rpm
Weight:	2,459 lb (1,117 kg)
Economy:	19.9 mpg (7 km/l)

Panther Solo

The Solo was overdue, as it was to be launched in 1985, but Toyota brought out their MR2. As such, the car was delayed until 1989 when a newer, more complex chassis could be produced which incorporated 4WD. A steel floorpan was joined to front and rear subframes while the centre cockpit and bodywork was made in composite material. At the front the car used MacPherson struts, while at the rear double wishbones helped give the great cornering power. The engine was the same Cosworth unit which had been developed for the Sierra, though in the Panther it was mounted behind the driver. Up front was rack and pinion steering while brakes were 10-inch (254mm) ABS-assisted discs. The driving experience was good, but the looks weren't convincing enough and, after just 26 cars had been made, Panther gave in to the tough competition and stopped production in 1990.

Top speed:	142 mph (227 km/h)
0–60 mph (0–95 km/h):	7.0 sec
Engine type:	In-line four
Displacement:	122 ci (1,993 cc)
Transmission	5-speed manual
Max power:	204 bhp (152 kW) @ 6,000 rpm
Max torque:	198 lb ft (268 Nm) @ 4,500 rpm
Weight:	2,723 lb (1,237 kg)
Economy:	22 mpg (7.8 km/l)

Peugeot 205 T16

This was one of the infamous Group B rally contenders homologated for the road in the same vein as Ford's RS200 and MG's 6R4, but this car was the most successful rally machine, taking the constructors' championship in 1985 and 1986 and making world champions of Timo Salonnen and Juha Kankkunen. The T16 was a 205 two-door hatchback only in looks, because underneath it used a strong steel monocoque with rear tubular frame holding the transversely mounted engine and gearbox which was accessed by hinging rear bodywork. A centre differential split drive between the front and rear wheels, depending on conditions, from 25:75 to 45:55 front/rear. Double wishbones, anti-roll bars and coil-over-shocks made up the suspension. Powering the car was an all-alloy 16v engine with Bosch fuel injection, dry sump lubrication and an intercooled KKK turbo.

Top speed:	128 mph (205 km/h)
0–60 mph (0–95 km/h):	7.8 sec
Engine type:	In-line four
Displacement:	108 ci (1,775 cc)
Transmission:	5-speed manual
Max power:	200 bhp (149 kW) @ 6,750 rpm
Max torque:	188 lb ft (256 Nm) @ 4,000 rpm
Weight:	2,436 lb (1,107 kg)
Economy:	23 mpg (8.1 km/l)

Peugeot 406 Coupe

A rare beauty from a major car manufacture, the 406 Coupe had many people thinking it was from Italy and not France. Therein lies the truth, as the car was styled by Italian design firm Pininfarina. The Coupe was based on the 406 sedan and the top model used the silky 183ci (3-litre) 24-valve V6. The coupe managed to combine excellent street manners and a smooth ride with both sharp steering and fabulous handling. Even with front-wheel-drive, the chassis nonetheless coped with the V6's power exceptionally well, and the car could pull the speed down just as quickly, thanks to anti-lock Brembo disc brakes. Being the flagship model in the 406 range, the Coupe also has luxurious equipment with full electrics inside including seats, a 10-speaker CD system, while externally there were moisture-sensitive wipers and seven colour options unique to the Coupe.

Top speed:	146 mph (234 km/h)
0–60 mph (0–95 km/h):	7.9 sec
Engine type:	V6
Displacement:	180 ci (2,946 cc)
Transmission	5-speed manual
Max power:	194 bhp (145 kW) @ 5,500 rpm
Max torque:	197 lb ft (266 Nm) @ 4,000 rpm
Weight:	3,274 lb (1,488 kg)
Economy:	23 mpg (8.1 km/l)

Plymouth 'Cuda 383

The 'Cuda was another handsome example of Chrysler's E-body cars. These shared the front end with the larger B-body models so had room for the biggest V8s on offer in the Dodge/Plymouth stable. The 1971 'Cuda 383 had, as the name suggests, a 383ci (6.3-litre) V8 which shared the block, heads, exhaust and camshaft. Only the crankshaft was different, with less stroke and displacement. Although not the quickest of muscle cars, the 'Cuda 383 nevertheless pumped out massive torque and could still turn in mid-14 second quarter-mile. The chassis was conventional Chrysler, using torsion bars up front which drag racers often raised a couple of splines to transfer weight more to the rear tyres. Stiffer springs all around improved handling and the Sure-Grip Dana axle helped traction. Because of falling demand, the 'Cuda 383 was made for just two years, then axed.

Top speed:	120 mph (192 km/h)
0–60 mph (0–95 km/h):	7.8 sec
Engine type:	V8
Displacement:	383 ci (6,276 cc)
Transmission	3-speed auto
Max power:	300 bhp (224 kW) @ 4,800 rpm
Max torque:	410 lb ft (555 Nm) @ 3,400 rpm
Weight:	3,475 lb (1,579 kg)
Economy:	12 mpg (4.2 km/l)

Plymouth Duster 340

Towards the end of the 1960s, with muscle cars getting out of reach financially to many buyers, the Chrysler Corporation decided to bring in a new entry-level performance machine. It was achieved by combining the 340ci (5.6-litre) small-block engine with a lightweight, two-door version of their Valiant bodyshell. The result was the 1970 Duster 340 and although regarded as a budget racer, it could easily hold its own against bigger-engined cars. Chrysler's trusted torsion bar front suspension meant it was comfortable (and cheap to produce), and leaf springs out back held the live axle in place, the latter coming with 3.23:1 gears and optional Sure Grip limited-slip differential. The standard transmission was a three-speed manual, though a four-speed was on the option list, as was the Torqueflite automatic. Externally the car had a matt black hood with '340 Wedge' graphic.

Top speed:	120 mph (192 km/h)
0–60 mph (0–95 km/h):	6.0 sec
Engine type:	V8
Displacement:	340 ci (5,571 cc)
Transmission	3-speed auto
Max power:	275 bhp (205 kW) @ 5,000 rpm
Max torque:	340 lb ft (460 Nm) @ 3,200 rpm
Weight:	3,500 lb (1,590 kg)
Economy:	16 mpg (5.7 km/l)

Plymouth Fury

It was Fury by name and fury by nature for the 1958 two-door from Plymouth, because while it looked like it had more style than substance, it was quicker than most in its day. Furys had always been fitted with Chrysler's biggest powerplant available since their launch in 1956, and the 1957 cars' 318ci (5.2-litre) engine disappeared after a year to be replaced by a more powerful 350ci (5.7-litre) V8. The Fury got the reputation for being Detroit's best-handling car in 1957, and this was mostly down to Chrysler's new-for-1957 'Torsion Air Ride' suspension which had longitudinal torsion bar springs up front. The design was so good it lasted through until 1980 in the Volaire. The car handled well also because it had a low centre of gravity due to the car's low stance. Styling was typical for the era, with high fins on the rear, wraparound front and rear windshields, and pillarless side windows.

Top speed:	122 mph (195 km/h)
0–60 mph (0–95 km/h):	8.0 sec
Engine type:	V8
Displacement:	350 ci (5,735 cc)
Transmission	3-speed auto
Max power:	305 bhp (227 kW) @ 5,000 rpm
Max torque:	370 lb ft (501 Nm) @ 3,600 rpm
Weight:	3,510 lb (1,595 kg)
Economy:	13 mpg (4.6 km/l)

Plymouth GTX 426 Hemi

In direct competition to Pontiac's GTO, Plymouth brought out the Hemi-powered GTX. More of a luxury vehicle with an awesome powerplant than out-and-out racer, the car nonetheless dominated on the track or street. The Hemi engine, which had arrived in 1964, was specially de-tuned with a new cam and lower compression (10.25:1) to make it better at low revs, but kept two four-barrel carbs. Chrysler's torsion bar front end was assisted by tubular shocks and an anti-roll bar. The brakes were heavy-duty drums, with 11-inch (279mm) front discs as options. The gearbox had its shift points altered to better suit the Hemi's power, but there was a manual available. Inside, the seats were thickly padded and the dash hinted of what could be achieved with its 150mph (241km/h) speedometer. The GTX was all about speed, because it could easily run the quarter-mile in 13 seconds (12 with racing tyres).

Top speed:	127 mph (203 km/h)
0—60 mph (0–95 km/h):	4.8 sec
Engine type:	V8
Displacement:	426 ci (6,980 cc)
Transmission	3-speed auto
Max power:	425 bhp (317 kW) @ 5,000 rpm
Max torque:	490 lb ft (663 Nm) @ 4,000 rpm
Weight:	3,535 lb (1,606 kg)
Economy:	12 mpg (4.2 km/l)

Plymouth Hemi 'Cuda

This model represented one of the best of all Chrysler muscle cars, having a handsome bodystyle and the awesome Hemi V8. In standard form the car used a monocoque centre section with chassis subframes front and rear, but this particular machine has been through what is known as 'back-halving' which means the back half of the car has had its stock suspension cut out to be replaced by a drag-racing four-link and coil-over-shocks. Also, to house the 18.5-inch (470mm) wide Mickey Thompson street/strip racing tyres, the car has been fitted with aluminium 'tubs' for inner arches which means the back seat and most of the trunk space has gone. The engine here has been modified by Dick Landy Industries and output is up by around half over the standard Hemi. A four-speed manual and 4.56:1 geared rear end put it down the quarter-mile in 11 seconds.

Top speed:	137 mph (219 km/h)
0–60 mph (0–95 km/h):	4.3 sec
Engine type:	V8
Displacement:	432 ci (7,079 cc)
Transmission	3-speed auto
Max power:	620 bhp (462 kW) @ 6,500 rpm
Max torque:	655 lb ft (887 Nm) @ 5,100 rpm
Weight:	3,945 lb (1,793 kg)
Economy:	9.4 mpg (3.3 km/l)

Plymouth Prowler

Massively popular as a concept, the Prowler took three years to make production but when it did, demand was huge, to the point where its $40,000 price quickly doubled on the second-hand market. It was headed by Chrysler design head Tom Gale, himself a hot rodder, who wanted to give the public a new slant on a 1930s hot rod. The idea was to keep it light, with an aluminium chassis to which slender A-arms were attached either end for full independent suspension. At the front, the coilovers were mounted inboard as per race cars, while the rear had a multi-link arrangement. To distribute weight evenly the gearbox was mounted out back. It all added up to neutral handling and supercar cornering. The only slight let down was the power – although the 24v engine was linear in output, it didn't have enough torque to make the Prowler a true hot rod.

Top speed:	140 mph (224 km/h)
0–60 mph (0–95 km/h):	7.0 sec
Engine type:	V6
Displacement:	215 ci (3,523 cc)
Transmission:	4–speed auto
Max power:	214 bhp (159 kW) @ 5,850 rpm
Max torque:	221 lb ft @ 3,100 rpm (300 Nm)
Weight:	2,862 lb (1,300 kg)
Economy:	20 mpg (7.1 km/l)

Plymouth Road Runner

When Chrysler realized muscle-car fans of the 1960s wanted a high-power, no-frills car at reasonable costs, they responded and came up with the Road Runner. The company paid Warner Bros $50,000 to use the cartoon character's name and logo on the car, and although the forecast was sales of 2,500, the Road Runner was such a success it sold 44,589. It used uprated torsion bars at the front and leaf springs on the live axle, which had 3.23:1 gears though higher ratios for better acceleration were available. The engine was the basic cast-iron big-block which had been in production since the 1950s, in this form displacing 383ci (6,276cc) but putting out tremendous torque. The heads, camshaft, and exhaust were all from the 440ci (7.2-litre) motor. Despite its size, the Road Runner in basic form was relatively lightweight and performed well, making it an instant classic.

Top speed:	130 mph (208 km/h)
0–60 mph (0–95 km/h):	6.7 sec
Engine type:	V8
Displacement:	383 ci (6,276 cc)
Transmission	3-speed auto
Max power:	335 bhp (250 kW) @ 5,200 rpm
Max torque:	425 lb ft (575 Nm) @ 3,400 rpm
Weight:	3,400 lb (1,545 kg)
Economy:	12 mpg (4.2 km/l)

Plymouth Superbird

Plymouth built the 1970 Superbird to win NASCAR. Ford had been dominating the races in the 1960s with their Talladegas and even the 1969 Dodge Daytona couldn't defeat them. So, in 1970 the 'Bird came out with better aerodynamics and enough downforce for 200mph (320km/h). Under the hood the by-then legendary 426ci (6.9-litre) Hemi was fitted. This engine was so-called because of its hemispherical combustion chambers, which meant it could use bigger valves and thus let more fuel in. The Superbird was so fast that it won 21 races and the championship in its first season but NASCAR rules to keep competition even imposed engine restrictions on cars with rear wings, and so it was banned. Plymouth had trouble selling the street versions because of its looks, so many had the nose cones and rear spoilers stripped to be sold as standard Dodge Chargers.

Top speed:	140 mph (224 km/h)
0–60 mph (0–95 km/h):	6.1 sec
Engine type:	V8
Displacement:	426 ci (6,980 cc)
Transmission	4-speed manual
Max power:	425 bhp (317 kW) @ 5,000 rpm
Max torque:	490 lb ft (663 Nm) @ 4,000 rpm
Weight:	3,841 lb (1,745 kg)
Economy:	13.8 mpg (4.9 km/l)

Pontiac Firebird Firehawk

Ex-drag racer Ed Hamburger formed his company Street Legal Performance (SLP) in 1987 and negotiated a deal with GM whereby he'd design a performance package for the Pontiac Firebird. The first SLP 'Firehawk' hit the market in 1992 and by 1995 it was using the 315bhp (235kW) LT1 engine in coupe and convertible bodies. In 1998 this new Firehawk was revealed, featuring the Corvette's all-alloy LS1 engine, only available with the six-speed manual, as this was the only gearbox which could cope with the power. SLP options offered Bilstein Ultra Performance Suspension which got the Firehawk to 0.91g on the skidpad. The styling cleverly incorporated heat-extracting vents in the top of the hood with functional ram air nostrils in the nose. The 9x17-inch (229x432mm) alloys hid 11.8-inch (299mm) vented discs, ABS assisted and completing the car as a devastating all–rounder.

Top speed:	157 mph (251 km/h)
0–60 mph (0–95 km/h):	5.1 sec
Engine type:	V8
Displacement:	350 ci (5,735 cc)
Transmission:	6–speed manual
Max power:	327 bhp (244 kW) @ 5,200 rpm
Max torque:	345 lb ft (467 Nm) @ 4,400 rpm
Weight:	3,520 lb (1,600 kg)
Economy:	22 mpg (7.8 km/l)

Pontiac Firebird H.O.

The Pontiac Firebird was not regarded as a major contender in the muscle-cars wars, being overshadowed by the Camaro from which it was derived. Arriving in 1968, the base Firebird came with manual steering and brakes, though most buyers opted for power versions of both, which totally transformed the car. Inside it used buckets seats and extra deep-set gauges for a sporty feel. The H.O. model wasn't the most powerful engine available (the 400ci/6.5-litre took that crown) but the 350ci (5.7-litre) did have a long duration camshaft, 10.25:1 compression and big valves to achieve its impressive power. While it was barely slower than the bigger-engined car, it was much cheaper, so was a good seller. The four-speed manual was the gearbox to have, while at the rear the 10-bolt, leaf-sprung axle could be ordered with the Safe-T-Track limited-slip differential and a variety of gear ratios.

Top speed:	114 mph (182 km/h)
0-60 mph (0–95 km/h):	6.9 sec
Engine type:	V8
Displacement:	350 ci (5,735 cc)
Transmission	4-speed manual
Max power:	320 bhp (239 kW) @ 5,000 rpm
Max torque:	380 lb ft (514 Nm) @ 3,400 rpm
Weight:	3,740 lb (1,700 kg)
Economy:	12 mpg (4.2 km/l)

Pontiac GTO 1964

Thismodel is often referred to as the one which started the muscle-car wars, and it combined a 1964 Tempest body with a 389ci (6.3-litre) V8 to be the 'GTO'. In creating the new model, designers got around a GM ruling which limited its intermediate cars to a maximum engine size of 330ci (5.4 litres). Thus the trend for shoehorning big engines into medium cars began, lasting for almost 10 years before the fuel crisis of 1973. The GTO had a thicker anti-roll bar, stiffer springs, uprated shocks and higher speed rated tyres. The top-option gearbox was the four-speed 'Muncie' that made the most of the huge power output. Drum brakes weren't the greatest attribute of the GTO, but they could be ordered with sintered lining, which helped a little. The biggest advantage was the weight, some 300lb (136kg) lighter than most later muscle cars, making the car very quick off the line.

Top speed:	120 mph (192 km/h)
0–60 mph (0–95 km/h):	6.6 sec
Engine type:	V8
Displacement:	389 ci (6,374 cc)
Transmission	4-speed manual
Max power:	348 bhp (259 kW) @ 4,900 rpm
Max torque:	428 lb ft (579 Nm) @ 3,600 rpm
Weight:	3,126 lb (1,420 kg)
Economy:	14 mpg (5 km/l)

Pontiac GTO 1968

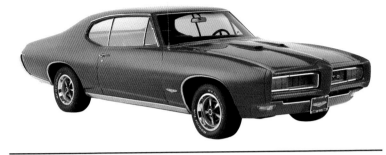

Using what was previously a Ferrari model name, Pontiac created the GTO (Grand Turismo Omologato) and by 1968 it had more power than anything Italian and the handling to match. The torquey 400ci (6.6-litre) engine meant the Safe-T-Track limited-slip differential was essential. For 1968 the GTO, having been out since 1964, had a new body style which improved looks while retaining an aggressive look. It was also slighter shorter in the wheelbase than its predecessor, but kept the separate chassis and body. At the front it used unequal-length A-arms, while the live rear axle used trailing arms and coil springs with separate shocks. Three versions of the engine were available in 1968, the base having 350bhp (261kW), the second featuring a higher lift cam and 360bhp (268kW), and third, the Ram Air II with improved heads and hood cold-air feed, giving 366bhp (273kW).

Top speed:	120 mph (192 km/h)
0–60 mph (0–95 km/h):	6.4 sec
Engine type:	V8
Displacement:	400 ci (6,554 cc)
Transmission	5-speed manual
Max power:	360 bhp (268 kW) @ 5,400 rpm
Max torque:	445 lb ft (602 Nm) @ 3,800 rpm
Weight:	3,506 lb (1,595 kg)
Economy:	11 mpg (3.9 km/l)

Pontiac GTO Judge

Launched in Carousel Red only paint with 'The Judge' logos on the hood and fenders, you couldn't miss this new GTO. Looks were backed up with a regular 350bhp (261kW) 400ci (6.6-litre) on the base model,while the best Judges got the 366bhp (273kW) Ram Air III engine. Also provided with the car was heavy-duty suspension with stiffer springs and shocks. The standard gear ratio in the rear axle was 3.90:1 with a Safe-T-Track differential, though steeper gears for better acceleration could be ordered. Externally the car was one of the first to use energy-absorbing fenders which would cope with any low-speed knocks. The car was raved about for its interior style, with a very clear dash layout and a useful hood-mounted rev counter. The buckets seats gave good support and the Hurst shifter could bang the four-speed Muncie gearbox into gear without missing a shift.

Top speed:	123 mph (197 km/h)
0–60 mph (0–95 km/h):	6.2 sec
Engine type:	V8
Displacement:	400 ci (6,555 cc)
Transmission	4-speed manual
Max power:	366 bhp (273 kW) @ 5,400 rpm
Max torque:	445 lb ft (603 Nm) @ 3,600 rpm
Weight:	3,503 lb (1,592 kg)
Economy:	11 mpg (3.9 km/l)

Pontiac Turbo Trans Am 1989

Pontiac wanted a car to commemorate the first Trans Am put into production in 1969. It had to be powerful, it had to be ground-breaking and, most of all, it had to be a driver's machine. They came up with the Turbo Trans Am, loaded with electrics inside plus a wealth of performance extras. All these 20th anniversary models came with the WS6 handling package which consisted of uprated shocks and springs plus fatter anti-roll bars front and rear. Also fitted was a torque arm for better rear tyre grip and Panhard rod to locate the axle in a sideways direction, both of which benefited the car because it could pull 0.89g in cornering. The powerplant was straight from the not-long departed Buick Grand National and used a Garrett turbo, air-to-air intercooler and electronic ignition for massive power which could only be compared to a big V8, though the V6 was much lighter.

Top speed:	157 mph (251 km/h)
0–60 mph (0–95 km/h):	5.1 sec
Engine type:	V6
Displacement:	231 ci (3,785 cc)
Transmission	4-speed auto
Max power:	255 bhp (190 kW) @ 4,000 rpm
Max torque:	340 lb ft (460 Nm) @ 2,800 rpm
Weight:	3,406 lb (1,548 kg)
Economy:	27 mpg (9.6 km/l)

Porsche 356

Ferry Porsche started something big with the 356. Being the first Porsche-badged car, the prototype first hit the street in 1948 using a VW engine. It made a spring debut at the Geneva Motor Show in 1949 and in 1951 it won its class at Le Mans. An updated 356A appeared with Speedster and Carrera versions in 1955, then came the 356B in 1959 with a facelift and more powerful engines, while the final 356C made an appearance in 1963, only to be replaced by the 911 two years later. The 356 has, like the Beetle, a floorpan chassis with swing axles and torsion bars at the rear, while at the nose, torsion bars are again used with trailing arms. The engine might also have its roots in the air-cooled VW unit, but it's more sophisticated with better balancing, improved flow and the ability to rev more freely. The ultimate variant was the Carrera which came with four cams for 125mph (201km/h) performance.

Top speed:	103 mph (165 km/h)
0–60 mph (0–95 km/h):	13.0 sec
Engine type:	Flat four
Displacement:	96 ci (1,582 cc)
Transmission	4-speed manual
Max power:	75 bhp (56 kW) @ 5,000 rpm
Max torque:	85 lb ft (115 Nm) @ 3,700 rpm
Weight:	2,059 lb (936 kg)
Economy:	25 mpg (8.8 km/l)

Porsche 356 Speedster

In 1952 Porsche produced a few stripped-out 356 American Roadsters which were mainly for racing, but later in 1954 they resurrected the idea in the lightweight Speedster. In 1956 the car received a bigger engine which made it quite a performance model: indeed, it attracted many serious drivers because it was lighter than the hardtop. It used the same pressed-steel floorpan as the 356 Cabriolet, with the rear-mounted engine and transaxle plus torsion bar front suspension and swing axle rear end. The engine in base form produced 70bhp (52kW) but a 'Super Tune' version was available which took it to 88bhp (66kW), but best of all was the Carrera four-cam engine with twin spark plugs which pushed out 115bhp (86kW). The Speedster windshield was around 3 inches (76mm) shorter to save weight, and there was no side glass, plus a very light folding roof.

Top speed:	100 mph (160 km/h)
0–60 mph (0–95 km/h):	11.2 sec
Engine type:	Flat four
Displacement:	96 ci (1,582 cc)
Transmission:	4-speed manual
Max power:	70 bhp (52 kW) @ 4,500 rpm
Max torque:	82 lb ft (11 Nm) @ 2,700 rpm
Weight:	1,790 lb (813 kg)
Economy:	26 mpg (9.2 km/l)

Porsche 911 (901 model)

The very first 911 was model was launched at the Frankfurt Motor Show in 1963, but was penned in 1959 to replace what was considered the ageing 'upturned bath' 356 design. Engineers wanted the power of the 356 Carrera engine, so the new car could comfortably top 100mph (160km/h), but without the complexity and expense of multiple cams, so added two cylinders instead. The resultant 122ci (2-litre) flat-six '901' engine was innovative in design, featuring dry sump lubrication and hemispherical combustion chambers. With carburettors it made a reliable 145bhp (108kW). The 1963 911 needed more strength to cope with the bigger, more powerful engine and the designers stiffened the floorpan, added large box-section sills and made the roof a stressed section. MacPherson struts and torsion bars took care of the front while the rear used a trailing-arm layout. It lasted until the 1990s.

Top speed:	132 mph (211 km/h)
0–60 mph (0–95 km/h):	9.0 sec
Engine type:	Flat six
Displacement:	122 ci (1,991 cc)
Transmission:	5-speed manual
Max power:	145 bhp (108 kW) @ 6,100 rpm
Max torque:	143 lb ft (194 Nm) @ 4,200 rpm
Weight:	2,360 lb (1,073 kg)
Economy:	19 mpg (6.7 km/l)

Porsche 911 Carrera RS 2.7

Regarded by many Porsche fans as the best-handling 911 ever, the RS 2.7 is one of the finest fettled cars ever to come out of Stuttgart, Germany. Originally there were to be just 500 built for homologation purposes, though this went to 1,500. The car was so radically modified compared to the regular 911 that it had to be built on a separate production line, having a delete list of items like the carpet, sealer, glovebox door and even the coat hooks. Also, the body received treatment with the engine cover and fenders being glass-fibre, while the steel panels and window glass were thinner. Bilsten gas shocks were fitted, along with thicker anti-roll bar, and the RS was given wider Fuchs alloys. The engine was taken out to 164ci (2.7 litres) from 146ci (2.4 litres) and flat top pistons plus fuel injection was fitted. A close-ratio gearbox helped keep the motor in the power band.

Top speed:	148 mph (237 km/h)
0–60 mph (0–95 km/h):	5.9 sec
Engine type:	Flat six
Displacement:	164 ci (2,687 cc)
Transmission	5-speed manual
Max power:	210 bhp (156 kW) @ 6,300 rpm
Max torque:	188 lb ft (255 Nm) @ 5,100 rpm
Weight:	2,160 lb (982 kg)
Economy:	14.7 mpg (5.2 km/l)

Porsche 911 1998

Introduced in 1997, the new 911 followed a tradition dating back to 1963, of a rear-engined sports car with an emphasis on quality and driving pleasure. The sixth-generation version featured an all-new body and a water-cooled flat-six for the first time. While being 122ci (200cc) larger than the former air-cooled unit, it boasted more power and was far quieter, in fact Porsche claimed it took 20 new 911s to make the same noise as one older model. To keep rear weight bias to a minimum and neutralize the handling, the unit was all-alloy and used dual overhead cams with variable valve timing. The platform is a stretched version of the Boxster's and uses Porsche's high-tech MacPherson type struts at the front, with rear double track control arms and multi-link suspension. A stronger bodyshell helped with the torsional rigidity and made the handling the best ever in a 911.

Top speed:	174 mph (278 km/h)
0–60 mph (0–95 km/h):	5.0 sec
Engine type:	Flat six
Displacement:	207 ci (3,387 cc)
Transmission	6-speed manual
Max power:	296 bhp (200 kW) @ 6,800 rpm
Max torque:	258 lb ft (349 Nm) @ 4,600 rpm
Weight:	3,081 lb (1,400 kg)
Economy:	23.3 mpg (8.3 km/l)

Porsche 911 Ruf 1997

Alois Ruf began modifying Porsche 911s in 1977, turning them into the fastest road cars available. In 1987 a Ruf CTR (based on a 911) broke the World Speed Record for a production car by going 211mph (339km/h), and the company has since grown. Ruf specialize in modfying all areas, therefore a 911 from them is a Ruf production car, not a Porsche. This 1997 example got 1.5-inch (38mm) lower suspension, Bilstein shocks, stiffer anti-roll bars and a strut brace. Drive was still via Porsche's permanent 4WD system with viscous coupling and traction control. The flat-six engine had different pistons, modified cylinder heads, more aggressive cams and special KKK turbochargers. Also changed was the stock exhaust for custom Ruf pipes, while a re-mapped engine management system took care of the running. Optional was an electronic clutch, permitting fingertip gear changes.

Top speed:	192 mph (307 km/h)
0–60 mph (0–95 km/h):	3.8 sec
Engine type:	Flat six
Displacement:	220 ci (3,600 cc)
Transmission:	6-speed manual
Max power:	490 bhp (365 kW) @ 5,500 rpm
Max torque:	480 lb ft (650 Nm) @ 4,800 rpm
Weight:	3,090 lb (1,404 kg)
Economy:	11 mpg (3.9 km/l)

Porsche 911 Turbo 1976–1977

The Turbo version of the 1976–1977 911 was for the rich performance enthusiast after a challenging drive. It was a brave move by Porsche to install the turbo, as only BMW and Chevrolet had tried it on a production model before, though the Stuttgart, Germany-based company did know the turbocharging had strong appeal in its own race programme. It was a single KKK turbo with 12psi boost, but it made the engine so much more punchy that a stronger transmission was required. To get the power down, wider rear arches were also needed in order to get sufficient rubber under them. After 1977 the car's displacement was upped to 201ci (3,293cc) for 300bhp (224kW), but the Turbo had developed a reputation for being a monster, well deserved given the performance and sudden oversteer. The 'whaletail' spoiler, where the intercooler was mounted, also provided downforce at speed.

Top speed:	156 mph (250 km/h)
0–60 mph (0–95 km/h):	4.9 sec
Engine type:	Flat six
Displacement:	183 ci (2,993 cc)
Transmission	4-speed manual
Max power:	234 bhp (174 kW) @ 5,500 rpm
Max torque:	245 lb ft (332 Nm) @ 4,000 rpm
Weight:	2,514 lb (1,143 kg)
Economy:	19 mpg (6.7 km/l)

Porsche 911 Turbo 1990–1995

A new 911 bodystyle in 1989 saw the Turbo re-launched a year later. It remained rear-wheel drive only, though traction was good because of the engine's weight being over the rear wheels. The new model still demanded respect, however, especially in the wet, even though development engineers at Porsche tamed these later models a little by stiffening the rear suspension and revising the rear trailing arm set-up. Also much better was the MacPherson strut front end, a carry-over from the Carrera 2 of 1989. The brakes were huge for this year, being 12-inch (305mm) vented items with four-piston callipers. Power-assisted steering was required on this model, because despite the weight being at the rear, the wide tyres still made the steering heavy. The engine was still air-cooled with Bosch K-Tronic fuel injection plus a single KKK turbo, with intercooler mounted in the 'whale tail' spoiler.

Top speed:	168 mph (269 km/h)
0–60 mph (0–95 km/h):	4.9 sec
Engine type:	Flat six
Displacement:	201 ci (3,299 cc)
Transmission:	5-speed manual
Max power:	315 bhp (235 kW) @ 5,750 rpm
Max torque:	332 lb ft (449 Nm) @ 4,500 rpm
Weight:	3,274 lb (1,488 kg)
Economy:	12.4 mpg (4.4 km/l)

Porsche 911 Turbo 3.3 SE

While the 1980s Porsche Turbo was phenomenally quick, Porsche went one better with the 1985 SE (Special Equipment). Visual upgrades included the nose with an aerodynamic flat front, deep spoiler and pop-up lamps, while the rear aches had functional engine-cooling vents. The suspension of the standard car was left alone, apart from Bilstein shocks, but the Fuchs alloys were up to 16 inches (406mm) in diameter. The engine received high-performance camshafts, bigger intercooler, re-mapped engine management, and a modified exhaust system for an extra 30bhp (22kW) over the regular Turbo model. Inside, the SE was given air-conditioning, full leather trim, heated adjustable Recaro seats and Blaupunkt sound. The SE had a strictly limited production run so ended in 1986, though in the USA, the SE package remained as a $23,244 option on the Turbo model in 1987.

Top speed:	170 mph (272 km/h)
0–60 mph (0–95 km/h):	5.0 sec
Engine type:	Flat six
Displacement:	201 ci (3,299 cc)
Transmission	4-speed manual
Max power:	330 bhp (246 kW) @ 5,750 rpm
Max torque:	318 lb ft (430 Nm) @ 4,000 rpm
Weight:	3,000 lb (1,363 kg)
Economy:	18 mpg (6.4 km/l)

Porsche 924 Turbo

While the 924 had been the first Porsche to run with a front-engine, rear-wheel drive layout, purists didn't like it because of the involvement with VW/Audi. The car used a 122ci (2-litre) Audi 100 engine, itself was derived from a VW LT van, and didn't look like a Porsche, nor did it go like one. Porsche addressed the car's shortcomings and made it a driver's machine. They fitted a KKK 26 turbocharger and though, like many other turbo cars of the era it suffered from turbo lag, when the boost came in the acceleration was good. Better still was the handling and braking, the former helped by perfect 50:50 weight distribution with the gearbox in the rear transaxle, while the latter was incredible, thanks to massive 11-inch (279mm) discs all around. The body changes were subtle with a NACA-style duct in the hood for the turbo, grilles in the front spoiler and a discreet rear spoiler.

Top speed:	134 mph (214 km/h)
0–60 mph (0–95 km/h):	8.9 sec
Engine type:	In-line four
Displacement:	121 ci (1,985 cc)
Transmission	5-speed manual
Max power:	143 bhp (107 k/W) @ 5,500 rpm
Max torque:	147 lb ft (199 Nm) @ 3,000 rpm
Weight:	2,719 lb (1,236 kg)
Economy:	19.5 mpg (6.9 km/l)

Porsche 928

Intended as a replacement for the 911, the 1977 928 seemed to offer more space, grace and pace. Indeed it did offer the first two, but not in the latter with just 240bhp (179kW) at launch in a much heavier car than the 911. A jump to 300bhp (224kW) in 1979 cured the situation somewhat, but by then it was obvious the 928 wasn't so much a replacement as an extra model in Porsche's line-up. To balance the car, the transmission was put at the rear, while up front an all-new 90-degree V8 started off with single-overhead cams, eventually progressing to a dual-overhead set-up with 32v and 305ci (4,998cc) displacement, in the 1986 S4. Suspension was double wishbones at the front and semi-trailing arms at the rear with diagonal links. The body blended flexible polyurethane fenders into the bodywork, giving the car a smooth look and excellent drag coefficient of 0.39 in 1977.

Top speed:	165 mph (264 km/h)
0–60 mph (0–95 km/h):	5.8 sec
Engine type:	V8
Displacement:	302 ci (4,957 cc)
Transmission:	5-speed manual
Max power:	330 bhp (246 kW) @ 4,100 rpm
Max torque:	317 lb ft (429 Nm) @ 4,100 rpm
Weight:	3,449 lb (1,568 kg)
Economy:	12.4 mpg (4.4 km/l)

Porsche 993 Turbo

The 1997 993 Turbo was the last of the 911-shaped cars to use the famous air-cooled flat six, and by then it been bored out to the limit, yet still used just two valves per cylinder. The key to its enormous output was, as ever, turbocharging, though this model was the first to use twin turbos, Porsche again choosing KKK for two smaller units, which virtually eliminated the turbo lag which had been associated with previous models. Aside from the engine refinement, Porsche had also made the power far more useable, thanks to four-wheel drive which had first appeared in the Carrera 4 model of 1989. Cleverly, to make it feel like the old cars, the rear wheels would be driven only in normal situations, but when sensors detected traction was being lost, drive would be fed to the front wheels as well. The 993 goes down as one of many Porsche fans' favourites.

Top speed:	180 mph (288 km/h)
0–60 mph (0–95 km/h):	3.8 sec
Engine type:	Flat six
Displacement:	220 ci (3,600 cc)
Transmission:	6-speed manual
Max power:	400 bhp (298 kW) @ 5,750 rpm
Max torque:	400 lb ft (542 Nm) @ 4,500 rpm
Weight:	3,307 lb (1,503 kg)
Economy:	18 mpg (6.4 km/l)

Porsche 968

Carrying on a tradition which had been started by the 924 25 years earlier, the 1991 Porsche 968 offered a budget-priced Porsche to the enthusiast which was far more refined and civilized than any of its ancestors. Too refined and too well-honed for some Porsche's fans' liking, in fact. It used one of the biggest displacement four-cylinder engines in recent production history, which had balancer shafts to run smoothly, plus 16 valves for more performance, in fact over 30bhp (22kW) more than the 944 S2's similar engine. The gearbox was set at the rear to maximize weight-distribution and it balanced the car beautifully. So good was the handling that people remarked it required less driver involvement and hence wasn't a real Porsche. This Club Sport model rectified that, with 17-inch (432mm) wheels, no back seat nor power windows thus saving 117lb (53kg) weight.

Top speed:	150 mph (240 km/h)
0–60 mph (0–95 km/h):	6.1 sec
Engine type:	In-line four
Displacement:	182 ci (2,990 cc)
Transmission	6-speed manual
Max power:	240 bhp (179 kW) @ 6,200 rpm
Max torque:	224 lb ft (303 Nm) @ 4,100 rpm
Weight:	2,943 lb (1,338 kg)
Economy:	19.4 mpg (6.9 km/l)

Porsche Boxster

Porsche's first new car in 20 years had to do two things: boost the company's flagging profits, and bring a supercar to the masses. It did both successfully, and remained a strong seller into the 21st century. Using Porsche's famed engine layout of six horizontally opposed cylinders, the Boxster's was slightly different being mid-ships, giving near perfect weight distribution. With an output of 204bhp (152kW) at 6,000rpm, the Boxster needs to be revved, and is at its best with the motor near the redline. Being relatively lightweight made the car very responsive in corners and the brilliant steering further enhanced this. The car wasn't just a great driver's machine, however, because with good trunk and hood space, it was practical. The interior went way beyond the dated ergonomics of the 911, while the convertible roof felt like a hardtop in reality, such was the build quality.

Top speed:	149 mph (238 km/h)
0–60 mph (0–95 km/h):	6.9 sec
Engine type:	Flat six
Displacement:	151 ci (2,480 cc)
Transmission	6-speed manual
Max power:	204 bhp (152 kW) @ 6,000 rpm
Max torque:	181 lb ft (245 Nm) @ 4,500 rpm
Weight:	2,756 lb (1,252 kg)
Economy:	23.5 mpg (8.3 km/l)

Range Rover

The original luxury off-roader was launched in 1970 to massive acclaim from the world's press. Not only did it have more agility off road than the Land Rover, thanks to long-travel coil springs instead of leaf springs front and rear, it had much better road manners than anything else in its class, plus it looked and felt almost limo-like inside. At first it was only available as a two-door, but the impracticalities of this soon showed, and by 1981 all models had four doors. The underside was brutally strong, using a separate ladder-style chassis which protected all the major components. Telescopic shocks sat up front while the rear had self-levelling Boge units, and disc brakes were used all around. The engine was the all-aluminium Buick V8, for which Rover had bought the rights back in the 1960s, and it offered the perfect combination of lightweight and plenty of torque.

Top speed:	99 mph (158 km/h)
0–60 mph (0–95 km/h):	12.9 sec
Engine type:	V8
Displacement:	215 ci (3,528 cc)
Transmission	4-speed manual
Max power:	130 bhp (97 kW) @ 5,000 rpm
Max torque:	205 lb ft (277 Nm) @ 3,000 rpm
Weight:	3,864 lb (1,756 kg)
Economy:	17 mpg (6 km/l)

Range Rover Overfinch

While the Range Rover was good, it wasn't quick, for all its V8 thirst. The Rover engine, while being lightweight, just didn't have the torque needed. Under the name Schuler, Overfinch created its first modified Range Rover as early as 1975, but it wasn't until 1982 that production proper began, with the 570T being Overfinch's first Chevy-powered vehicle. As time went by and technology increased, Overfinch added injection on the 570TPi model using Chevrolet's Tuned Port Injection, then produced a very special limited edition 20th Anniversary model with a 380bhp (283 kW) 400ci (6.5-litre) GM V8. In 1998 came the car shown, the 570 HSE, with firmer air suspension, seven seats (the stock had five), a quicker steering ratio, and Bentley turbo tyres. While it has all the extra power, the Overfinch remarkably can achieve the same fuel economy as the stock Range Rover.

Top speed:	130 mph (208 km/h)
0–60 mph (0–95 km/h):	7.2 sec
Engine type:	V8
Displacement:	350 ci (5,733 cc)
Transmission	4-speed auto
Max power:	330 bhp (246 kW) @ 4,700 rpm
Max torque:	425 lb ft (573 Nm) @ 3,150 rpm
Weight:	4,960 lb (2,254 kg)
Economy:	17 mpg (6 km/l)

Renault 5 Turbo 2

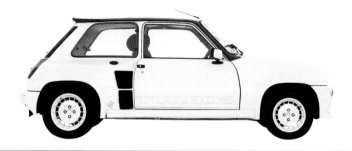

Renault did two important things with the 1980 R5 Turbo 2. It immediately raised the profile of its brand, plus gave itself a formidable rally car to tackle the Group B class. Just 1,000 road cars homologated the R5 Turbo for competition but 1,300 were made. It had little in common with the standard R5; the suspension was all-new with double wishbones at each end, using torsion bars springs up front but regular rear coils. The engine used the gearbox from the larger Renault 30, but turned around allowing the four-cylinder unit to be mounted midships. The motor featured an alloy head with hemispherical combustion chambers and a Garrett turbo running 12.2psi for the road but more boost and 300bhp (224kW) on rally cars and up to 500bhp (373kW) in the R5 Turbo Evolution. Sensational handling helped give the car great rally success: 250 international wins in four years.

Top speed:	124 mph (198 km/h)
0–60 mph (0–95 km/h):	7.7 sec
Engine type:	In-line four
Displacement:	85 ci (1,397 cc)
Transmission:	5-speed manual
Max power:	160 bhp (119 kW) @ 6,000 rpm
Max torque:	158 lb ft (214 Nm) @ 3,500 rpm
Weight:	2,138 lb (972 kg)
Economy:	22 mpg (7.8 km/l)

Renault Alpine A110

The Alpine 110 started as a simple lightweight coupe and by sticking to that ideal, with a few tweaks, Renault topped rallying for 10 years. The low weight was partly due to a skinny, yet strong, chassis, made in alloy and using a single spine design with a subframe for the front suspension and more substantial cage for the drive train/suspension out back. Unequal length wishbones were used at the front in conjunction with coil-over-shocks, where the rear again used wishbones but with two coil-over-shocks per side because of the extra weight. Four wheel 10-inch (254mm) disc brakes ensured great stopping power. Because of the low production run, it was only ever produced in lightweight glass-fibre and with the small all-alloy hemi-chambered engine on twin Weber carburettors, was rapid through the bends. It won the World Rally Championship in both 1971 and 1973.

Top speed:	127 mph (203 km/h)
0–60 mph (0–95 km/h):	6.3 sec
Engine type:	In-line four
Displacement:	98 ci (1,605 cc)
Transmission:	5-speed manual
Max power:	138 bhp (103 kW) @ 6,000 rpm
Max torque:	106 lb ft (144 Nm) @ 5,000 rpm
Weight:	1,566 lb (712 kg)
Economy:	23.5 mpg (8.3 km/l)

Renault Alpine V6 GT/Turbo

The GT's origins can be traced back to the early 1970s and the A110 two-seater sportscars which also excelled in racing and rallying. And with Renault's manufacturing might behind the new model, it had everything going for it in 1985, except image. The car used a separate steel backbone chassis with subframes at the front and rear carrying the suspension/steering and engine/'box. Suspension was double wishbone all around which gave very good handling even with rear weight bias split 37:63. The all-aluminium engine had a cam-per-bank and two valves per cylinder in the hemispherical combustion chambers. A short-stroke crankshaft meant the V6 was rev happy, but its real power came through the turbo, which gave great torque at low rpm. This was a great driver's machine, having very controllable handling and a near-perfect driving position.

Top speed:	152 mph (243 km/h)
0–60 mph (0–95 km/h):	6.3 sec
Engine type:	V6
Displacement:	150 ci (2,458 cc)
Transmission	5-speed manual
Max power:	200 bhp (149 kW) @ 5,750 rpm
Max torque:	214 lb ft (289 Nm) @ 2,500 rpm
Weight:	2,600 lb (1,182 kg)
Economy:	25 mpg (8.8 km/l)

Renault Sport Spider

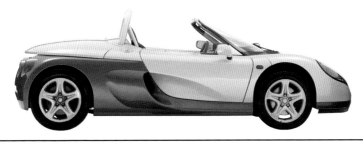

Prior to the Spider's production in 1996, Renault had never produced an open-top two-seater sportscar. The Spider was originally a race machine designed to run in a one-make endurance series across Europe, but such was the demand for it, even without a windscreen to begin with, the decision was made to produce a street-going version. An light chassis of just 176lb (80kg) was made in extruded alloy sheet boxes, while the body panels were all glass-fibre. All suspension joints dismissed rubber bushes in favour of Heim joints, yet the car still managed an above-average ride quality. For power Renault used the 122ci (2-litre) 16-valve unit also used in the Megane, and the long-stroked engine produced impressive torque which the chassis easily handled. The small screen eventually fitted was deemed to ineffective for regular use, so a conventional screen was fitted to 1997 models.

Top speed:	124 mph (198 km/h)
0–60 mph (0–95 km/h):	7.7 sec
Engine type:	In-line four
Displacement:	122 ci (1,998 cc)
Transmission:	5-speed manual
Max power:	150 bhp (112 kW) @ 6,000 rpm
Max torque:	140 lb ft (190 Nm) @ 4,500 rpm
Weight:	2,106 lb (957 kg)
Economy:	23.5 mpg (8.3 km/l)

Roush Mustang 1999

Roush and Mustang go back to 1988, when Jack Roush built a 351ci (5.8-litre) twin turbo 400bhp (298kW) Mustang as a 25th Anniversary edition. Due to costs, Ford rejected selling it, but seven years later Roush Performance was formed as an offshoot of Roush Racing, and attention turned to the Mustang again, with thoughts of a high-performance GT for the street. With the advent of the 1999 Mustang, Roush had developed a number of models in various stages of tune and prices. Shown is the Stage II car, which had minor but effective tweaks for more driver involvement. The shocks and springs were uprated and lowered, stiffer anti-roll bars were fitted and Roush control arms bolted in to locate the live rear axle. Brembo13-inch (330mm) vented discs were added at the front and, with the stock ASB, work extremely well. Finishing it off was a full skirt body kit with side exits for exhaust.

Top speed:	150 mph (240 km/h)
0–60 mph (0–95 km/h):	5.8 sec
Engine type:	V8
Displacement:	281 ci (4,606 cc)
Transmission	5-speed manual
Max power:	260 bhp (194 kW) @ 5,250 rpm
Max torque:	302 lb ft (409 Nm) @ 4,000 rpm
Weight:	3,471 lb (1,578 kg)
Economy:	16 mpg (5.7 km/l)

Rover SD1 Vitesse

As part of the British Leyland group, Rover launched the SD1 in 1976 and gave it handsome fastback styling which years later was admitted as being inspired by the Ferrari Daytona. The car initially used the Rover V8 engine, which was a version of Buick's all-aluminium unit which had been bought in the early 1960s. While the SD1 sold well into the 1980s, by then it had started to look dated, so it was facelifted in 1982. The following year saw a substantial increase in power with the launch of the Vitesse, which was French for 'speed'. The Vitesse ran the same SD1 layout of front-engine, rear-wheel drive via a live axle, but had lowered and stiffened suspension, uprated front disc brakes, larger alloys and re-calibrated steering. The engine received Lucas electronic fuel injection and the heads had gas flow improvements. In 1986 a Twin Plenum intake upped power over 200bhp (149kW).

Top speed:	135 mph (216 km/h)
0–60 mph (0–95 km/h):	7.1 sec
Engine type:	V8
Displacement:	215 ci (3,528 cc)
Transmission	5-speed manual
Max power:	190 bhp (142 kW) @ 5,280 rpm
Max torque:	220 lb ft (298 Nm) @ 4,000 rpm
Weight:	3,175 lb (1,443 kg)
Economy:	22 mpg (7.8 km/l)

SAAB

Saab 99 Turbo

As a standard sedan, the 99 was rather dull and uninviting, but with the clever addition of a turbo, Saab created a cult car. Looking typically heavy (which it was) and clumsy in design, the 99 turbo was surprisingly good to drive with a great ride quality and even inspiring handling. The engine was from, of all places, the Triumph Dolomite range, and for turbocharging Saab simply dropped the compression ratio, fitted a Garrett T3 turbo, and added electronic fuel injection. A five main bearing crank kept it reliable while the driven went through a tough three-row Triplex chain. Suspension comprised a wishbone front end and beam rear located with the aid of a Panhard rod. The set-up was good enough in uprated form for Stig Blomquist to take the Swedish Rally in 1979, in the first turbocharged car to do so. The 99 was later replaced by the even more successful 900 Turbo.

Top speed:	120 mph (192 km/h)
0–60 mph (0–95 km/h):	9.1 sec
Engine type:	In-line four
Displacement:	121 ci (1,985 cc)
Transmission:	4-speed manual
Max power:	145 bhp (108 kW) @ 5,000 rpm
Max torque:	174 lb ft (236 Nm) @ 3,000 rpm
Weight:	2,715 lb (1,234 kg)
Economy:	22 mpg (7.8 km/l)

Saleen Explorer

Steve Saleen's company had been modifying and selling its own Mustang for years before the Explorer came to light in 1990, so it was natural for the company to take on Ford's S.U.V. It was 1996 when they did, after the launch of the Ford Explorer V8 which used the pushrod 5.0L engine. Saleen launched their version in 1998 and concentrated on giving it enhanced driver appeal and a more dynamic road presence, where most 4WD S.U.Vs spent their time. The separate steel chassis and live axle were retained, but stiffer bushes were added throughout the suspension, plus the springs were both lowered and uprated and the shocks re-valved. Thicker anti-roll bars replaced the stock items, and with lightweight magnesium 18-inch (457mm) rims and low-profile tyres, the car could pull 0.80g on the skidpad. Finishing off was a spoiler and, on this model, a supercharger.

Top speed:	125 mph (200 km/h)
0–60 mph (0–95 km/h):	7.9 sec
Engine type:	V8
Displacement:	302 ci (4,948 cc)
Transmission	4-speed auto
Max power:	286 bhp (213 kW) @ 4,500 rpm
Max torque:	333 lb ft (451 Nm) @ 3,200 rpm
Weight:	4,500 lb (2,045 kg)
Economy:	15 mpg (5.3 km/l)

Saleen Mustang (racer)

With an established name on the racing circuit and street in the 1980s, Steve Saleen continued to develop his company. In 1997 his SR Mustang became a force to be reckoned with at Le Mans, then in 1998 in the US Speedvision World Challenge Series, Saleen, in conjunction with Tim Allen from 'Home Improvement', dominated with the 1998 Mustang RRR. Using a stock SN 95 stripped bare, the car received a full tubular spaceframe chassis with double A-arm suspension with Howe springs and Bilstein shocks. The engine was a bored-out Windsor 351ci (5.7-litre) with GT40 aluminium heads, 10:1 compression and a Holley 600cfm carburettor. Carbon-fibre was abundant on the doors, trunk lid, hood, fenders and nose. A brute Jerico gearbox handled the power and remained, and was reliable. In 1998 Terry Borcheller won five races, winning Saleen the manufacturer's trophy.

Top speed:	210 mph (336 km/h)
0–60 mph (0–95 km/h):	3.2 sec
Engine type:	V8
Displacement:	357 ci (5,850 cc)
Transmission	4-speed manual
Max power:	525 bhp (391 kW) @ 6,800 rpm
Max torque:	N/A
Weight:	N/A
Economy:	N/A

Saleen Mustang SSC

Steve Saleen made his name in 1984 racing his own modified Mustang. He produced three examples which got sold, then in 1985 modified and sold a further 139 hatchbacks and two convertibles. In 1986 sales continued to grow so Saleen formed a racing team. By 1989 the race and road experience led to the production of the SSC, or Saleen Super Car. Based on the 5.0L LX, Saleen had modified the suspension by adding stiffer springs and adjustable shocks, and improved the chassis rigidity by fitting a strut brace and 4-point roll cage. A special Saleen leather interior and bodykit finished it all off. In the drive train Saleen took the standard 5.0L and re-worked the heads, increased the throttle body size, got more lift from the cam and increased exhaust flow. The gearbox remained, but the rear end gears were changed for 3.55:1 ratio and discs were added to the rear.

Top speed:	156 mph (250 km/h)
0–60 mph (0–95 km/h):	5.6 sec
Engine type:	V8
Displacement:	302 ci (4,948 cc)
Transmission:	5-speed manual
Max power:	290 bhp (216 kW) @ 5,200 rpm
Max torque:	325 lb ft (440 Nm) @ 3,500 rpm
Weight:	3,425 lb (1,556 kg)
Economy:	22 mpg (7.8 km/l)

Shelby Charger GLH-S

The name Carroll Shelby is synonymous with performance cars, so as power became important again in the 1980s, he was called upon by Chrysler to inject some life into the rather lame Charger range of 1986 and 1987, which were by then devoid of a V8 and rear-wheel drive in favour of a four-cylinder and front-wheel drive, thus leaving them in direct competition with the compact imports. Shelby took the 146bhp (109kW) engine and added an air-to-air intercooler to the turbo plus equal-length intake runners. Koni shocks were fitted at each corner with lowering springs, and alloys with low-profiles were added for improved handling. The owner of this car has gone a step further with the engine by changing the pistons, strengthening the rotating assembly, gas-flowing the head and adding four extra injectors. Power is sufficient to give 13-second quarter-miles times.

Top speed:	125 mph (200 km/h)
0–60 mph (0–95 km/h):	5.4 sec
Engine type:	In-line four
Displacement:	134 ci (2,200 cc)
Transmission:	5-speed manual
Max power:	289 bhp (215 kW) @ 6,200 rpm
Max torque:	274 lb ft (371 Nm) @ 3,700 rpm
Weight:	2,483 lb (1,128 kg)
Economy:	18 mpg (6.4 km/l)

Shelby Dakota

For the majority of the 1980s the compact Dodge Ram Mini pick-up was actually a Mitsubishi truck, simply re-badged for sale in the USA. That changed in 1987 when Dodge brought out their home-grown Dakota to replace it. It was bigger than most of its rivals plus ran a 238ci (3.9-litre) V6. Two years later Dodge offered a Sport version of the same truck, with blacked-out trim and alloys. Carroll Shelby decided to go one further when he offered his Shelby Dakota later that same year, by removing the V6 and squeezing in Chrysler's 318ci (5.4-litre) V8, giving it way more power. But it wasn't all about acceleration, because Shelby also added stiffer springs and dampers, Goodyear Eagle tyres and a limited-slip differential for the rear live axle. A sport steering wheel plus Shelby trim inside finished it off as a new breed of sport truck.

Top speed:	119 mph (190 km/h)
0–60 mph (0–95 km/h):	8.5 sec
Engine type:	V8
Displacement:	318 ci (5,211 cc)
Transmission	4-speed auto
Max power:	175 bhp (130 kW) @ 4,000 rpm
Max torque:	270 lb ft (366 Nm) @ 2,000 rpm
Weight:	3,610 lb (1,641 kg)
Economy:	15 mpg (5.3 km/l)

Shelby Mustang GT350

Carroll Shelby's started with the powerful Cobra two-seater roadster, but in 1965 he turned his attention to the Mustang at Ford's request. He took the powerful 271bhp (202kW) Mustang as a base and created the GT350. Shelby improved the handling by re-locating the front suspension control arms, fitting stiffer springs and re-valved Koni shocks, and adding rear traction bars. To provide extra stopping power, he used Kelsey-Hayes front discs, and while the rears were drums, they were cooled by air from the functional side scoops. The 289ci (4.7-litre) V8 engine was upped in power with higher compression, a high-lift camshaft, larger valves and a bigger carburettor. The Shelby R was more powerful, but only 37 racers were built, though they did win Sports Car Club of Americas B-production class against Corvettes, Cobras, Ferraris, Cobras, Lotuses and Jaguar E-Types.

Top speed:	131 mph (210 km/h)
0–60 mph (0–95 km/h):	6.2 sec
Engine type:	V8
Displacement:	302 ci (4,948 cc)
Transmission	4-speed manual
Max power:	335 bhp (250 kW) @ 5,200 rpm
Max torque:	325 lb ft (440 Nm) @ 3,200 rpm
Weight:	3,340 lb (1,518 kg)
Economy:	14 mpg (5 km/l)

Shelby Mustang GT500

The Shelby GT500 joined the GT350 in production in 1967 and was instantly a hit, outselling its brethren two to one. The car differed from the standard Mach 1 Mustang visually with a new grille, different tail lights, Shelby stripes and a pair of square centre-exit tailpipes which caused several fires through being so close to the pop-open filler cap. Like the Mach 1, the Shelby used the same 428 Cobra Jet V8, but the biggest difference was handling. Heavy-duty springs and shocks, wider tyres, thicker anti-roll bars and an in-built roll cage to stiffen the shell meant the Shelby was well balanced. The handling was its biggest attraction alongside exclusivity, for which you had to pay three times the cost of the Mach 1. Although the factory rated the Cobra Jet motor at 335bhp (250kW) to appease insurance companies who were charging $1000 to insure young males, the output was closer to 400bhp (298kW).

Top speed:	130 mph (208 km/h)
0–60 mph (0–95 km/h):	5.5 sec
Engine type:	V8
Displacement:	428 ci (7,013 cc)
Transmission:	3-speed auto
Max power:	335 bhp (250 kW) @ 5,200 rpm
Max torque:	440 lb ft (596 Nm) @ 3,400 rpm
Weight:	3,100 lb (1,409 kg)
Economy:	8 mpg (2.8 km/l)

Shelby/Cooper King Cobra

British racer John Cooper had introduced his mid-engined race car in 1958, but it wasn't until 1963 that Carroll Shelby, in his search for the quintessential race-car design, chose it to shoehorn in an American V8. The chassis was strong but very light being of tubular construction, with the engine and transmission forming part of the structure for extra rigidity. Double A-arms, anti-roll bars and disc brakes sat at either end and the whole body was hand-formed in aluminium. The engine was massively tuned, and a full balancing and blueprinting job was carried out to cope with the racing use. Compression was raised to 10.5:1 for more power, and four twin Weber downdraught carburettors gave the car immense pulling power, even from low rpm. In the space of 2 years, just 12 cars were made and only 3 are known to survive, making them incredibly valuable today.

Top speed:	176 mph (282 km/h)
0–60 mph (0–95 km/h):	3.5 sec
Engine type:	V8
Displacement:	289 ci (4,735 cc)
Transmission	4-speed manual
Max power:	400 bhp (298 kW)@ 6,800 rpm
Max torque:	345 lb ft (467 Nm) @ 4,000 rpm
Weight:	1,400 lb (636 kg)
Economy:	10 mpg (3.5 km/l)

Subaru Impreza Turbo

For many the Impreza Turbo was the car of the 1990s. It made its debut in Japan in 1992, with the engine from the bigger Legacy, a car which had already proven itself in rally competition. The Impreza hit the UK market in 1994 , the same time as Colin McRae romped home to win the World Rally Championship in one. From there the model has gone from strength to strength, and it's easy to see why. Though the interior is bland and the exterior barely more dynamic, the driving experience has sold this car to thousands. With limpet-like grip in corners, the handling is nothing short of sensational, while the punch from the turbo is virtually lag-free, partly down to the high compression ratio of 9.5:1. Four-wheel discs with ABS make for excellent braking, while the 4WD split torque evenly front/rear, unless conditions change, whereby it alters the split to where the grip is best.

Top speed:	143 mph (229 km/h)
0–60 mph (0–95 km/h):	6.4 sec
Engine type:	Flat four
Displacement:	122 ci (1,994 cc)
Transmission:	5-speed manual
Max power:	208 bhp (155 kW) @ 5,600 rpm
Max torque:	214 lb ft (289 Nm) @ 4,000 rpm
Weight:	2,879 lb (1,308 kg)
Economy:	29 mpg (10.35 km/l)

SUBARU

Subaru Impreza rally car

Subaru started making an impression on the World Rally Championship with its 1990 4WD turbo Legacy. When the 1994 Impreza was introduced, they used it because it was both lighter and smaller, thus more nimble. The road was so good that the rally car remained very similar in layout, having MacPherson struts all around but fully adjustable. Vented discs with four-pot callipers at each corner ensured superb braking while the 4WD system remained 50:50 split in torque. A tubular roll cage strengthened up the stock body and gave the required safety. The flat-four engine received new engine management but was limited to 300bhp (223kW) as per the FIA World Rally regulations, and used a three-way catalytic converter to conform to emissions standards. This car is Colin McRae's WRC-winning car which made him the first British champion and Subaru's first. champion also.

Top speed:	140 mph (224 km/h)
0–60 mph (0–95 km/h):	3.2 sec
Engine type:	Flat four
Displacement:	122 ci (1,994 cc)
Transmission	6-speed sequential
Max power:	300 bhp (223 kW) @ 5,500 rpm
Max torque:	348 lb ft (471 Nm) @ 4000 rpm
Weight:	2,711 lb (1,232 kg)
Economy:	N/A

Subaru SVX

The SVX is a curious car in that it came out of the blue from Subaru. Though the company had previously produced their XT Coupe which ran from 1985 to 1990, the car was not a beauty, yet in most ways the 1991 SVX made up for that with Italian styling. Uniquely it used glass all around with hidden pillars, which gave it great visibility for such a low-slung supercar. The SVX's drive train was another one-off, featuring a flat-six engine mounted at the front and driving all four wheels. The torque was automatically split between front and rear wheels depending on grip, and MacPherson struts at each corner helped with space allocation for the 4WD set-up. Handling was superb and the traction phenomenal, with minimal body roll in corners. Alas, sales weren't good for the car, even when cheaper models were introduced, and by 1996 it had gone.

Top speed:	144 mph (230 km/h)
0–60 mph (0–95 km/h):	7.6 sec
Engine type:	Flat six
Displacement:	202 ci (3,318 cc)
Transmission	4-speed auto
Max power:	230 bhp (172 kW) @ 5,400 rpm
Max torque:	228 lb ft (309 Nm) @ 4,400 rpm
Weight:	3,614 lb (1,642 kg)
Economy:	22 mpg (7.8 km/l)

Sunbeam Tiger

With V8s being fitted to many sportscars, Sunbeam were only trying what many others had done by 1964. They took their four-cylinder Alpine, which usually had a 91ci (1.4-litre) engine, and fitted a Ford V8. Being a British company, Ford had no problem selling their Mustang's 260ci (4.6-litre) V8 and the unit fitted well. The Alpine bodyshell needed little work   in order to take the new larger engine, the most notable change being a switch to rack and pinion steering, as the standard recirculating ball system got in the way. Also, the engine left no room for the battery so that had to be mounted in the trunk. The chassis was very strong, featuring an X-brace design welded to the body and carrying wishbone suspension at the front and a live axle rear on leaf springs. All the spring rates and shocks were uprated, but on twisty streets, the car would show its limitations.

Top speed:	117 mph (187 km/h)
0–60 mph (0-95 km/h):	9.7 sec
Engine type:	V8
Displacement:	289 ci (4,735 cc)
Transmission	4-speed manual
Max power:	164 bhp (122 kW) @ 4,400 rpm
Max torque:	258 lb ft (349 Nm) @ 2,200 rpm
Weight:	2,644 lb (1,201 kg)
Economy:	14.7 mpg (5.2 km/l)

Talbot Sunbeam Lotus

Chrysler bought the British Rootes and French Simca groups in 1967 as part of its foray into Europe. It produced the Avenger from 1976 to 1979 and it was a shorter version of that car's wheelbase under the Talbot Sunbeam. It was called a Talbot by then because Chrysler sold its Europe operation to Peugeot in 1978, and Talbot was part of Simca. As a celebration of the takeover, in conjunction with Lotus, Peugeot produced this new hot hatch in 1979. Lotus used the all-alloy, twin-cam from their own Elite, but with extra crank stroke for another 10.5ci (172cc), plus twin Weber carbs. Uprated and lowered springs and shocks were added to the simple MacPherson strut front and trailing arm-located live rear axle, and 6x13-inch (152x330mm) alloys added. Also fitted were bucket seats and 5-speed gearbox. This very capable car won the 1981 World Rally Championship, beating Audi's Quattro.

Top speed:	121 mph (194 km/h)
0–60 mph (0-95 km/h):	7.4 sec
Engine type:	In-line four
Displacement:	133 ci (2,174 cc)
Transmission:	5-speed manual
Max power:	150 bhp (112 kW) @ 5,750 rpm
Max torque:	150 lb ft (203 Nm) @ 4,500 rpm
Weight:	2,116 lb (962 kg)
Economy:	22 mpg (7.8 km/l)

Toyota Celica GT

The Celica went from a live axle rear-wheel drive configuration to front-wheel drive in 1986. Toyota also slotted in a high-revving, smooth four-cylinder motor which in US version put out just 130bhp (97kW) but in Europe had 147bhp (110kW). In 1990 the car was updated, then again in 1994 with the swoopy shape shown here. By the mid-1990s the car's sporting prowess had been well established as Carlos Sainz had taken home the World Rally Championship in a Celica earlier that decade. The independent suspension layout, being MacPherson struts all around with anti-roll bars, was retained for the new model, as were the 10-inch (254mm) four-wheel disc brakes with ABS. New alloys with low-profile tyres ensured excellent cornering speed. The 16v engine used dual-phase intake system, which used a shorter intake once the revs climbed above 5,000rpm, for extra power.

Top speed:	131 mph (210 km/h)
0–60 mph (0–95 km/h):	8.3 sec
Engine type:	In-line four
Displacement:	134 ci (2,200 cc)
Transmission:	5-speed manual
Max power:	130 bhp (97kW) @ 5,400 rpm
Max torque:	145 lb ft (196 Nm) @ 4,400 rpm
Weight:	2,580 lb (1,173 kg)
Economy:	26 mpg (9.2 km/l)

Toyota Celica All-Trac

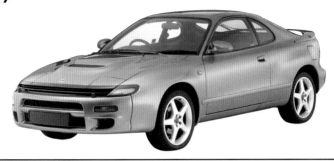

Toyota built a 4WD turbo version of their Celica in order to homologate it for world rallying. It first appeared in 1988 as the GT-Four, which in street-going form produced 185bhp (138kW) with its boosted 16v four-cylinder. The Celica was already a great handling front-wheel drive vehicle, and the extra two wheels driving made it even more memorable, if expensive. In 1990 Toyota launched the All-Trac, with more power and active suspension. This did very well in rallying in the early 1990s, winning many races and eventually taking the World Rally Championship in 1993. By then the car was both quick and very reassuring on fast, twisty streets. The hood had a huge intake for the intercooler and the turbo used a clever method of smoothing flow with two different-sized ports for the exhaust. Power on street cars could be 300bhp (224kW); the excellent chassis easily coped.

Top speed:	136 mph (218 km/h)
0–60 mph (0–95 km/h):	6.7 sec
Engine type:	In-line four
Displacement:	122 ci (1,998 cc)
Transmission	5-speed manual
Max power:	200 bhp (149 kW) @ 6,000 rpm
Max torque:	200 lb ft (271 Nm) @ 3,200 rpm
Weight:	3,218 lb (1,463 kg)
Economy:	24 mpg (8.5 km/l)

Toyota MR2

When Toyota first debuted their mid-engined Toyota MR2 to the world's press in 1984, journalists couldn't believe something with such basic suspension could handle so well. But it did, and was incredibly nimble because of its lightweight construction. When the second-generation car hit the market in 1990, it was heavier so lost that razor-sharp feel of the early car, but at the same time became more civilized and was, ultimately, built better. The new car retained the handling of the first through use of MacPherson struts all around, but was less twitchy on the limit as mid-engined cars are prone to be. The 122ci (2-litre) engine used twin camshafts and a variable induction system to increase high rpm output whilst retaining reasonable low rpm power. Discs that were slightly larger at the rear accompanied slightly larger rear tyres too, all in an effort to balance the car perfectly.

Top speed:	128 mph (205 km/h)
0–60 mph (0-95 km/h):	8.1 sec
Engine type:	In-line four
Displacement:	122 ci (1,998 cc)
Transmission	5-speed manual
Max power:	173 bhp (129 kW) @ 7,000 rpm
Max torque:	137 lb ft (185 Nm) @ 4,800 rpm
Weight:	2,833 lb (1,288 kg)
Economy:	23.5 mpg (8.3 km/l)

Toyota MR2 Turbo

The 1990 version of the MR2 was further improved with more refinement and power, and with a turbocharger attached to the 122ci (2-litre) 16v four-cylinder unit, output was 200bhp (149kW) and 200lb ft (279Nm) torque, making the car more like a mini Ferrari. Yet the engine remained very useable throughout, thanks to a variable induction system, and of course being a Toyota, it was ultra-reliable. All the power was put down by capably by a limited-slip differential. The 1990 MR2 Turbo used MacPherson struts and anti-roll bars front and rear, and to overcome twitchy handling experienced on earlier models, later cars were fitted with both taller tyres and fatter rears, which worked well with the 42:58 front/rear weight distribution. The car was very controllable even in hard acceleration out of corners. Vented discs all around meant braking was also superb, with no fade under heavy use.

Top speed:	144 mph (230 km/h)
0–60 mph (0-95 km/h):	6.2 sec
Engine type:	In-line four
Displacement:	122 ci (1,998 cc)
Transmission:	5-speed manual
Max power:	200 bhp (149k kW) @ 6,000 rpm
Max torque:	200 lb ft (271 Nm) @ 3,200 rpm
Weight:	2,888 lb (1,313 kg)
Economy:	27 mpg (9.6 km/l)

Toyota Supra Turbo

The Supra name first appeared in the Celica range on the Celica Supra, which unlike the other four-cylinder cars in the range had a 171ci (2.8-litre) straight six twin-cam motor with 168bhp (125kW). By 1986 the two names had separated again and the Supra was completely re-styled. Its engine was taken out to 183ci (3 litres) and with 24 valves, power was up to 200bhp (149kW). Three years later Toyota hotted the car up with an intercooled turbo for 232bhp (173kW) and much improved mid-range torque. This turned the car from cruising GT to street monster; Toyota had well and truly put the Supra into supercar territory. Wishbone suspension plus fattened anti-roll bars gave it good handling. The brakes were 11-inch (279mm) vented discs with ABS. Power steering was essential, and the car was better with the standard five-speed manual, though four-speed auto was popular.

Top speed:	144 mph (230 km/h)
0–60 mph (0-95 km/h):	6.5 sec
Engine type:	In-line six
Displacement:	180 ci (2,954 cc)
Transmission	4-speed auto
Max power:	232 bhp (173 kW) @ 5,600 rpm
Max torque:	254 lb ft (344 Nm) @ 4,000 rpm
Weight:	3,535 lb (1,606 kg)
Economy:	24 mpg (8.5 km/l)

Triumph Dolomite Sprint

In 1965 Triumph brought out their one and only front-wheel drive car, the 1300, and though it was styled by Italian House Michelotti it looked rather dumpy, but inside was at least luxurious for the money and so sold well. The car was re-styled for 1970 and given rear-wheel drive, and it came in both Toledo and 1500 guises, the 1500 being slightly longer in the tail and featuring double headlamps. The 1973 Dolomite was simply an upgraded 1500 and came with had the new generation 113ci (1.8-litre) four cylinder, which for the Sprint only was given a 16-valve head working with one camshaft. The TR6's gearbox was needed to cope with the extra power made. The Dolomite had firmer suspension which made it into a good quality sports saloon, and it won the 1974 British Saloon Car Championship with Andy Rouse behind the wheel. Production ended in 1980, with just short of 23,000 made.

Top speed:	115 mph (184 km/h)
0–60 mph (0–95 km/h):	8.8 sec
Engine type:	In-line four
Displacement:	122 ci (1,998 cc)
Transmission	5-speed manual
Max power:	127 bhp (95 kW) @ 5,700 rpm
Max torque:	122 lb ft (165 Nm) @ 4,500 rpm
Weight:	2,300 lb (1,045 kg)
Economy:	25 mpg (8.8 km/l)

Triumph Stag

The Triumph Stag was out on its own in the market when it appeared in 1970. There was nothing quite like the grand touring four-seater convertible, but it embodied the British Leyland spirit of setting trends and not following them. The theory behind the car worked well, in that it used a new, small-capacity SOHC V8, unitary construction for extra chassis strength, independent front and rear suspension and an Italian-involved design. Unfortunately, reliability problems on the engine with overheating and head gasket failures meant many replacement motors under warranty, and when the car hit the US market in 1971, its reputation had already started to tarnish. Two years on saw a MkII version produced with a more refined V8, better steering, five-spoke alloys and improved seating, but by then the damage was done, and the Stag was doomed by 1977.

Top speed:	118 mph (189 km/h)
0–60 mph (0-95 km/h):	9.3 sec
Engine type:	V8
Displacement:	183 ci (2,997 cc)
Transmission:	4-speed manual
Max power:	145 bhp (108 kW) @ 5,500 rpm
Max torque:	170 lb ft (230 Nm) @ 3,500 rpm
Weight:	2,795 lb (1,270 kg)
Economy:	22 mpg (7.8 km/l)

Triumph TR6

For many enthusiasts the 1969 TR6 was the last Triumph TR. It might have been crude and old fashioned, but it rewarded drivers who knew its limits. The styling was by Karmann of Germany, and now enthusiasts regard this as a classic look thanks to wraparound rear lights and the bold, aggressive front. Underneath it had a separate chassis with double wishbones at the front and a trailing arm independent rear which, though better than previous live axles TRs, still wasn't that great so Triumph gave the TR6 wide tyres to help. The straight-six engine was a development of the former four-cylinder cast-iron unit from the early 1960s and hence was no technical revelation in design; however, it did use Lucas mechanical fuel injection which improved power, but at the cost of reliability at low speeds. The TR6 lasted until 1976, and remained on the market when the TR7 was launched.

Top speed:	119 mph (190 km/h)
0–60 mph (0–95 km/h):	8.4 sec
Engine type:	In-line six
Displacement:	152 ci (2,498 cc)
Transmission	4-speed manual
Max power:	150 bhp (112 kW) @ 5,500 rpm
Max torque:	164 lb ft (222 Nm) @ 3,500 rpm
Weight:	2,473 lb (1,124 kg)
Economy:	16.8 mpg (5.9 km/l)

Triumph TR8

In the same way that British Leyland (BL) livened up the MGB by fitting a V8, so the Triumph TR7 was improved with one. The TR7 appeared in 1975 but with the 122ci (2-litre) only producing 92bhp (69kW). In the US market, for which the TR8 was intended, the car needed more power. To satisfy demand, British Leyland slotted in their Rover V8, which was all-aluminium, so weighed a similar amount to the four-cylinder TR7 engine. The new car used MacPherson strut front and a four-link rear suspension which improved handling over the TR6 model. The spring rates were slightly too soft, giving more of a leisurely touring ride quality than firm sportscar feel, but there was no doubt about performance, as the V8 made the car 12 seconds quicker to 100mph (160km/h) than the 2-litre. Due to BL strikes and production delays it was two years late, never making the impact it should have.

Top speed:	120 mph (192 km/h)
0–60 mph (0–95 km/h):	8.4 sec
Engine type:	V8
Displacement:	215 ci (3,528 cc)
Transmission	5-speed manual
Max power:	148 bhp (110 kW) @ 5,100 rpm
Max torque:	180 lb ft (243 Nm) @ 3,250 rpm
Weight:	2,620 lb (1,190 kg)
Economy:	20 mpg (7.1 km/l)

TVR 450 SEAC

TVR's theory of putting a lot of power into a relatively lightweight body has won many fans and produced some stunning machines. The 450 SEAC, one of their most brutal-looking cars with performance to match, was produced from 1988 to 1991. In TVR tradition the chassis is tubular steel with a central backbone and outriggers along the sills to provide side impact protection. Independent suspension all around using double wishbones at the front and lower wishbones at the rear provided a nimble, if firm, ride. The body was made from glass-fibre composite and the engine is all-aluminium; as such the car is only just over a ton so has an excellent power-to-weight ratio. The powerplant is a heavily modified version of the Rover V8, the TVR's being bored and stroked to give an extra litre displacement and fitted with Lucas L-Type electronic fuel injection.

Top speed:	165 mph (264 km/h)
0–60 mph (0–95 km/h):	4.7 sec
Engine type:	V8
Displacement:	271 ci (4,441 cc)
Transmission	5-speed manual
Max power:	320 bhp (239 kW) @ 5,700 rpm
Max torque:	310 lb ft (420 Nm) @ 4,000 rpm
Weight:	2,315 lb (1,052 kg)
Economy:	16 mpg (5.7 km/l)

TVR Cerbera 4.5

The 1997 Cerbera continued in TVR's tradition of producing lightweight sportscars and developed their modern range, started with the Griffith in 1991. Conventional underneath, it used TVR's strong backbone chassis with double wishbones and anti-roll bars front and rear, though softer spring rates were used to make it more comfortable than former models. At first the car had a 224ci (4-litre) straight-six producing 365bhp (272kW). This new engine was quickly followed by a new all-alloy V8, with a flat plane crank to promote rpm, one camshaft per bank and dry sump lubrication. There were two versions of the V8: 256ci (4.2-litre) with 349bhp (260kW); and this 275ci (4.5-litre) with 420bhp (313kW). Huge vented discs with racing four-piston callipers could stop the car from 60mph (95km/h) in just 2.8 seconds. The body had electronic door buttons under the door mirror.

Top speed:	168 mph (269 km/h)
0–60 mph (0–95 km/h):	4.1 sec
Engine type:	V8
Displacement:	273 ci (4,475 cc)
Transmission	5-speed manual
Max power:	420 bhp (313 kW) @ 6,750 rpm
Max torque:	380 lb ft (514 Nm) @ 5,500 rpm
Weight:	2,598 lb (1,180 kg)
Economy:	19.3 mpg (6.8 km/l)

TVR Chimaera

The 1993 Chimaera was built as a milder version of the Griffith, but was still a formidable roadster thanks to the lightweight construction. It used a steel backbone chassis with side rails to provide impact protection which was strong and transmitted no cowl shake. Wishbone suspension was used front and rear as were four-wheel discs brakes, but the handling was good, thanks to 50:50 weight distribution, achieved by setting the engine well back. The steering was, like other TVRs, a very quick rack and pinion. The engine was a developed version of Rover's all-aluminium V8, and TVR modified theirs by increasing the compression ratio to 9.8:1, then mapping their own engine management to help power delivery. By 1995 there was a 305ci (5-litre) version of the Chimaera available, which took power up to 340bhp (253kW) and the 0–60mph (0–95km/h) down to 4.1 seconds.

Top speed:	158 mph (253 km/h)
0–60 mph (0–95 km/h):	5.2 sec
Engine type:	V8
Displacement:	241 ci (3,950 cc)
Transmission	5-speed manual
Max power:	240 bhp (179 kW) @ 5,250 rpm
Max torque:	270 lb ft (366 Nm) @ 4,000 rpm
Weight:	2,260 lb (1,027 kg)
Economy:	23 mpg (8.1 km/l)

TVR Griffith

The 1992 Griffith's rounded and smooth shape took over the wedge-shaped TVRs of the 1980s to much public enthusiasm. Underneath it used the ultra-stiff steel backbone chassis which extended to the side sills, with the entire frame being plastic-coated to prevent corrosion. Twin wishbones front and rear created an independent suspension which was a marvel, though the TVR took some taming thanks to a heavy clutch and no power steering at first. Ever-accessible oversteer was just a prod of the throttle away despite a Quaife limited-slip differential used in a beefed-up Sierra rear housing. The latest tune of Rover V8 up front was by then sporting (in the 1993 Griffith 500) over double the original engine's 1960's output and an equally spectacular torque figure. Cleverly, the motor was mounted far back in the chassis to provide a near equal front/rear weight distribution.

Top speed:	161 mph (258 km/h)
0–60 mph (0–95 km/h):	4.3 sec
Engine type:	V8
Displacement:	305 ci (4,997 cc)
Transmission	5-speed manual
Max power:	340 bhp (253 kW) @ 5,500 rpm
Max torque:	351 lb ft (475 Nm) @ 4,000 rpm
Weight:	2,370 lb (1,077 kg)
Economy:	13.1 mpg (4.6 km/l)

TVR Tuscan (racer)

Chairman of TVR, Peter Wheeler, described the Tuscan racer as 'very frightening', which was no understatement, given its incredible power. The car came about as the 420 SEC was banned from competition because it was beating all its competition. TVR responded by creating its own one-make racer series, with the Tuscan announced as the new car everyone would compete in. The first meeting was in 1989 and was deemed a huge success because of the close racing and the skill required from the drivers. The Tuscan used a backbone chassis, but with double wishbones at the rear instead of trailing arms. Huge disc brakes were fitted to withstand hard use, and racers were allowed changes only to the spring rates, anti-roll bars and shocks. The mandatory engine was TVR's modified version of a Rover V8, using four Dellorto carbs and a strengthened bottom end.

Top speed:	165 mph (264 km/h)
0–60 mph (0–95 km/h):	3.6 sec
Engine type:	V8
Displacement:	271 ci (4,441 cc)
Transmission	5-speed manual
Max power:	400 bhp (298 kW) @ 7,000 rpm
Max torque:	361 lb ft (489 Nm) @ 5,500 rpm
Weight:	1,765 lb (802 kg)
Economy:	N/A

ULTIMA

Ultima Spyder

The first Ultima was built in 1986 and entered the British Kit Car Championship, which it won twice. By 1992 the car had been so finely honed in MkIII guise that it made sense for Ultima to offer it as a road car for track day/autocross use. The inspiration for the Ultima was Group C2 racing cars of the 1980s, used at events like Le Mans 24 hours. In 1993, once the MkIV Ultima was thoroughly proven, it was re-bodied with the new Spyder roadster. The car was mid-engined, as per all Ultimas, and ran a tubular steel perimeter chassis with integral roll bar and composite bodywork. Double wishbone suspension was fitted at either end, along with a low-geared steering rack and 12-inch (305mm) four-wheel AP racing vented discs. Though various engine options were available, the one to go for was the small-block Chevy. This one has Chevy's H.O. unit, with a Porsche 911 transaxle.

Top speed:	170 mph (272 km/h)
0–60 mph (0–95 km/h):	3.8 sec
Engine type:	V8
Displacement:	350 ci (5,733 cc)
Transmission	5-speed manual
Max power:	345 bhp (257 kW) @ 5,600 rpm
Max torque:	379 lb ft (513 Nm) @ 3,600 rpm
Weight:	2,180 lb (991 kg)
Economy:	18 mpg (6.4 km/l)

Vauxhall/Opel Calibra Turbo

The Calibra was welcomed by all when it debuted at the Frankfurt Motor Show, Germany, in 1989. It was a clever piece of design too, as Vauxhall had simply based it on their Vectra/Cavalier sedan yet managed to create one of the most aerodynamic production cars in the world. The range-topper that came early in 1990 was the 122ci (2-litre) 16-valve 150bhp (112kW) model, which finally brought the former dull-driving model to life. With the Cavalier/Vectra having been successful with 4WD, the company decided to install it on the Calibra and to distance the car from the sedan, they added a turbo which pushed power beyond 200bhp (149kW). The chassis handled it well, and the grip from the 4WD system was incredible, though it would start to understeer on the limit. While other turbo 4WD rally refugees were faster, none could match the bargain price of the Calibra.

Top speed:	150 mph (240 km/h)
0–60 mph (0–95 km/h):	6.3 sec
Engine type:	In-line four
Displacement:	122 ci (1,998 cc)
Transmission	6-speed manual
Max power:	201 bhp (150 kW) @ 5,600 rpm
Max torque:	207 lb ft (280 Nm) @ 2,400 rpm
Weight:	3,100 lb (1,409 kg)
Economy:	25 mpg (8.8 km/l)

Vector W8

America's answer to the likes of Lamborghini and Ferrari was a long time in the making. Debuted in Los Angeles in 1977 as 'the fastest car in the world', the Vector W2 eventually saw launch in 1990 as the W8, with a Donovan-designed aluminium small-block V8 displacing 348ci (5,703cc) based on Chevrolet's Corvette engine. Two years later came the WX3 model, which utilized twin turbos on the same engine to produce an astonishing 1100bhp (820kW). Sadly, the tiny company never did enjoy particularly spectacular success and the total built to date numbers less than 50. What a package you got though, with a mid-engined aerodynamic body, lightweight composite panels, an aluminium chassis and huge ABS-assisted disc brakes to pull the car down from its top speed of 218mph (350km/h). This was a hypercar in the true sense, being fast, expensive and extremely rare.

Top speed:	195 mph (312 km/h)
0–60 mph (0–95 km/h):	4.1 sec
Engine type:	V12
Displacement:	348 ci (5,707 cc)
Transmission:	3-speed auto
Max power:	492 bhp (367 kW) @ 7,000 rpm
Max torque:	428 lb ft (580 Nm) @ 5,200 rpm
Weight:	3,308 lb (1,504 kg)
Economy:	8.4 mpg (3 km/l)

Venturi 260

France's only supercar manufacturer, Venturi, started manufacturing in 1984 and tested Peugeot's four-cylinder turbo engines at first. However, they eventually went for Renault's GTA V6, and full production began in 1986 with two models, the 210 and 260 (bhp output). The 260 used a backbone chassis with the glass-fibre composite body bonded to it to form a stiff monocoque. The suspension had double wishbones up front and a sophisticated multi-link rear. The PRV V6, so called because both Peugeot, Renault and Volvo use it, started off as a 153ci (2.5-litre) but was increased in 1990 then again to 183ci (3 litres) in 1994. Venturi modified the all-alloy unit with new pistons, camshafts, high compression and a new exhaust. Extra power came through an intercooled Garrett turbo. The car combined leech-like grip, controllable oversteer, sharp steering and incredible braking power.

Top speed:	168 mph (269 km/h)
0–60 mph (0–95 km/h):	5.3 sec
Engine type:	V6
Displacement:	174 ci (2,849 cc)
Transmission	5-speed manual
Max power:	260 bhp (194 kW) @ 5,500 rpm
Max torque:	318 lb ft (431 Nm) @ 2,000 rpm
Weight:	2,867 lb (1,303 kg)
Economy:	19.6 mpg (6.9 km/l)

Venturi Atlantique

The Atlantique was produced after a Thai consortium took over Venturi in 1996. It used a similar layout to most mid-engined cars, with a backbone steel chassis supporting double wishbones at the front and a multi-link rear, plus coil springs and telescopic shocks all around. Large vented discs handled the braking and anti-lock was standard. The car developed quickly, thanks to composite plastic bodywork, which is one of the strongest of its kind. It also boasts a very slippery drag coefficient of just 0.31. While the V6 was familiar to Venturis of the past, the Atlantique's owed little to the previous motor except in layout. It is all-aluminium and has quad cams plus 24 valves. Sequential fuel injection is state-of-the-art, but the real key to the V6's power is the twin intercooled turbos which have variable internal geometry to maintain near-maximum power across the rev range.

Top speed:	174 mph (278 km/h)
0–60 mph (0–95 km/h):	5.3 sec
Engine type:	V6
Displacement:	180 ci (2,946 cc)
Transmission:	5-speed manual
Max power:	302 bhp (225 kW) @ 5,500 rpm
Max torque:	298 lb ft (403 Nm) @ 2,500 rpm
Weight:	2,750 lb (1,250 kg)
Economy:	24 mpg (8.5 km/l)

Volvo C70 T5

Debuted in 1996 at the Paris Motor Show, the C70 a demonstrated a radical departure from regular Volvos. It used the same five-cylinder drive train as the V70 T5, and although much of the suspension hardware was derived from the V70 sedan also, F1 racing team TWR were commissioned to fine-tune the set-up for its new purpose. It retained Volvo's Delta Link rear which allowed the back wheels to turn fractionally to aid handling. The engine was all-aluminium and featured Motronic fuel injection plus a high-pressure turbo. The only gearbox available was an auto but it had settings for sports, economy and winter. As always with Volvos there were several safety features such as EBD (electronic brake distribution) and SIPS (side impact protection system), but it managed to combine luxury as well with wood, leather and a very quiet interior, thanks to a drag coefficient of just 0.29.

Top speed:	155 mph (248 km/h)
0–60 mph (0–95 km/h):	6.3 sec
Engine type:	In-line five
Displacement:	141 ci (2,319 cc)
Transmission	5-speed manual
Max power:	236 bhp (176 kW) @ 5,100 rpm
Max torque:	243 lb ft (329 Nm) @ 2,700 rpm
Weight:	3,365 lb (1,529 kg)
Economy:	18 mpg (6.4 km/l)

VOLVO

Volvo S80 T6

Volvo's reputation for building boxy tanks belongs in the history books. The handsome S80, with its high sculptured waistline, was one of the finest vehicles ever to come out of the Gothenburg, Sweden, factory and its performance variant, the T6, looked more dynamic than any Volvo previous. Launched in 1998, the car was strong and safe in Volvo tradition, and handled well, thanks to MacPherson front struts and a multi-link rear. Its cornering and ride-quality was superb, enough to prove competition to BMW and Mercedes. Unusually, the straight-six 171ci (2.8-litre) engine was mounted transversely, the first car to use such a layout in over a decade. It used twin turbos for the incredible power output, with 280lb ft (379Nm) torque at 2,000–5,000rpm. This power was helped down by traction control and a limited-slip differential with viscous coupling. Top speed was electronically limited.

Top speed:	150 mph (240 km/h)
0–60 mph (0–95 km/h):	6.7 sec
Engine type:	In-line five
Displacement:	170 ci (2,783 cc)
Transmission	4-speed auto
Max power:	268 bhp (200 kW) @ 5,400 rpm
Max torque:	280 lb ft (379 Nm) @ 2,000 rpm
Weight:	3,580 lb (1,627 kg)
Economy:	26 mpg (9.2 km/l)

Volvo V70 T5

When the 850 arrived in 1992 it dispelled the myth that Volvos were boring, especially in the case of the T5. That car quickly became a commercial success, but in the fast-changing 1990s a new shape was needed just four years later and Volvo came up with the S70 and V70, 'S' for 'sedan' and 'V' for 'vagen', or wagon. The body was of unitary construction and had a rubber-mounted subframe to isolate major components such as the engine, transmission, strut suspension and steering. The rear used a multi-link arrangement, while the brakes were 11-inch (279mm) discs all around. Few companies use five-cylinder engines but Volvo has mastered it and in the smooth V70 this was obvious. Power was upped through twin camshafts, four valves per cylinder and sequential fuel injection. The compression was low to allow for the turbo which pushed power to 247bhp (184kW) in Europe.

Top speed:	152 mph (243 km/h)
0–60 mph (0–95 km/h):	6.9 sec
Engine type:	In-line five
Displacement:	141 ci (2,319 cc)
Transmission	5-speed manual
Max power:	236 bhp (176 kW) @ 5,100 rpm
Max torque:	244 lb ft (330 Nm) @ 2,100 rpm
Weight:	3,371 lb (1,532 kg)
Economy:	25 mpg (8.8 km/l)

VW Beetle

During the 1970s when the drag-racing scene of the USA was dominated by muscle cars, VWs began to make an appearance on the West Coast tracks. With companies such as Empi and Scat providing aftermarket VW performance parts, and individuals like Gene Berg who was at the forefront of tuning the flat four, the VWs started to embarrass many quick muscle cars with crazy quarter-miles times of 12 seconds. This was almost unheard from engines as small as 122ci (2 litres), but it sparked a craze in tuning VWs. That craze continues today and this Beetle is a British street/strip racer. It retains the Beetle floorpan, but has lowered suspension and uprated shocks. The all-alloy engine comprises a custom-machined block, race spec heads, dual 2-inch (52mm) carbs and a custom grind cam, all driving through a modified gearbox. With slick tyres the car can run low 12-second quarter-miles.

Top speed:	133 mph (212 km/h)
0–60 mph (0–95 km/h):	5.2 sec
Engine type:	Flat four
Displacement:	146 ci (2,398 cc)
Transmission	4-speed manual
Max power:	210 bhp (157 kW) @ 7,000 rpm
Max torque:	180 lb ft (244 Nm) @ 4,800 rpm
Weight:	1,629 lb (740 kg)
Economy:	18 mpg (6.4 km/l)

VW Corrado VR6

Volkswagen's Corrado was one of the best-handling front-wheel drive cars in the world. Based on the excellent Golf MkII platform, it was never intended as a replacement for the VW's ailing Scirocco because it was far too good for that. The Corrado got revised spring and shock rates and with its front heavy weight bias (64:36) was brilliant through corners, suffering virtually no understeer. The chassis was so good that it easily handled the powerful VR6, launched in 1992. The engine used a very narrow 'V' (15 degrees) to make it compact, and although it had been used in the Golf before, for the Corrado it was bored out an extra 4.2ci (70cc) for more power, plus the compression was raised to 10:1. A subtle form of traction-control was used, so when a wheel was spinning, the brake on it would come on until its speed matched the other side. Other tricks included a self-raising spoiler.

Top speed:	140 mph (224 km/h)
0–60 mph (0–95 km/h):	6.8 sec
Engine type:	V6
Displacement:	170 ci (2,792 cc)
Transmission	5-speed manual
Max power:	178 bhp (132 kW) @ 5,800 rpm
Max torque:	177 lb ft (240 Nm) @ 4,200 rpm
Weight:	2,810 lb (1,277 kg)
Economy:	28 mpg (9.9 km/l)

VW Golf GTi

When Volkswagen launched the Golf GTi in 1975, it created a new breed of car called the hot hatch, or sport compact. VW combined serious performance – the GTi could out-pace and out-handle most sportscars of the time – with the practicality of a small family car and thus opened a very lucrative market. The GTi looked different from the regular Golf by fitting wider wheels and tyres, which necessitated flared plastic arches, plus it had slightly lowered suspension all around and used a front chin spoiler. Bilstein shocks and a rear anti-roll bar made for terrific handling while the brakes were simple but effective with discs front and drums rear. The engine started out as a 91ci (1.5-litre) four-cylinder, transversely mounted for front-wheel drive, but soon went to 109ci (1.7 litres). Bosch fuel injection allowed the power to be developed while retaining excellent refinement.

Top speed:	107 mph (171 km/h)
0–60 mph (0–95 km/h):	9.8 sec
Engine type:	In-line four
Displacement:	97 ci (1,588 cc)
Transmission	5-speed manual
Max power:	110 bhp (82 kW) @ 6,100 rpm
Max torque:	100 lb ft (135 Nm) @ 5,000 rpm
Weight:	1,904 lb (865 kg)
Economy:	25 mpg (8.8 km/l)

Westfield SEiGHT

Chris Smith started Westfield in the UK in 1982, building a one-off Lotus XI replica for a US customer which later went into production as the Westfield XI. Though a Lotus Seven replica followed in 1984, a lawsuit filed by Caterham Cars, which had the rights to the Lotus Seven, forced him to re-style his cars, and by 1988 he'd created the SE and SEi. In 1991 his models had developed further and the ultimate SE variant was born: the SEiGHT. The chassis for this car was made in square section steel tubing which was heavily triangulated, and it ran high up inside the bodywork as there was no requirement for doors. The V8 was an all-aluminium Rover, stroked to 238ci (3,900cc) and at first featuring SU carbs, though later versions had fuel injection and either 198bhp (148kW) or 273bhp (203kW). Double wishbones suspension front and rear and quick steering made it a driver's machine.

Top speed:	139 mph (222 km/h)
0–60 mph (0–95 km/h):	4.3 sec
Engine type:	V8
Displacement:	240 ci (3,946 cc)
Transmission:	5-speed manual
Max power:	273 bhp (203 kW) @ 5,750 rpm
Max torque:	265 lb ft (359 Nm) @ 4,750 rpm
Weight:	1,521 lb (691 kg)
Economy:	24 mpg (8.5 km/l)

Willys Coupe

In the 1960s when drag-racing really caught on in the USA, pre-war cars were cheap and plentiful and popular as a basis for 'Gassers'. These used large V8s run on pump gas and ran high in order to fit both large wheel in the rear and the big motor up front without any body modifications. The 1940–1941 Willys was a Gasser favourite, but as drag-racing came on, aerodynamics became more important and so the cars sat lower. Street rodders started using the Willys body from the 1960s, but they became most popular in the 1980s and 1990s. This car is typical of the best produced, using a strong ladder frame style chassis, off of which a custom double wishbone suspension hangs at the front, and a four-bar linked live axle sits at the rear. A blown Chrysler Hemi engine gives power for 10-second quarters.

Top speed:	150 mph (240 km/h)
0–60 mph (0–95 km/h):	3.4 sec
Engine type:	V8
Displacement:	392 ci (6,423 cc)
Transmission:	3-speed auto
Max power:	700 bhp (522 kW) @ 6,800 rpm
Max torque:	509 lb ft (689 Nm) @ 3,200 rpm
Weight:	2,872 lb (1,305 kg)
Economy:	5 mpg (1.8 km/l)

Glossary

9-inch (228mm) axle: Size of ring gear within axle housing; also a popular Ford high-performance axle.

Alloys: Aluminium wheel rims, used as lightweight alternatives to pressed steel rims.

Bhp (bhp): Brake horsepower, measurement used for engine power output. Power output can also be measured in kW (kilowatts).

Big-block: Generic term given to large-displacement American V8 engines, usually 383 ci (6,276 cc) or under. Also refers to larger physical size of engine compared to small-block.

Cam: Abbreviation of camshaft, the component which controls the opening and closing of valves, thus controlling air/fuel flow into an engine.

Coilovers: Type of spring and shock-absorber suspension arrangement, whereby the shock is located within the coil spring.

Crank: Abbreviation of crankshaft, the main component in an engine's rotating assembly which, via connecting rods, is attached to pistons.

Ci (ci): Cubic inches – measurement of engine displacement most commonly used in the USA.

Cc (cc): Cubic centimetres – measurement of engine displacement as used throughout Europe and Japan.

Diff: Abbreviation of differential, this being the unit which turns drive (via gears in the axle) into rotation of the wheels.

Fourbar: Four parallel arms used, two per side, to locate the front or rear axle on a car.

Hot rod: Car which is stripped and tuned for speed (usually associated with pre-1949 American cars). A Hot rodder is person who does such work.

Inline four: Engine configuration whereby the engine's four cylinders sit in a straight line. Such engines can be mounted longitudinally in a car or transversely, the latter in the case of most frontwheel-drive vehicles.

Intercooler: Radiator which cools intake charge of air to an engine, therefore creating denser air for more power.

Lb ft (lb ft): Measurement of engine torque output, representing pounds per feet force. Torque outputs can also be measured in Nm (Newton Metres).

Leaf spring: Strip (or strips) of spring steel used to support a car's weight. Development of 19th-century horseless carriage cart spring. Often referred to as semi-elliptical spring because of shape.

Live axle: Solid rear axle through which rearwheel-drive is provided.

Lowrider: Car which sits very low to the ground and uses hydraulic suspension rams for radical changes in body height/angles.

Muscle car: Car built in the era between 1964 and 1972, when large-displacement V8 engines were put into medium-sized sedans for high power-to-weight ratios and fast acceleration.

Pro Street: Style of street car whereby drag-racing suspension and wide rear tyres are used under stock bodywork.

Quarter-mile: Measured distance over which drag cars are raced in a straight line to determine speed.

Rear end: Generic term for rear axle or suspension arrangement on a car.

Small-block: Generic term given to small displacement American V8 engines, usually 380 ci (6,227 cc) or under.

Supercharger/turbocharger: Device which forces more air and fuel into an engine, the supercharger being crankshaft driven, while the turbo is spun via exhaust gas.

Traction bars: Modification bars which attach to the rear axle to prevent wheel hop on leaf sprung, rearwheel-drive cars.

Transaxle: A transmission combined in the same housing as the rear axle.

V8: Engine configuration whereby eight cylinders sit in a V fashion, usually at 60 degrees in the case of the V8 engines from the US.

Wheel hop: Bouncing of wheel under hard acceleration, usually suffered on leaf spring-equipped, rearwheel-drive cars.

Wishbone: Suspension locating arm, name deriving from chicken wishbone shape. Also referred to as A-arm.

Index